T0373401

INTERNATIONAL
THEMES AND ISSUES

VOLUME
6

CAMPS

INTERNATIONAL THEMES AND ISSUES
A joint series of the Canadian Historical Association
and the University of Toronto Press

SERIES EDITOR | Pierre-Yves Saunier

Canadian
Historical Association

Société historique
du Canada

UNIVERSITY OF TORONTO PRESS

INTERNATIONAL THEMES AND ISSUES
A joint series of the Canadian Historical Association
and the University of Toronto Press

SERIES EDITOR │ Pierre-Yves Saunier

CAMPS

A Global History of Mass Confinement

AIDAN FORTH

UNIVERSITY OF TORONTO PRESS
Toronto Buffalo London

© University of Toronto Press 2024
Toronto Buffalo London
utorontopress.com

ISBN 978-1-4875-8828-1 (paper)   ISBN 978-1-4875-8830-4 (EPUB)
                                   ISBN 978-1-4875-8831-1 (PDF)

Library and Archives Canada Cataloguing in Publication

Title: Camps : a global history of mass confinement / Aidan Forth.
Names: Forth, Aidan, author.
Series: International themes and issues (Toronto, Ont.) ; v. 6.
Description: Series statement: International themes and issues ; 6 | Includes
    bibliographical references and index.
Identifiers: Canadiana (print) 2024030957X | Canadiana (ebook) 20240309634 |
    ISBN 9781487588281 (paper) | ISBN 9781487588311 (PDF) |
    ISBN 9781487588304 (EPUB)
Subjects: LCSH: Imprisonment – History.
Classification: LCC HV8705 .F67 2024 | DDC 365/.9 – dc23

Cover design: Black Eye Design
Cover image: Molly Crabapple

We welcome comments and suggestions regarding any aspect of our publications – please feel free to contact us at news@utorontopress.com or visit us at utorontopress.com.

Every effort has been made to contact copyright holders; in the event of an error or omission, please notify the publisher.

We wish to acknowledge the land on which the University of Toronto Press operates. This land is the traditional territory of the Wendat, the Anishnaabeg, the Haudenosaunee, the Métis, and the Mississaugas of the Credit First Nation.

University of Toronto Press acknowledges the financial support of the Government of Canada and the Ontario Arts Council, an agency of the Government of Ontario, for its publishing activities.

ONTARIO ARTS COUNCIL
CONSEIL DES ARTS DE L'ONTARIO
an Ontario government agency
un organisme du gouvernement de l'Ontario

Funded by the   Financé par le
Government   gouvernement
of Canada   du Canada   Canadä

Contents

Illustrations

Figures

Maps

Acknowledgments

All authors rely on the expertise of others – but this is especially true for a book of this nature. At many points, the breadth and scope of *Camps* threatened to overwhelm me, and I fear my efforts to master – or even scratch the surface of – so many diverse fields have often been inadequate. Errors and shortcomings, whether of fact or interpretation, are entirely my own. I am nonetheless grateful to Laura Belik, Wilson Bell, Kjersti Gravelsæter Berg, Michael Carroll, Christopher Holdridge, Rob Falconer, Timothy Gilfoyle, Dan Gorman, Sean Hannan, Julia Hoth, Jennifer Hyndman, Matthew Wm Kennedy, Michael Khodarkovsky, Jonas Kreienbaum, Robert Irwin, Benjamin Johnson, Steven Lee, Joseph Patrouch, Mezna Qato, Zandi Sherman, Andreas Stucki, Michelle Tusan, Christina Twomey, Robert Jan van Pelt, Barrington Walker, Jeff Wasserstrom, Alice Weinreb, and Craig Whittall for providing suggestions, advice, and support along the way. Hai-Ching Du, Aya Okamoto, Elena Krevsky, and Calvin Kha provided helpful translations of foreign language material. At MacEwan my research assistant Courtney Webber helped me tackle a vast array of camp memoirs and pointed out useful passages I would otherwise have missed. Engagement with students in multiple classes on the global history of camps at Loyola University (HIST 300C and 300E), Charles University in Prague (where Jan Stoloda and Dáša Ejemová of the University Studies Abroad Consortium were gracious hosts), and MacEwan University (HIST 442, 490, and 491) have enriched the book immeasurably. Students in HIST 491 during winter 2023 even read and commented on draft chapters; their research projects, likewise, enriched my understanding of the material and gave me great ideas. A well-timed research trip to Britain in fall 2022, facilitated by funding from both MacEwan and Loyola Universities, was fundamental to completing this project. I am grateful to my London hosts, Kathryn Müller (as well as James, Alfie, and Mikey) and Katherine McDonough, for putting up with me. Librarians at the British Library and National Archives as well as Valla McLean and Eva Revitt at MacEwan University Library have been indispensable in helping me gather such a diverse source base. At the University of Toronto Press, my editors, Pierre Yves Saunier and Natalie Fingerhut, provided patience, insight, and good-humored support throughout the journey. I am grateful to the five peer reviewers at the University of Toronto Press for challenging me to clarify key parts of the argument, while my diligent copy editor Eileen Eckert and the rest of the editorial team prevented multiple errors from going into print. Erik Goosmann's maps are testaments to his patience and expertise. My greatest debt of gratitude, however, goes to my family: to my parents, Christine and Gregory Forth; to my parents-in-law, Susan and Gordon Summers; to my children, Rupert and Beatrice; and above all to my wife, Dr. Kelly Summers. From beginning to end, from putting me in touch with the University of Toronto Press in the first place to a keen-sighted edit of the final draft – and all the love and support in between – she has been my guiding light.

Kelly, this book is dedicated to you.

Introduction

After reprimanding Hermann Göring for Germany's burgeoning network of concentration camps on the eve of World War II, the British Ambassador to Berlin, Sir Nevile Henderson, received a sharp rebuke. Walking to his bookshelf, the Nazi leader pulled out the "K" volume of a German encyclopedia and read *"Konzentrationslager:* first used by Britain in the South African War [1899–1902]."[1] However twisted his logic in justifying German crimes by equating them with those of Great Britain, Göring was correct: the mass confinement of socially or racially marginalized populations extends far beyond the history of Nazi Germany. Enslaved Africans toiled in segregated plantations; vigilante militias rounded up native populations and corralled them onto reservations; and colonial armies concentrated suspect and racialized groups *en masse*, not only in British South Africa but in German South-West Africa (where Göring's father was colonial governor), Cuba, the Philippines, Palestine, India, Malaya, Vietnam, Kenya, Algeria, and beyond. Total war in the twentieth century entailed the confinement of prisoners of war (POWs) and enemy aliens, including Japanese Canadians and Americans, alongside "racial enemies" like Jews and Roma/Sinti in Nazi Germany and "class enemies" in the Soviet Union. Amid a global "war on terror," the United States today holds "suspects" at extrajudicial enclaves like Guantanamo Bay, while Myanmar and Xi Jinping's China intern Muslim minorities on an indiscriminate basis. And while camps remain icons of twentieth-century brutality, the twenty-first century now witnesses the mass detention of forced migrants on isolated islands and in barbed-wire holding pens, some administered by the United Nations, others by hostile states who regard refugees and asylum-seekers with suspicion and disdain.

The horrific nature of totalitarian crimes, of which camps are symbols and warnings, testify to humanity's capacity for evil. Philosophers like

1

Wolfgang Sofsky define Nazi *Konzentrationslager* as typologies of terror that crystallized an ideal essence of inhumanity.[2] For the political theorist Hannah Arendt, camps "seal off" human masses from the world of the living.[3] Yet the habitual dominance of Nazi Germany and the Soviet Union in efforts to define or describe concentration camps has obscured a more diverse and complex reality. Emblematic sites like Auschwitz, extreme even by Nazi standards, are murderous but unrepresentative models to understand the global history of mass confinement – a history that predated and outlasted World War II, and that spread far beyond the confines of Europe. And while liberal democracies have commonly associated camps with the "evil empires" of fascism and communism, incompatible with freedom or human rights, countries like Canada, Britain, France, and the United States have together concentrated millions of innocent, racialized, and colonized populations. This book examines concentration camps, refugee camps, internment camps, and other carceral venues through a global and comparative lens, one that treats the atrocities of Hitler or Stalin, or of Mao Zedong and the Khmer Rouge, as emanations of a more diverse and pervasive repertoire of modern statecraft. In doing so, it presents the camp, broadly conceived, as a truly global phenomenon, one that has made (and is still making) the modern world.

What Are Camps?

Perhaps because they represent an antithesis to cherished notions of human freedom, perhaps because they spotlight the struggles of individuals within impersonal bureaucracies, perhaps because they reveal something about the modern state and our conception of citizenship and belonging, or perhaps because inmates, from the Nobel laureate and Soviet dissident Alexandr Solzhenitsyn to the Kikuyu feminist Wambui Otieno, have written poignant memoirs of their experiences, camps have attracted great interest from philosophers, literary critics, and social theorists. Indeed, camps are reflections of the societies that create them, revealing dark truths about fascism, communism, racialized capitalism, and colonial exploitation. Camps, put simply, are demarcated institutions that contain or confine categories of people – enemy aliens, racial minorities, social outcasts, POWs, non-citizens – as a preventive measure, often in a moment of perceived emergency: war, revolution, or economic crisis. Temporary installations that often become permanent, camps are spaces of disempowerment that concentrate arbitrary power in the hands of authorities, while stripping inmates of agency and freedom. Wooden barracks and barbed-wire fences symbolize the infamous camps of Nazi Germany, while Solzhenitsyn described "walls and fences made of rotting wood, rammed earth, brick, concrete, [and] iron railings."[4] The global history of camps, however, indicates the sheer diversity of architectural form and function: bamboo stakes, mud walls, thorn hedges, or simply vast expanses of mountains, desert, or ocean have also served the purposes of mass confinement. And at times, social dislocation, economic disempowerment, and police surveillance have concentrated and confined as effectively as fences or walls.

According to the political theorist Giorgio Agamben, camps exist within a "state of exception" that suspends the ordinary judicial order. Nazi camps established under emergency decree; internment camps governed by Canada's War Measures Act (1914) and Britain's Defense of the Realm Act (1914); or the American enclave at Guantanamo Bay, located outside the jurisdiction of US law, are prime examples. Since sovereignty, according to Agamben, rests on the ability to "decide the exception," to suspend individual rights and political norms, camps, in theory, are undiluted emblems of state power, even if, in practice, their management is often marked by administrative chaos and inefficiency. In contrast to prisons, which incarcerate guilty individuals who have been lawfully convicted of specific crimes, camps hold suspects and enemies conceived collectively, not for what they have necessarily done, but for who they are or for the real or imagined threat they pose. As such, camps often operate on a larger scale than prisons, and their collective logic incarcerates broad categories of humanity, including large numbers of women and children. And while prisoners typically retain constitutional rights and their administrative status as human beings, camps detain those reduced to what Agamben calls "bare life," a raw physiological existence stripped of legal rights and social status.[5] For such populations, innocent of any crime yet totally dependent on the whim and will of presiding (and often hostile) authorities, "life or death could be lightly decided," the Holocaust survivor Primo Levi observed.[6]

Distinctions between prisons and camps are less absolute in practice than in theory. As this book's opening chapter maintains, prisons, workhouses, and penal colonies laid important logistical and ideological foundations for future camps – if not as legal constructs, then as material sites of surveillance, social control, and political power. Meanwhile, institutions like the Soviet Gulag (chap. 4) and Communist China's *laogai* (chap. 6) combined the functions of camp and penal colony, incarcerating those convicted of murder, theft, and assault alongside "counterrevolutionary" suspects; they thus fit awkwardly with the state of exception paradigm. Even Nazi

Konzentrationslager (chap. 5), Agamben's archetypal case, detained German criminal convicts alongside racial enemies and political suspects. In such regimes, legislation, however unfair or illegitimate, was often deployed as a political tool to deny basic rights to ethnic and political groupings, who were detained *en masse*. As critics of American prisons, which confine racial minorities in disproportionate numbers (often without trial), might attest, the line between prisons and camps is sometimes fine and sometimes crossed.

Nonetheless, an emphasis on "bare life" and the emergency and extrajudicial nature of encampment usefully captures the rightless and dependent status of inmates – an interpretive thread that ties together the multiple episodes of encampment this book examines. Moreover, it suggests intriguing connections and ambiguities, blurred lines and hidden solidarities, between concentration camps – Agamben's prime referent – and other forms of mass confinement. If "bare life" could be arbitrarily taken, it could also be arbitrarily saved, like at modern refugee camps, where the lives of inmates, deprived (if not entirely devoid) of rights, also depend on the mercy (in this case usually granted) of authorities.[7] As such, the various categories of camp – containing refugees, political prisoners, POWs, enemy aliens, terror suspects, racial outcasts, or other captives deemed inferior, undesirable, or potentially dangerous – should not necessarily be understood as discrete or monolithic entities enclosed by clear definitional barriers, but as species of a common genus of containment and control. Highlighting a shared genealogy – the terms "concentration camp," "refugee camp," "POW camp," and "internment camp" remained largely interchangeable until the end of World War II – this book examines a diverse and flexible carceral continuum, one that both complicates and confirms prevailing visions of the camp. It considers cultural, political, and geographic differences between multiple camps in multiple regimes while weaving common narratives exhibited at camps and camplike structures across the world. In the process, it highlights suggestive, upsetting, and possibly contentious – yet hopefully thought-provoking – connections and continuities.

Imperial Dimensions

We often associate camps with the violent extremes of twentieth-century Europe. But camps developed in a global arena, and recent scholarship led by postcolonial critics has revealed a more diverse, more pervasive, and more complex history of encampment than previously appreciated.[8]

Göring's reminder that concentration camps were tools of conquest in colonial Africa should not beguile us into false equivalencies. Revolutionary upheaval, modern technology, and an emphasis on ideological purity radically accelerated the violent capacity of twentieth-century dictatorships. Nonetheless, this book's attention to colonial motivations and colonized voices offers a preliminary effort to decolonize the history of camps – previously the subject of Eurocentric narratives – by examining the shared dynamics of imperial conquest and military occupation that spawned camps in multiple regimes. In particular, colonial or asymmetric warfare against partisans, brigands, guerrillas, and "terrorists" has offered a recurring but sometimes forgotten context for the development of camps and the domination of ethnic or racial minorities, not only in the British, Spanish, French, and American empires, but in Nazi Germany, the Soviet Union, and Communist China.

For Hannah Arendt, herself interned in France during World War II as a German-Jewish refugee, and for anticolonial activists like Frantz Fanon and George Padmore, who "saw but shades of difference between fascism and imperialism,"[9] European colonies were laboratories that assembled many of the basic ingredients of modern violence and mass encampment. European imperialists fetishized violence – for Winston Churchill, the Maxim gun was a "beautiful white devil,"[10] a sublime instrument of conquest. Embracing an authoritarian will to power, meanwhile, colonists divided the world into a white and "civilized" West and an abject, dark-skinned other. Concentrating those denied political status or the rights of citizenship, camps were material manifestations of this primal partition. And in a world where nation-states emerged as the prime guarantors of human rights, colonial subjects, who lacked their own representative state, shared a similar status to Jews, kulaks, and other marginalized groups. Like stateless refugees today, they were cast out as dangerous outsiders or detained as internal others.

Despite invocations to the rule of law, the dynamics of military conquest and a regular resort to emergency powers rendered colonial spaces enduring states of exception. Multiple wars of colonial occupation fostered processes of professionalization that endowed modern militaries with logistical capacities to confine and control large populations, while doctrines of instrumental rationality, which legitimized mass violence in order to accomplish specific goals set by professional bureaucracies, framed the European conquest of Asia and Africa. If Hitler and Stalin discovered in their camps an instrument of total power, a belief that "everything is possible," as Arendt put it,[11] then European colonies were places, in the words of the imperial novelist Joseph Conrad, where "anything – anything could be done."[12] Though nineteenth-century developments in international law guaranteed protections for both soldiers and civilians, such distinctions rarely applied to "uncivilized" colonials, much as twentieth-century total war suspended the norms of civilization and rendered civilians legitimate military targets.

Colonial attitudes toward race and space also laid the foundations for early camps. In particular, imperial powers viewed territories in North America, Australia, and temperate regions of Africa as *tabula rasa*, empty spaces (what Germans called *Lebensraum*) that could be occupied and cultivated. "Settler colonialism," Patrick Wolfe and Lorenzo Veracini note, is a distinct form of domination premised on the "elimination of the native."[13] Whether in Africa or America, conquest and settlement entailed violent roundups of Indigenous people and their subsequent concentration in reservations, compounds, and residential schools (chap. 2). Mobile and nomadic tribes were especially vulnerable to removal and resettlement. Yet as postcolonial historians like David Olusoga, Dirk Moses, and Jürgen Zimmerer contend,[14] settler colonialism also generated camps in eastern Europe (chap. 5), which Nazi functionaries viewed, by some measures, as a colonial space filled with itinerant wanderers and racially inferior "savages" who lacked a settled homeland. Further extending the colonial paradigm, this book suggests comparable dynamics have framed encampment in the Soviet Union (chap. 4), China (chaps. 6 and 7), and elsewhere.

Colonial labor demands also generated camps. New World plantations represented significant advances in the organization of unfree labor (chap. 2), though even after the formal end of slavery, enclosed compounds exploited captive workers at South African diamond mines, Congolese rubber plantations, and at factories attached to shipping facilities in South-West Africa, where German authorities in 1905 enforced a work-or-starve policy against prisoners from the Nama and Herero Wars (chap. 3). Along with factories and workhouses in metropolitan Europe, such institutions pioneered the logistics of corralling unfree labor, enforcing time discipline, and regulating productivity according to standardized measures – a precedent for future concentration camps, where slave labor became an organizing motif, from the gold mines of Siberia (chap. 4) to the cotton fields of Xinjiang (chap. 7). The flip side of exploitation, meanwhile, was welfare and rehabilitation, a justifying logic rooted in the "civilizing missions" of European empires, which cast work as both a disciplinary device – one that would instill modern industrial habits – *and* a vehicle for "liberation." However hollow Nazi slogans like *Arbeit Macht Frei* ("Work Makes You Free") were, developmentalist agendas motivated many camps, from Kenya to the Soviet Union, and from Victorian workhouses (chap. 1) to modern refugee facilities (chap. 8). Efforts to manufacture governable, hard-working subjects, however, existed in tension with physically destructive manual labor that built modern infrastructure but created sick, emaciated, and disempowered inmates.

Genealogical Origins

By examining the colonial dimensions of mass confinement, this book challenges common periodizations that assert a break between a long and imperial nineteenth century and a short twentieth century of world wars and ideological extremes. The twentieth century was indeed "a century of camps," as the sociologist Zygmunt Bauman put it.[15] But modern camps rested on political and logistical foundations assembled during an earlier age of empire and industry. Moreover, they reflected a basic Enlightenment premise, one shared between free market capitalists, Marxist revolutionaries, and even colonial racists – that humanity is pliable, that utopia (or dystopia?) could be achieved on earth rather than in heaven, and that human action rather than divine prescription could shape and reforge human societies. Emerging at the end of the eighteenth century, this intellectual reorientation precipitated dramatic administrative developments as governments took responsibility not only for acquiring new territory (an old priority of dynastic monarchies) but governing and actively intervening in the life of populations – what the philosopher Michel Foucault called biopolitics.[16] As products of colonial conquest, camps exhibited clear markers of military influence, whether in terms of motives, infrastructure – bell tents, A-frame huts, barbed wire – or personnel. Indeed, the term "camp" derives its ancient roots from the Roman *campus*, an originary site of military discipline and drill. But as artifacts of mass industrial society, of managing populations on a macro scale, hospitals, factories, prisons, and workhouses (chap. 1) also inspired future camps. Such institutions monitored and regulated security, health, economic production, and biological reproduction, with the aim of rendering inmates healthy, hygienic, and hard-working citizens, or else segregating – or "amputating" – them from the body politic according to ambitious social or political agendas. The development of democracy in the eighteenth and nineteenth centuries thus found its correlative in the emerging tactics of discipline and punishment, and in the concomitant exclusion, exile, or incarceration of social, political, or ethnic others.

As instruments of social transformation, camps also operated according to what Bauman deemed the defining allegories of modern politics: gardening and medicine.[17] Cultivating the "human garden" – an abiding colonial fantasy that presaged the employment of captive labor on plantations and irrigation canals – depended on the elimination of "weeds." Enforcing basic distinctions between insider and outsider, citizen and other, the fences and walls of nineteenth-century prisons and workhouses were early iterations of the modern "gardening state." The segregation of "noxious counterrevolutionaries" in Maoist China (chap. 6) and the use of napalm and Agent Orange to defoliate Malayan and Vietnamese jungles and flush suspected insurgents into barbed-wire pens (chap. 7) were iterations of the same discursive parameters. Conceiving society as a body, a common motif of eighteenth- and nineteenth-century politics, metaphors of disease likewise framed the "quarantine" (and in extreme cases, the "euthanasia") of demographics associated with dirt, viruses, or parasites. Dirt, of course, was largely allegorical, a symbol of disorder, of "matter out of place," as the anthropologist Mary Douglas argues.[18] Yet camps and other enclosures were very real, material manifestations designed to isolate and possibly "cure" unwanted bodily matter. Leper colonies, plague lazarettos, and lock hospitals for suspected prostitutes were products of this symbolic encounter – what the sociologist Judy Whitehead calls a "cosmic dualism" – between order and chaos, health and disease.[19] And they were precedents for the *cordons sanitaire* of colonial dirty wars; for ethnic cleansing and military "sweeps"; for apartheid South Africa's Soweto native location, which was built on a former sewage dump; and even for Nazi fantasies of "racial hygiene." The irony, however, was that by concentrating marginalized populations in crowded confines, camps spread epidemic diseases that killed millions. Occasionally on purpose, as in the Armenian genocide (chap. 3), but often as an unintended consequence, as at Congo's Mugunga refugee camp (chap. 8), disease killed more inmates in the global history of camps than willful extermination.

Once marginalized people were concentrated in camp, authorities embraced the epidemiological techniques of segregation and isolation to "quarantine" social, political, and sanitary "contagion." Relocating mobile bodies to fixed and regulated sites, camps also facilitate observation. As forms of information technology – relatively crude in the nineteenth century, incredibly sophisticated at Chinese "smart camps" today (chap. 7) – camps gather knowledge, and therefore power, over concentrated populations. Roll calls and registration numbers (whether issued on identity cards, as at enemy alien camps, or branded on raw skin, as at slave plantations) foster "legibility," as the political anthropologist James Scott puts it,[20] over inscrutable and possibly suspect groups that previously existed beyond the reach of the state. Meanwhile, spatial partitions divide inmates according to such criteria as race, social class, political affiliation, and labor capacity. Exhibiting a classificatory impulse shared across the world's multiple camp regimes, British colonial officials interrogated, tortured, and then segregated suspects during the Mau Mau rebellion according to the categories "white," "grey," and "black," while the Nazis preferred colored triangles: yellow, green, red, pink, brown, and black (chaps. 5 and 7). Reflecting the bird's-eye view of the planner, meanwhile, geometric plots, interchangeable huts, and perpendicular sightlines exhibit modernity's aspiration for order – one pioneered in the imperial world, where administrators dreamed of converting colonial chaos into cartesian regularity. Such themes, recurring with different intensities and variations across time and space, offer a common framework to understand the diverse array of camps showcased in the chapters that follow.

Connections and Continuities

To understand the history of camps, we must extend our spatial and temporal gaze. Accordingly, this book charts the history of mass confinement across a broad historical and geographical canvas. Scholars who treat camps as products of discrete national histories (many of which are cited in the annotated bibliography) are well attuned to local complexities and contextual specificities. But the rich historiography on Nazi *Konzentrationslager* and the Soviet Gulag, along with emerging scholarship on colonial and East Asian camps, has too often existed in conceptual and geographical silos that fail to make connections across time and space. Disciplinary divisions have likewise hampered understanding. Dominated by anthropologists, for example, studies of contemporary refugee and migrant detention camps in the Global South rarely place their studies within longer histories of refugees and ethnic suspects in wartime Europe or in colonial empires prior to World War II, while historians too often fail to connect their findings to a contemporary world divided by wire. *Camps: A Global History of Mass Confinement* builds on existing general histories of the camp as an institution, many of which are dominated by the conceptual tropes of Nazi or Soviet history.[21] But the chapters that follow are more global, more interdisciplinary, and more accessible to English-speaking audiences than

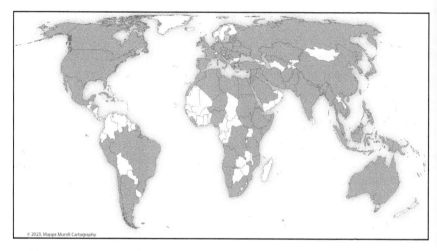

© 2023, Mappa Mundi Cartography

MAP 0.1 Countries specifically discussed in *Camps* are shaded gray.

previous narratives.[22] Moreover, *Camps* integrates scholarship on military history, forced labor, crime and punishment, and the comparative history of genocide into the theme of mass confinement.[23] Inspired by the methods of global, transnational, and comparative history, of studying processes and practices that transcend regions, states, and nations, the emphasis is on connection and circulation, on shared mindsets and mentalities, on charting global networks, on tracing continuity as well as change, and on identifying phenomenological affinities between institutions normally considered in isolation.

Common themes – hunger, labor, and the politics of soup; trauma and collaboration; the dehumanizing conditions inmates faced in cattle cars and livestock pens, branded or tattooed – stitch the chapters together, as do more concrete connections. Inmates like Wim Hopford (chap. 3) and Margarete Buber-Neumann (chaps. 4 and 5) found themselves encamped by multiple regimes. Technical experts experimented with hygiene and discipline, or with counterinsurgency doctrine and interrogation tactics, that contributed to a transnational learning curve from South Africa to the Philippines, from Malaya to Algeria, and from Britain to China. And politicians sought to justify their camps with reference to past precedents. As camps migrated from colony to metropole (during World War I) or from west to east (in interwar Asia), new cultures and new political formations adopted and actively adapted camps to their own purposes, injecting local variation into globally circulating technologies. Particularly in the case of postcolonial regimes, meanwhile, victims of one camp system sometimes became perpetrators in the next, as histories of Israel (chaps. 5 and 7), South Africa (chaps. 3 and 7), and Kenya (chaps. 7 and 8) attest. The material history of individual campsites likewise reveals continuities – between workhouse, concentration camp, and displaced persons camp in the case of Moringen, Germany, or between army camp, refugee camp, and detention camp at Guantanamo Bay.

More than concrete connections, however, the chapters that follow are framed by structural continuities and shared cultures of confinement as they spread and transformed across the modern world. No two regimes and no two circumstances are identical, and the camps and other enclosures examined in this book exhibit significant variations according to the purpose and politics that generated them. Yet in the interests of comparative and transnational history, *Camps* does more than identify differences and peculiarities, many of which are obvious, uncontested, or well-identified by specialist literature on individual regimes. The goal, rather, is to highlight patterns and regularities, familiar attitudes about race and space, shared priorities of discipline and labor, common languages of suspects and enemies, or viruses and weeds, or citizens and others, in the global history of mass confinement. In doing so, the aim is not to provide a definitive and comprehensive account of individual camp systems, but rather to provide an integrative history that provokes discussion and facilitates comparison.

Notes

1 Nevile Henderson, *Failure of a Mission: Berlin, 1937–1939* (New York: G.P. Putnam's Sons, 1940), 21.

2 Wolfgang Sofsky, *The Order of Terror: The Concentration Camp* (Princeton, NJ: Princeton University Press, 1993).

3 Hannah Arendt, *The Origins of Totalitarianism* (New York: Harcourt, 1968), 445.

4 Alexandr Solzhenitsyn, *The Gulag Archipelago: An Experiment in Literary Investigation, I–II*, trans. Thomas P. Whitney (New York: Harper Perennial, 1974), 4.

5 Giorgio Agamben, *State of Exception*, trans. Kevin Attell (Chicago: University of Chicago Press, 2005); Agamben, *Homo Sacer: Sovereign Power and Bare Life*, trans. Daniel Heller-Roazen (Stanford: Stanford University Press, 1998).

6 Primo Levi, *Survival in Auschwitz*, trans. Stuart Woolf (New York: Touchstone, 1996), 27.

7 Giorgio Agamben, "We Refugees," *Symposium* 49, no. 2 (1995): 114–19.

8 See, for example, Aidan Forth, *Barbed-Wire Imperialism: Britain's Empire of Camps, 1876–1903* (Berkeley: University of California, 2017); Jonas Kreienbaum, *A Sad Fiasco: Colonial Concentration Camps in Southern Africa, 1900–1908*, trans. Elizabeth Janik (New York: Berghahn, 2019); Elizabeth van Heyningen, *The Concentration Camps of the Anglo-Boer*

War: A Social History (Auckland Park: Jacana Media, 2013); David Olusoga and Casper W. Erichsen, *The Kaiser's Holocaust: Germany's Forgotten Genocide and the Colonial Roots of Nazism* (London: Faber and Faber, 2010); Caroline Elkins, *Imperial Reckoning: The Untold Story of Britain's Gulag in Kenya* (New York: Henry Holt, 2005).

9 Caroline Elkins, *Legacy of Violence: A History of the British Empire* (New York: Knopf, 2022), 297.

10 Winston Churchill quoted in Daniel R. Headrick, *The Tools of Empire: Technology and European Imperialism in the Nineteenth Century* (Oxford: Oxford University Press, 1981), 118–19.

11 Hannah Arendt, "On the Nature of Totalitarianism: An Essay in Understanding," in *Essays in Understanding: Formation, Exile, Totalitarianism, 1930–1954*, ed. Jerome Kohn (New York: Harcourt, 1994), 354.

12 Joseph Conrad, *Heart of Darkness* (Toronto: Penguin, 1988), 58.

13 Patrick Wolfe, "Settler Colonialism and the Elimination of the Native," *Journal of Genocide Research* 8, no. 4 (2006): 387–409; Lorenzo Veracini, *Settler Colonialism: A Theoretical Overview* (New York: Palgrave Macmillan, 2010).

14 Olusoga and Erichsen, *The Kaiser's Holocaust*; Jürgen Zimmerer, "The Birth of the *Ostland* Out of the Spirit of Colonialism: A Postcolonial Perspective on the Nazi Policy of Conquest and Extermination," *Patterns of Prejudice* 39, no. 2 (2005): 197–219; A. Dirk Moses, ed., *Empire, Colony, Genocide: Conquest, Occupation and Subaltern Resistance in World History* (New York: Berghahn, 2008).

15 Zygmunt Bauman, "The Century of Camps," in *The Bauman Reader*, ed. Peter Beilharz (Malden, MA: Blackwell, 2001), 266–81.

16 Michel Foucault, *The Birth of Biopolitics: Lectures at the Collège de France, 1978–9*, ed. Michel Senellart, trans. Graham Burchell (Basingstoke: Palgrave MacMillan, 2008).

17 Zygmunt Bauman, *Modernity and the Holocaust* (Ithaca: Cornell University Press, 1989), 70–3.

18 Mary Douglas, *Purity and Danger: An Analysis of the Concepts of Pollution and Taboo* (London: Routledge, 1966).

19 Judy Whitehead, "Bodies Clean and Unclean: Prostitution, Sanitary Legislation, and Respectable Femininity in Colonial North India," *Gender & History* 7, no. 1 (1995): 53.

20 James Scott, *Seeing Like a State: How Certain Schemes to Improve the Human Condition Have Failed* (New Haven, CT: Yale University Press, 1998), 2.

21 Dan Stone, *Concentration Camps: A Short History* (Oxford: Oxford University Press, 2017); Andrea Pitzer, *One Long Night: A Global History of Concentration Camps* (New York: Little, Brown and Company, 2017).

22 Joël Kotek and Pierre Rigoulot, *Le Siècle des Camps: detention, concentration, extermination, cent ans de mal radical* (Paris: JC Lattes, 2000); Andre Kaminski, *Konzentrationslager 1896 bis heute: Eine Analyse* (Stuttgart: W. Kohlhammer, 1982).

23 Examples include Laleh Khalili, *Time in the Shadows: Confinement in Counterinsurgencies* (Stanford: Stanford University Press, 2013); Christian De Vito and Alex Lichtenstein, eds., *Global Convict Labour* (Leiden: Brill, 2015); Frank Dikötter and Ian Brown, eds., *Cultures of Confinement: A History of the Prison in Africa, Asia, and Latin America* (Ithaca: Cornell University Press, 2007); Moses, *Empire, Colony, Genocide*.

1 | Industrial Enclosure: Prisons, Workhouses, and Labor Colonies

The nineteenth century was an age of both freedom and captivity, of buoy-ant optimism and repressive discipline. The geography of London, capital of the world's leading superpower, reflects the paradox. A shrine to pro-gress, the Crystal Palace (opened in 1851) was an impressive glass edifice in the city's west end, exhibiting the artifacts of industrialization to a popular audience, one that clamored for constitutional rights and democratic free-doms. Yet just a few miles away rested another monument to nineteenth-century ambitions, one enclosed by brick and iron rather than curtains of glass: the notorious Pentonville Prison. As Western civilization and the world it increasingly dominated forged societies based on national, social, or cultural belonging, those deemed undesirable faced exclusion or con-finement. To this end, prisons and penal colonies concentrated inmates con-victed of judicial crimes alongside vagrants, political prisoners, and others who blurred distinctions between "guilty" and "innocent," "criminal" and "suspect." In particular, the era witnessed a preemptive militarized assault on the "criminal poor," as social prejudices compromised the supposedly value-neutral character of criminal justice. Prisons, workhouses, and other carceral sites were registers of uprootedness, products of social and spa-tial dislocation inherent to changing times. By fixing marginal groups to monitored and immobile sites, their standardized, serialized architecture pioneered practices of discipline, punishment, and forced labor that would ultimately govern confined populations throughout the modern world.

Insurgency of the Poor

Whatever opportunities they afforded, the rapid social and economic changes of eighteenth- and nineteenth-century Europe – rapid population growth, capitalist boom-and-bust cycles, and the breakdown of traditional patronage networks – generated crime and social unrest. At times, industrial capitalism displaced peasant farmers as dramatically as war and famine: economic pressure drew them to urban areas, where repressive social policies concentrated them at confined sites. In particular, the privatization and physical enclosure of common land, of fields and forests previously accessible to the public, presaged a great uprooting, one that squeezed the peasantry out of the countryside. Starting in the sixteenth century, geometric lattices of hedge and stone partitioned Europe's landscape, consolidating small plots of land into large commercial estates while concentrating wealth into the hands of prominent landlords. Enclosure, by some accounts, was a form of internal colonization that codified property rights and enforced literal boundaries with fences and ditches between rich and poor. Tenant and subsistence farmers, who depended on common land for planting, pasture, and gleaning, found themselves displaced and dispossessed of their customary rights. Such practices drove thousands from rural areas, leading to social riots and radical movements like the seventeenth-century Levellers, so named because its proponents destroyed, or "levelled," enclosure fences in an attack on social inequality. Fortified by the ascendant ideology of private property, however, the period 1760–1850 witnessed a dramatic acceleration of enclosure, first in Britain and then across western and later eastern Europe.

Uprooted by the forces of an emergent capitalism, the urban poor and "barbarian" peasants – a "race as wild as the fens," as contemporaries called them[1] – evinced special fear. Social commentators expressed growing anxieties about alcoholism, violence, and exotic criminal underworlds populated by the displaced and dispossessed. And when they acted collectively, marginalized groups were more than social outcasts – they were potentially subversive. The French jurist Guillame-François Le Trosne (1728–80) disparaged the "malefactors" who "roam[ed] the countryside like swarms of locusts." These "voracious insects," he continued, "are, quite literally, enemy troops spreading over the surface of the territory, living as they wish, as in a conquered country, exacting levies under the name of alms."[2] English commentators also articulated the paradigm of military combat: "the working classes are now, in fact, at war with all the superior classes," one spokesman feared, before calling on police to "sweep the country" and clear out "those parts … that are most *infested*."[3]

In France, landless peasants and urban *sans-culottes* engaged in regular bouts of revolutionary violence from 1789 to 1848, while urban workers and rural agriculturalists in Britain embraced quasi-military forms of organization in the most traumatic years of industrialization. Followers of "General

Ludd" sabotaged industrial factory equipment in the 1810s as a form of political protest, while the "Captain Swing" riots saw small, armed units conduct incendiary raids against wealthy landlords in the same year that France's July Revolution (1830) witnessed looting and widespread riots. With the conviction that "small farmers and tenants … were waging a guerrilla-style resistance" against *nouveaux riches* estate holders,"[4] authorities turned to military force. As large mobs with blackened faces, armed with crowbars, sledgehammers, and pistols, protested enclosure at Otmoor in 1830, Lord Churchill (great uncle to the future prime minister) mobilized troops to occupy the district and arrest suspected rioters. Class warfare, then, was more than metaphorical: as in a military counterinsurgency, it entailed the detention and even execution of "enemy fighters." Such was a fitting context for new forms of mass confinement.

A MILLENNIAL HATE?

The persecution and concentration of Jewish populations holds a special place in the history of mass confinement. In the Middle Ages, religious persecution, combined with social, cultural, and economic resentments, concentrated Jews in specific neighborhoods like Prague's *Josefov* (1262) and Frankfurt's *Judengasse* (1460). In 1516, following an influx of refugees from the War of the League of Cambrai, municipal authorities in Venice formally segregated Jewish residents in a gated "ghetto" surrounded by walls and canals. And as Rome constructed magnificent Renaissance churches, Pope Paul IV (1555–59) concentrated Jews in a squalid "Hebrew enclosure." Conditions in ghettos – many were so crowded that "there was not enough floor space to allow all of its inhabitants the luxury of lying down at one time"[5] – forged links between Jews, poverty, dirt, and disease. Atributing their destitute living conditions to God's divine judgment, and associating them with greed, dishonesty, and political subversion, city governments forced many Jews to wear yellow badges as markers of identity. Nonetheless, Jewish residents often viewed their ghettos as safe havens from mob violence, and as autonomous zones and holy communities where they could sustain their own social, religious, and educational institutions. As alternatives to expulsion, ghettos even represented an uneasy equilibrium between hatred and interdependence, as Jewish merchants brought wealth and trade to the surrounding community.

The eighteenth and nineteenth centuries represent a paradox. Enlightenment-era discourses of universal human rights facilitated Jewish emancipation, and Napoleonic forces tore down the gates of the Venetian ghetto in 1797, thereby integrating Jews into the cultural and economic life of western Europe (though East European Jews continued to live in impoverished *shtetls*). Yet as ghettos disappeared, other walls proliferated: around prisons, workhouses, and penal colonies (see below); around native compounds and holding pens for captive slaves; and around wartime internment and colonial concentration camps. In 1939, Nazi Germany reinvented the ghetto and introduced other antisemitic measures, like yellow star-of-David armbands. Were these infamous measures an atavistic throwback to premodern times, products of "millennial anger," as the Holocaust survivor Primo Levi suggested?[6] Or did nineteenth- and twentieth-century developments in politics, racism, and social discrimination (as charted in the next three chapters) transform the potential of modern persecution and widen the targets of mass confinement to broader arrays of social and racial outsiders?

Carceral Archipelagos

Until the nineteenth century, exile and execution remained the most common forms of criminal punishment, both in Europe and the world. As class warfare intensified, Britain's infamous "Black Acts," originally conceived as "exceptional measures" in 1723, turned petty crimes like theft, arson, and poaching into capital offenses, punishable by death.[7] Yet as the forces of urbanization, enclosure, and population growth created large surplus populations, European countries embraced expansion overseas as a potential outlet to contain the rootless or displaced. The prolonged global conflicts of the eighteenth century – the Wars of Spanish and Austrian Succession (1701–15, 1740–48), the Seven Years' War (1756–63), and the French Revolutionary and Napoleonic Wars (1791–1815) – offered one solution. Not only could military force subdue class insurgents, it could recruit them as soldiers and discipline them in army camps at home and overseas (chap. 3). Indeed, military life provided structure to would-be criminals and to convicted felons who served in special penal battalions over the course of the eighteenth and nineteenth centuries. As captives of their own state, condemned to bleak barracks and menial labor, these subalterns were treated little better than the colonial subjects they were often tasked with subduing.

New colonial holdings, consolidated through war, also offered space to warehouse excess populations, particularly as European capitals witnessed renewed unrest following postwar demobilization. The outcome was an extensive archipelago of penal colonies and convict camps. British convicts sentenced to terms of indentured servitude first arrived in Virginia less than a decade after that colony's founding in 1607, though the process escalated markedly after the 1718 Transportation Act, as convict labor on farms and tobacco plantations set foundations for the future enslavement of African captives. The transportation of large numbers of women and their children likewise bolstered the settler population. In Paris, for example, an armed squad, the *Bandouliers du Mississippi*, founded in 1723, rounded up beggars and prostitutes for transportation to New World colonies. And as social and political upheaval intensified in the nineteenth century, France's overseas colonies presented a "final solution to the penal question," as authorities put it, that "weeded out ... certain tainted elements that ha[d] infiltrated the masses."[8] The cultivation of human society thus depended on the elimination of "weeds." For many, transportation was indeed final. Deportation to France's infamous "Devil's Island" in Guiana, which housed common criminals alongside socialist revolutionaries and republican opponents of Napoleon III, was little better than a death sentence: the majority died from tropical diseases compounded by forced labor. At France's Charvein labor colony, also in Guiana, inmates worked naked in mosquito-infested jungles. So deadly were conditions, they referred to the complex as a "dry guillotine" or a "*camp de la mort*" (camp of death).[9]

Within this global archipelago, Australia was emblematic. American independence in 1776, coupled with the growth of transatlantic slavery and the increasingly racialized division of forced labor in the Americas, shifted the gravity of British penal exile to the southern hemisphere, where the first convicts arrived in 1788. Encompassing an entire continent rather than a single island or enclave, New South Wales, Van Diemen's Land (Tasmania), and the remote but infamous Norfolk Island housed political prisoners and criminal convicts, ranging from socialist revolutionaries, Irish republicans, and anti-industrial saboteurs to vagrants, prostitutes, and thieves. As such, Australia became Britain's largest penal colony within an expansive carceral network stretching from Bermuda to Hong Kong, and from India to Tangiers.

Following lengthy journeys, during which shipboard routines accustomed inmates to health checks, prison rations, and military discipline, the regimented life and communal hammocks of Sydney's Hyde Park barracks awaited. After legislation in the 1820s, convicts were increasingly billeted behind government walls, while a system of police districts and passes regulated their movement to public works sites and extramural farms. Thus did the bureaucracies and logistics of mass confinement gradually develop – as did ideologies that placed labor at the center of criminal punishment and economic exploitation. If America's slave plantations produced cotton for Manchester textile mills (chap. 2), the wool came from Australia. Convicts also constructed Australia's physical infrastructure, placing penal colonies at the vanguard of colonization. From the start, the process rested on violence. Though depictions of "Auschwitzian horrors" "hardly to be rivalled until the era of the [Nazi] concentration camps" are unseemly twentieth-century exaggerations, inmates faced brutality and potential death.[10] Administrators on Norfolk Island ordered more than 136,000 floggings with the cat-o'-nine tails for an inmate population of a few thousand.[11] When their sentences expired, however, Australian convicts worked in the private sector and mingled with free settlers. And as chapter 2 indicates, their descendants would erect new systems of confinement directed at Australia's Indigenous population.

Following protest from British settlers, convict transport to Australia ended in 1868. Yet penal exile proved more enduring in colonies populated by disempowered racial others. After the 1857 Rebellion in British India, for example, colonial officials exiled some 20,000 "mutineers" and other convicts to the Andaman Islands, a remote archipelago in the Indian Ocean. And as India's independence movement intensified in the 1890s, the Andamans adopted a counterinsurgency function, removing potential rebels from the subcontinent. The journey itself was a mode of terror. Tattooed on the forehead with their name, crime, and date of sentence, Hindu prisoners regarded overseas penal camps as spaces of social disappearance: crossing the *Kala Pani*, the dreaded "black waters" of the Indian Ocean, entailed a loss of caste and hence a spiritual death. To that end, Britain outfitted the *SS Maharaja*, a high-security prison ship, for the voyage. Sentenced for political crimes, the memoirist Barindra Ghosh (1880–1959) described the hierarchical complex of prisons, barracks, and more open settlements of "mobile camps," huts, and tents he encountered, along with "red-turbaned wardens," bludgeons in hand, who assigned labor gangs with barked orders. Gunfire announced morning roll call, after which prisoners felled trees, grew crops, constructed roads, or twisted ropes. Such conditions reduced prisoners, Ghosh lamented, to brutish beasts and "flock[s] of terrified cattle," who felt "almost dead already."[12] Transformed into a POW camp by Japanese forces in World War II, the "Andaman gulag" lasted until Indian independence in 1947.

Britain and France, the eighteenth century's rival superpowers, maintained the largest carceral networks. But penal colonies spanned the globe. Convicts dredged harbors, loaded warships, and constructed Spanish and Portuguese fortifications in African enclaves like Fernando Po and Cueta, while South American convict stations set a precedent for twentieth-century Latin American states like Chile and Argentina, which exiled political suspects to the Islas Marina, the Juan Fernandez archipelago, or the forbidding Ushuaia peninsula. Starting in the seventeenth century, tsarist Russia likewise established penal colonies in Siberia and on the remote island of Sakhalin (from 1869 to 1906), which later inspired the Soviet Gulag (chap. 4). The Dutch East India Company also housed convicts and local *corvée* workers along with enslaved Indians and Southeast Asians in Jakarta's *kettinggangerskwartier*, or chain gang quarter, while Robben Island, off the coast of southern Africa, constituted a comprehensive carceral archipelago, with a prison, hospital, asylum, and leprosarium. A precursor to apartheid South Africa, which detained Black liberation fighters like Nelson Mandela, this geographically marginal but symbolically central site played a key role in the conquest of Cape Colony, as colonial powers imprisoned Black leaders, including those convicted during and after the Frontier Wars (1779–1879). It was thus a "symbolic container" for the social, medical, and racial "boundary drawing" of the nineteenth century, the historian Harriet Deacon observes.[13] Showcasing synergies between penal transport and other carceral practices, outposts like Mauritius – a Dutch, French, then British colony in the Indian Ocean – likewise exhibited a multilayered, overlapping disciplinary architecture. It served, successively, as a POW camp (1805–15), a convict station (1815–53), and then a vagrant depot for runaway indentured laborers (1864–68), not to mention, much later, as a site of internment for refugees from Hitler's Germany. Such sites, many of them islands demarcated by ocean barriers, thus offered important logistical foundations for the development of modern camps.

Floating Camps

Alongside penal colonies, which housed convicts, vagrants, and political suspects overseas, new domestic institutions concentrated them behind walls and, eventually, wire. As scholars like Michel Foucault have argued, confinement emerged in the eighteenth and nineteenth centuries as the normative method to manage criminality. In this process – longer, more gradual, and less absolute than Foucault acknowledged – ships offered transitional venues. Instruments of both fixity and fluidity, of detention and mobility, they combined ancient practices of exile with modern measures of confinement. Over the course of extended military campaigns, the claustrophobic lower decks of oar-propelled Mediterranean galleys concentrated sentenced criminals and POWs – from Iroquois Chiefs captured in New France in 1686 to "vagrants ... ruffians, rascals" and "all those who led an idle, wandering, and scandalous life" in metropolitan France whom the gendarmerie rounded up, often without due process or formal charge. And while technological advances rendered galley ships obsolete by the late eighteenth century, chain gangs continued to repair ships and construct port infrastructure across southern Europe. Galley slavery, then, was an important ancestor to the prison and the camp. Opened in 1748, the *bagnes* at Toulon, made famous by Victor Hugo's *Les Misérables*, confined some 4,000 prisoners, first on decommissioned galleys themselves and later in communal barracks. After sentencing, prisoners endured 800-kilometer forced marches; upon admission, their heads were shaved and their bodies bathed in communal basins, dressed in uniforms, shackled in chains, and branded *travaux forcés*, "hard labor," with hot iron. "We were made to strip nude so that all parts of our bodies could be examined" and "felt all over, more or less in the manner of a fatted calf one buys at market," a prisoner complained. In this way, barrack guards, organized into military squadrons, separated the "good specimens" from the "scum."[14]

The maritime powers of northern Europe also employed floating prisons. Decommissioned naval hulks moored in Britain and at colonial outposts like Gibraltar and Bermuda interned civilian convicts alongside American and French POWs from the Revolutionary, Seven Years', and Napoleonic Wars (chap. 3). In the words of Charles Dickens, the "black hulk[s]" moored along the river Thames resembled a "wicked Noah's ark," "cribbed and barred and moored by rusty chains."[15] Crowded confines afforded sleeping berths only 18 inches wide, while unsanitary conditions and meager rations caused the rapid outbreak of typhus – a disease that killed 28 percent of inmates in 1778 and that would visit concentrated camp confines for centuries to come. Indeed, more American POWs perished aboard British prison ships than in open battle, a pattern that would be repeated in the camps of future wars. As in southern Europe, however, ship inmates, both war captives and criminal convicts, offered a convenient labor pool for dockside public works, and their management suggested lessons – often by the negative example they set of corruption, inefficiency, and high mortality – in the sanitary regulation and disciplinary organization of space. Quarantine and regular medical inspections introduced in the 1800s would gradually make the "intolerable hulks" more sustainable expedients that Britain would deploy again for POWs during World War I, for Irish paramilitary groups in the 1970s, and even today, for 1,500 asylum-seekers currently billeted on a dilapidated fleet of ferries, barges, and cruise ships docked at Dorset and Liverpool.[16]

Birth of the Prison

Ships, however, were only temporary expedients. As prison hulks and galley barracks filled to capacity, new carceral spaces enclosed the dangerous, idle, and diseased. While modern capitalism, ascendant by the nineteenth century, fostered the mobility of money, labor, and people, anxiety about rootless masses – the so-called "dangerous classes" of an emerging sociological imagination – initiated a spatial reorganization of human life. As city walls crumbled amid flows of rural migrants, a new built environment fostered the modern state's ambitions to know, count, and regulate its population, particularly those from marginalized and subversive groups. The narrow, winding alleys of medieval towns – an environment that privileged local ways of knowing and moving – gave way to wide, straight, numbered roads and standard, serialized infrastructure. Urban planners refurbished disorderly conglomerations according to the meticulous logic of right angles, turning territory and populations into countable, calculable entities legible to state authority. The wide boulevards of Haussmann's Paris in the 1860s exemplified the process, as did slum clearances in colonial cities from Algiers to Bombay. The goal was to fix potentially criminal denizens within a grid of intelligibility. Complementing this new geography of surveillance, a nineteenth-century revolution in government ushered in new forms of expertise as professional bureaucrats and statisticians documented identity and movement, facilitating power and knowledge over bodies and space. As such, the concentration of power by modern governments mirrored the concentration of populations in cities and subsequently – and especially – in enclosed spaces.

Within this larger geography of surveillance and confinement, discrete carceral islands enacted new tactics of discipline and punishment. According to the "principle of agglomeration," problematic groups could be better controlled when organized into a single, concentrated space, where authorities could arrest or regulate movement, "clear up confusion," and "establish calculated distributions," as Foucault observed.[17] By the 1830s, meanwhile, new economies of scale relocated labor from the domestic workshop to the centralized factory, where large masses, crowded together, were organized like soldiers. As "cogs in a machine" and "privates of the industrial army," factory workers were "placed under the command of a perfect hierarchy of officers and sergeants," Karl Marx wrote in 1848, where they performed simple, segmented, and often demeaning tasks. Described by critics as "mitigated prisons" and "houses of terror," such arrangements facilitated discipline and regulation, while inducting workers into the mechanical patterns of the machine age.[18]

Driven into crime, the vagrant and unemployed presented a special danger. If they existed at all, prisons in the Middle Ages and early modern periods were temporary holding cells, detaining debtors along with criminals awaiting sentences of either transportation or execution. With corrupt wardens, porous boundaries, lax security, and onsite pubs and brothels, the general public could come and go as they pleased. Such arrangements changed dramatically, however, with the birth of modern prisons. As northern Europe and America's eastern seaboard industrialized, institutions like Ghent's Maison de Force (1772) and Philadelphia's Walnut Street jail (1790) transformed confinement into a lasting penal strategy. A building spree of brick walls and iron bars soon followed. If the ancient walls of a castle or city gate were once symbols of status and wealth, the new "meticulously sealed wall[s]" of the nineteenth century were "closed in upon the mysterious work of punishment."[19] Above all, the British philosopher Jeremy Bentham's (1748–1832) infamous "panopticon" (figure 1.2) suggested a new model for prison architecture that maximized surveillance and productive labor. State penitentiaries like Millbank (1816) and Pentonville (1842), which served as models for more than fifty similar institutions across Britain and its empire, were only imperfect reproductions of Bentham's blueprints, but their radial wings and central observation halls normalized a general emphasis on methodical observation, along with strict labor regimens that would supposedly facilitate the gradual rehabilitation of inmates. Appropriating the ascetic environment, time discipline, and cellular isolation of the Christian monastery, such facilities dressed prisoners in uniforms and emphasized "thought reform" – a priority at many future concentration camps – through religious instruction and the tight regulation of time.

Enlightenment thinkers and religious reformers favored prisons as humane alternatives to execution and torture – much as future regimes would favor the mass confinement of POWs and captured enemies over wholesale slaughter. In place of bloody spectacles in the open square, governments thus moved punishment behind the rational and regulated walls of state institutions, where humanitarian reformers like Elizabeth Fry (1780–1845), who inaugurated a long tradition of female activists investigating camp and prison conditions, hoped schools and industrial training would transform inmates into productive members of society (or, at the least, into docile factory workers). Nonetheless, an emphasis on deterrence mandated harsh conditions, highlighting tensions between rehabilitation and coercion that would recur throughout the history of twentieth-century camps. Pentonville operated "like a machine," with every minute of the day, from morning bell at 5:30 a.m. to lights out at 9 p.m. precisely regimented. Prisoners were forbidden to speak to each other, and when out on exercise, they tramped in silent rows, wearing brown cloth hoods. At chapel, likewise, separate cubicles, described by inmates as "coffins," further isolated them. Intended to foster individuality and self-reflection, such conditions instead inflicted intense mental trauma. Charles Dickens considered prisons that "tamper[ed] with the mysteries of the brain" to be "worse than any torture of the body."[20] And instead of forging rational subjects, visiting physicians documented delusions, depression, and anxiety among prisoners, who declared "they were visited by the spirits of the dead," that they were being poisoned, or that "there were snakes coiled around the bars of their cells."[21]

Despite the psychological toll, however, prisons, like convict camps and galley slavery, offered ready sources of captive labor. Why, after all, would society banish or execute a body that could "serve the state in a slavery that would be more or less extended according to the nature of his crime," the French legal reformer Antoine-Gaspard Boucher d'Argis reflected in 1781.[22] Like an industrial factory, then, the economic rationalities of work discipline and maximal efficiency governed the prison. Lasting from 6 a.m. to 7 p.m., labor at the Middlesex House of Correction (figure 1.1) consisted of repetitive, menial tasks that prepared inmates for industrial mines or the factory floor.

Harnessing captive labor may have served the economic interests of early capitalism, as prisoners sewed mailbags, broke stones for use in construction work, or picked oakum (unwinding old rope for use in various nautical and industrial applications). But logistical challenges meant labor was often more punitive than productive. The infamous treadwheel, a dour apparatus that compelled inmates to march, incessantly, for five hours a day, suggested continuities with more ancient torture devices. In this way, human labor lost its creative or redemptive qualities: it became a form of punishment and torture. And after long days of work, prison rations, one pound of bread or potatoes and half a pint of soup per day, along with hard wooden planks in place of mattresses, hardly replenished weary bodies.

FIGURE 1.1 The Middlesex House of Correction (*left*) set a template for menial, repetitive taskwork at modern sweatshops and reeducation camps, like those in Xinjiang, China (*right*), where inmates likewise work under regimes of enforced silence (chap. 7). (Source: Henry Mayhew and John Binny, *The Criminal Prisons of London* [1862]; Azamat Imanaliev/Shutterstock.)

Nineteenth-century prisons, then, offer glimpses into the dark side of Enlightenment-era experiments. While prisons differed from concentration camps in key respects, particularly regarding the legal status of inmates, who were usually criminals convicted according to established (albeit sometimes unjust) legal processes, they laid logistical and ideological foundations for future institutions of mass confinement in terms of disciplinary management, professional bureaucracy, economic rationalization, and the supposedly rehabilitative but often punitive and dehumanizing specter of forced labor. Some critics even argue that Bentham's panopticon, with its emphasis on social engineering and its affinity for unrestrained and mechanized power, served as a model for despotic regimes in the twentieth century. Like modern concentration camps, which represented a central institution of authoritarian polities (chaps. 4–6), the industrial prison was a "mechanism of power reduced to its ideal form."[23] And if prisons "tame[d] the fiercest of animals," as the prison reformer Charles Pearson boasted, their utilitarian efficiency left little room for humanity.[24]

BODY POLITICS

The body has long served as a metaphor for society and the state. Drawing from the sociologist Claude Lévi-Strauss, Zygmunt Bauman argues that modern societies pursue two strategies to manage deviance. One is *anthropoemic*, by which outsiders, suspects, or criminals are "vomit[ed] ... from the limits of the orderly world." By contrast, an *anthropophagic* strategy entails "devouring [strangers, internal or external] and then metabolically transforming [them] into a tissue indistinguishable from one's own."[25] While penal colonies pursued the former strategy through spatial banishment, prisons and workhouses temporarily excluded inmates from the body politic, through fences and walls, in order to transform or assimilate them back into society. Concentration camps in the twentieth century would pursue both tactics. The Soviet and Chinese gulags arguably promised reeducation and thus redemption (chaps. 4 and 6). Yet death, whether through Nazi gas chambers (chap. 5) or wanton neglect, also eliminated unwanted matter from the body politic, especially once the settlement of colonial frontiers had closed off any outlets for exile. Do all cultures seek either to assimilate or exclude difference? Are assimilation and elimination two components of a single equation? Can pluralist and multicultural societies accept difference and thus avoid camps and mass confinement?

Workhouses

If prisons accommodated those sentenced by ordinary judicial processes, workhouses detained a more ambiguous group – the suspect, the undesirable, and the potentially dangerous. Early nineteenth-century German states endowed police with extrajudicial powers to detain vagrants, loafers, and jobless wanderers,[26] while in France and Britain vagrancy laws were "coercive mechanisms of questionable legality" that gave state authorities discretionary, even arbitrary, powers to round up "deviants" without formal legal proceedings.[27] Targeting the "criminal poor" as a social rather than juridical category, they thus exhibited a preemptive logic "beyond the frontiers of criminal law."[28] Broad anxieties about the mobility of the "mob" rather than actual evidence submitted before a court of law thus framed efforts to detain vagrants, mendicants, and other rootless or wandering populations, including refugees from the Irish Famine (1845–52) and East European Jews fleeing antisemitic riots in the Russian Empire (1881–82). In an age when political citizenship – the right to vote – extended only to those who owned property, the poor existed in a semicolonial relationship to the rich. Amid the pervasive class warfare of the industrial age, then, workhouses offered tools of counterinsurgency against Europe's own poor. The *Book of the Bastiles*, an 1841 publication condemning workhouses as instruments of "that unholy war against the old, the helpless, the bedridden, the broken-hearted," speaks to their coercive function.[29] Or, as the playwright and social reformer George Bernard Shaw put it, workhouses took the "insurrectionary edge" off poverty.[30]

London's Bridewell Palace, refurbished in 1553 as a "house of correction" for homeless children and "disorderly women," was one of Europe's oldest workhouses. As authorities conceived vagrancy and unemployment as social problems, German towns like Württemberg followed suit, converting monasteries and abandoned castles into collection points for beggars and prostitutes, while Nuremberg repurposed an old pesthouse, used to accommodate medieval lepers and bubonic plague victims, to combat a "pandemic" of beggars.[31] Such arrangements existed across the continent, though in the early modern period they were especially common in northern European states, which did not employ galley slaves and which lacked access to overseas colonies for transportation. In landlocked eighteenth-century Vienna, for example, a "committee of chastity" arrested "a wide variety of deviants," including "beggars, thieves, poachers, [and] gypsies," as well as prostitutes and "unruly children," removing them to what contemporaries called a "human dump."[32] But similar institutions emerged across the continent, from Barcelona's Royal Hospice, which rounded up able-bodied vagrants, to Moscow's workhouse, founded by Catherine the Great in 1782.

As rapid industrialization and urbanization in the first decades of the nineteenth century presaged intensified counteroffensives against the impoverished and displaced, workhouses expanded. Emerging social vocabularies like "dangerous classes" and "habitual criminals" marked vagrants and prostitutes for social exclusion, while growing bureaucratic sophistication replaced earlier, ad hoc almshouses, normally managed by parishes or Christian charities, with new, centrally organized, and professionally managed institutions. By eliminating "outdoor" charity, landmark legislation like Britain's 1834 New Poor Law, established in the wake of industrial riots and revolutionary violence across Europe in the 1830s, concentrated all public assistance within the onerous confines of the "union workhouse." In the next decade, Britain built more than five hundred such structures according to standardized blueprints. Other countries, from the United States to Austria-Hungary and from Mexico to Japan, built similar facilities, though arrangements were often more improvised than in Britain. Germany's largest workhouse, located in the east Berlin suburb of

Rummelsburg and built in 1879, consisted of purpose-built brick barracks enclosed by a perimeter wall, though others, like Dresden's workhouse, appropriated old farm buildings and stockades.[33]

Along with human bodies, nineteenth-century workhouses concentrated administrative control in the hands of professional boards of guardians, who regulated inmates with military discipline. Indeed, ex-army officers, with their experience giving orders and their "ability to control large numbers of barely subordinate paupers," were favored superintendents.[34] The use of workhouses as POW camps in World War I, Nazi concentration camps in World War II, and Gulag outposts in Soviet-occupied East Germany suggest further continuities. According to the principle of "less eligibility," meanwhile, Victorian workhouses were uncomfortable by conscious design. "Our intention," proponents maintained, "is to make the workhouses as like prisons as possible" and "to establish therein a discipline so severe and repulsive as to make them a terror to the poor."[35] Rituals of admission initiated inmates into lives of discipline and dehumanization. After walking through the "archway of tears," as workhouse gates were known, inmates entered an austere space of sober slogans: "My Hand is Severe but my Intention Benevolent" (in Amsterdam), "I live by work, I am punished by work" (in Hamburg), or simply "God is Good."

A compartmentalized architecture classified inmates according to age, sex, and ability to work. Families were separated in the process: mothers and children were punished for attempting to find and speak to each other outside permitted "daily interviews." Segregated from society, regimes of silence at mealtimes and during work further isolated inmates from each other, though at night workhouse residents slept in communal quarters modeled on army barracks – an arrangement that existed in tension with the individualism of the age and that presaged the denial of rights to those considered unworthy of their responsibility. After intrusive lice inspections, inmates bathed in communal tubs, a baptism of sorts into new disciplinary regimes. Children's hair was cut short, and uniforms of coarse material prevented inmates from leaving without being identified. Typically, however, residents could leave upon formal application, an important distinction from prisons and other carceral institutions. In some cases, uniforms were also markers of moral and sexual shame – in Bristol, for example, unmarried pregnant women wore red dresses, while prostitutes wore yellow. Such policies revived practices of previous centuries that forced poor relief recipients to wear identifiable armbands or badges in public.

Pervading metaphors of disease, galvanized by the ascendant authority of professional medicine, helped contemporaries conceive workhouse

confinement as a social cleansing operation. "Society is ... like a popu-
lous city where signs of the plague have appeared," one French reformer
feared: "it cries out loudly for a lazaretto." Workhouses, accordingly,
would place the "*bacillus* of vice" under social and medical quarantine;
its walls would be a "cordon sanitaire" against "criminal contagion."[36]
Yet while strict moral dualisms – between clean and unclean, industrious and idle, healthy and diseased – patterned workhouse management,
and while inmates complained they were treated "well-nigh like lepers,"
crowded workhouse confines proved remarkably unhealthy. Dampness
and cold caused consumption and respiratory ailments, particularly,
one observer in Britain remarked, for the "many poor blacks" and other
racial minorities interned.[37] At Andover, rations in the 1840s were so
inadequate that inmates were forced to gnaw marrow from putrid bones
they were crushing to make fertilizer, while in North Dublin an appalling
63 percent of workhouse children died in 1841 – a mortality rate that
compared unfavorably, critics contended, to the "pestilential hold of a
slave ship."[38]

Physical and sexual assault also prevailed. A 13-year-old girl confined
at Hoo Union was forced to "lie upon a table," and "t[ake] her clothes off"
while a master "beat her with a rod made of a birch broom."[39] Some entered
the workhouse as "fallen women"; for others, moral debasement was the
result rather than the cause of their internment. Elsewhere, superintendents
punished children by hanging them in burlap sacks from the ceiling or
thrashing them with stinging nettles. Such horrors, products of both sad-
ism and neglect, indicate the abuses that often occur in what the sociologist
Erving Goffman called "total institutions," isolated and enclosed social
systems where inmates, marked as abject or inferior, are placed under the
absolute power of presiding authorities.[40] Similar atrocities would occur in
many future camps and other carceral venues, not least in residential schools
in North America (chap. 2).

THE CLEAN AND UNCLEAN

Metaphors of contagion framed the detention of workhouse inmates.
But fears of disease generated their own carceral outposts. Victorian hospitals concentrated medical care away from the home, often holding patients against their will, while lock hospitals, both in Europe and across

the colonial world, detained suspected prostitutes as a preemptive measure, subjecting them to invasive cavity searches. In a culture that likened
"cleanliness to godliness," diseased bodies also recalled the social exclusion of more ancient sites of confinement, such as leper colonies.

Camps were also tools of epidemiological policing. Canvas tents,
arranged geometrically, accommodated tuberculosis patients, where
they could recover in the open air, while the army habitually segregated
cholera "suspects" (to use an official term) in tented quarantine camps
where they could be monitored for disease. Much later, "medical
concentration camps," as they were called in the 1930s, also helped
contain and monitor sleeping sickness in colonial Africa. Bubonic
plague, however, generated the nineteenth century's most expansive
quarantine camps, particularly in the colonial world, which Europeans
classified as especially dirty and disordered. Likening plague to "an
invading army," the surgeon-general of British India seconded six army
regiments to perform urban cleansing operations during the 1896
outbreak in Bombay. Conducting house searches "like surprise military
raids," flying columns captured potentially infectious "suspects" and
marched them to purpose-built suburban camps consisting of tents
and barracks surrounded by guardhouses and bramble fences. And as
plague reached South Africa, soldiers with "fixed bayonets" encircled
"a mass of aborigines, numbering nearly a thousand, with the glitter of
steel." Though medical science ostensibly mandated the quarantine of
"fugitives" and "fleeing pestifiers," European residents (equally capable
of carrying plague) were categorically exempt from health regulations,
while natives "known to live in a style of superior civilization" were
trusted simply to isolate at home. Less than 1 percent of those detained
in quarantine camps exhibited actual plague symptoms; rather, they
were interned "by reason of their appearance."[41]

Plague camps provided logistical inspiration for future concentration
camps during the South African (or Anglo-Boer) War (chap. 3); campsites
in places like Soweto would form the nucleus for racially segregated
apartheid-era townships (chap. 7); and the racist dimensions of disease
mitigation motivated the detention of Haitian refugees at Guantanamo
Bay under the suspicion they carried AIDS (chap. 8). How, ultimately, does
medical quarantine, and the attendant politics of race and class, relate to
other camps discussed in this book?

Detention Colonies

As prisons and workhouses proliferated, anxieties about demoralization in crowded urban settings generated new experiments in the final decades of the nineteenth century in removing the "dangerous classes" to open-air villages and camplike communities. In the 1890s, the industrial philanthropist George Pullman billeted workers in a planned suburb attached to his factory in Chicago, while social reformers, including women like Jane Addams and Octavia Hill, enforced strict behavioral standards in return for sanitary accommodation at inner-city housing blocks. Yet the perceived benefits of fresh air and outdoor living, coupled with a stress on personal hygiene and self-discipline, motivated a move away from claustrophobic industrial centers. Dispersal to the countryside thus complemented the dynamic of concentration.

Founded in 1840, France's agricultural penal colony at Mettray pioneered efforts to transform "ignorant and dangerous boys into good industrious and useful members of society."[42] Modeled on an army camp — authorities organized the day with bugle calls and required inmates to shave their heads, salute wardens, and parade in uniform every Sunday — the facility contracted agricultural labor to outside firms by day, while workers returned to their barracks at night. Studied closely by a transnational network of penal experts, Mettray offered a model for similar arrangements in Europe and North America. Following national unification in 1871, Germany likewise established a network of "detention colonies," which incarcerated vagrants at rates eight times higher than in Britain,[43] while Belgium's Merxplas complex, replete with factories and workshops built with "vagabond labor," enforced military surveillance over 5,000 inmates in a "penitentiary atmosphere." "An absolute despot," the superintendent governed with "severe paternalism," one observer noted.[44] Concentrating young men and boys, labor colonies disseminated a militarized version of masculinity premised on strength, honor, and obedience. Redeployed to domestic territory, they also fulfilled colonial fantasies to cultivate and occupy marginal land while "civilizing" their inhabitants, the anthropologist Ann Stoler points out.[45]

The rehabilitative agenda stemmed from modern Enlightenment notions that humanity was pliable, that social environments could improve the individual. Self-contained communities like the "phalanstery," conceived in the 1830s by the French socialist Charles Fourier and inspired by rectangular military formations, or phalanxes, stemmed from utopian efforts to improve human life. Yet by the end of the nineteenth century, reformist optimism gave way to darker visions. Economic crises in the 1880s radicalized social commentary. Soon, an "insurgent multitude, … an army of the unemployed, … prey[ed] on the community, infesting our roads, damaging our property, … assaulting our women, [and] breeding disease," the American criminologist Edmond Kelly wrote.[46] To prevent crime and forestall revolutionary socialism, proponents advocated preemptive segregation in strictly bounded colonies. Meanwhile, a creeping xenophobia, marked by immigration restrictions like America's Chinese Exclusion Act (1882) and Britain's Aliens Act (1905), associated vagrants and paupers with "dirty, destitute, diseased, verminous, and criminal foreigner[s]" – including large numbers of Jews who had fled religious violence in the Russian Empire in 1881–82 and 1903–6.[47] As racist tropes increasingly described Europe's social underclass, the emerging "sciences" of eugenics and social Darwinism prompted social investigators like Henry Mayhew to identify "criminal races" with defective intelligence and distinctive physiognomy, while William Booth, founder of the Salvation Army, conflated race and class in 1890 when he compared London's "urban jungle," inhabited by "primitive" and "savage tribes," with the "dark continent" of Africa. In France, the "savage customs" of urban gangs like the "Apache" apparently resembled those of Native Americans, while the Italian criminologist Cesare Lombroso described "street Arabs" as "born criminals" driven by innate violence.[48] German psychiatrists likewise used the term *asozial* in the late 1890s to describe genetically defective "parasites" who existed in enmity with society. Many of them, the noted sociologist Max Weber observed, were ethnic Poles and Slavs, who resembled the "half-breed" populations of colonial North America.[49]

As Europe's social vocabulary forged existential distinctions between "us" and "them," "civilized" and "savage," "friend" and "enemy" (to quote the German political theorist Carl Schmidt[50]), authorities embraced harsher measures. Recognizing that "all men are not equal," the "militant pastor" Osborn Jay called for preventive measures in 1896 to segregate London's "peculiar [and] separate class" of "semi-criminals."[51] The British criminologist Wilson Dawson concurred: "social parasites" should, in his words, be "exterminated," if not through actual genocide – though that possibility remained latent – then by forced relocation to "detention colonies" where they would be compelled to labor under a severer discipline than prisons and workhouses.[52] Opened in the 1890s, British facilities at Hadleigh and Hollesley Bay detained the "incorrigibly lazy,"[53] while Mettray, once "a

progressive and utilitarian project, ... grew increasingly carceral and punitive," by the *fin de siècle*.[54]

As doubts spread about the limits of liberal reform and rehabilitation,
Germany also embraced more strident language. To prevent a "plague of
beggars" from "roam[ing] about" in "small troops" and "plundering the
... village as well as the ... city," early-twentieth-century criminologists
recommended "asocials" be detained indefinitely and treated as "serfs or
slaves," regardless of "whether [such measures] offended against the penal
law."[55] The segregation of problem groups, who were criminalized but not
necessarily convicted, thus embraced the extrajudicial logic of preventive detention, while the use of temporary, open-air barracks, located at
a distance from towns and cities, departed from metropolitan prisons but
foreshadowed future concentration camps. Such schemes also facilitated
internal colonization: in Prussia, work colonies appropriated the land of
30,000 Polish peasants, who were forcibly deported in 1885.[56] German legal
policy did not change significantly until 1933, but the tangible radicaliza-
tion of discourse paved the way for more menacing developments. In the
future, nineteenth-century workhouses and labor colonies would be transformed into Nazi *Konzentrationslager*, while "police camps" in Italy, like
Tre Fontane, which detained vagabonds in chains, would form the basis for
Mussolini's concentration camps (chap. 5).[57]

Global Confinement

As European ambitions spread overseas, so did carceral infrastructure. By the
end of the nineteenth century, at the high noon of European Empire, confinement was an essential feature of colonial rule, strung together in an expansive
penal chain from Australia to Algiers. The writer George Orwell, himself
a police official in British Burma in the 1920s, noted that prisons, as both
outposts of European civilization and symbols of colonial repression, were
the most central and impressive structures of any colonial town.[58] In Africa,
where Indigenous punishments included banishment, mutilation, or tying
offenders to logs or trees, but where confinement traditionally was unknown,
prisons were often the earliest examples of colonial architecture. In French
Indochina (1887–1954), likewise, prisons appeared "prior to virtually any
other colonial institution" – a fact twentieth-century communist and anticolonial leaders would condemn, even as they appropriated them for their own use
(chap. 6).[59] In 1904, American colonizers in the Philippines likewise erected
a model penal farm at Iwahig island, previously a place of banishment under

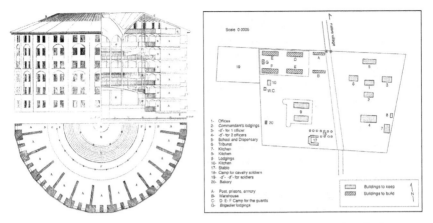

FIGURE 1.2 In contrast to the European panopticon (*left*), prisons in colonial Africa and Asia resembled "camps," with perimeter walls enclosing standalone communal barracks, like at Dori, Niger (*right*). (Source: Wikimedia Commons; Bernault, *History of Prison in Africa*, 17.)

Spanish occupation. Divided into three classes and apportioned privileges or restraints accordingly, convicts grew cash crops for export.

In some cases, these "colonial bastilles" appropriated the architecture of Bentham's panopticon. Complementing its open-air huts and compounds, the Andaman Islands' "cellular jail," opened in 1906 to incarcerate India's most prominent political prisoners, followed a classic panoptic design with solitary cells, a central tower, and radial wings. As the proliferation of carceral institutions became an iconic, though ironic, symbol of civilizational progress, modernizing administrations in Asia and Latin America also adopted Western models. Inspired by French templates, the Ottoman Empire constructed Benthamite cells and agricultural labor colonies, while Beijing Prison No. 1 explicitly emulated London's Pentonville: it enforced silence during meals, emphasized reform through industrial training, and provided lectures on moral and religious topics. Behind the lecturer's platform were portraits of Confucius, Laozi, Mohammed, Jesus, and the British prison reformer John Howard (1726–90) – a striking example of cultural syncretism. Foreign visitors were impressed by the ability of Chinese officials to establish and manage industrial institutions, and they lauded the prison's "point system," which added or removed privileges based on assessed behavior – an early basis for the "social credit system" that exercises totalitarian control over China today (chaps. 6 and 7).[60]

Colonial confinement, however, differed from metropolitan models. Instead of brick-and-mortar panopticons, most Indian prisons consisted of sheds and barracks, constructed with cheap, local material and surrounded by guardhouses and perimeter walls. The single-story dormitories of Jamaican workhouses likewise exhibited a distinctly tropical architecture, while prisons in Mauritius placed inmates in open-air huts of dried grass and mud walls scattered across the island. Such architectural arrangements, approximating "camps" more than prisons, reflected local priorities and colonial dynamics. Though France was a leader of nineteenth-century penal reform, its colonial prisons (like Dori, Niger, figure 1.2) never employed cellular or panoptic structures, and they held the majority of inmates in undifferentiated communal barracks. Political economies help explain the difference: in the absence of disciplined proletarian workers and cash economies, convict laborers, billeted in *al fresco* camps on public works projects, proved more compatible with labor demands in the developing and colonial world. Herbert Horatio Kitchener (1850–1916), a man who would play a prominent role in the formation of wartime "concentration camps" in South Africa (chap. 3), criticized panoptic penitentiaries in Egypt because they deprived authorities of extramural labor for canal work, road construction, and cotton plantations. Drawing inspiration from "standing prison camps in India" along with traditional practices of *corvée*, however, mobile work camps offered convict labor pools for the infrastructure projects of a modernizing colonial regime.[61]

The authoritarian context of colonial rule likewise obviated any objective to reform or rehabilitate inmates or forge rational, self-governing citizens. Indeed, economic profit, empire's *raison d'etre*, depended upon political despotism, while the tactics of "divide and rule" motivated authorities to maintain an "enduring antagonism between different segments of colonial society." In Europe's Asian and African colonies, the distinction between "us" and "them," the resort to arbitrary detention, and the use of corporal punishment were norms rather than exceptions. The tropical prison, then, "did not seek to separate lawful citizens from marginals and delinquents" but "aimed to reinforce the social and political separation of the races." If European society criminalized the idle and itinerant, often denigrating them with racial and imperial tropes, colonial rule "assigned the mark of illegality" to entire races dominated on a collective basis.[62] As such, paramilitary police forces rounded up populations in restive districts that resisted the political, economic, and military domination of white society, while legal courts facilitated the hegemony of the ruling power more than the rights of the individual. Though European workhouses and agricultural colonies applied dubious vagrancy laws to incarcerate social suspects, the despotism of empire enabled a wholesale denial of rights. Once confined, inmates found communal barracks rather than individual cells, along with traditional forms of bodily punishment like whipping and public shaming that had long been abandoned in European jails. In Nigeria, for example, women were stripped naked and beaten in a gendered display of colonial power, while in Kenya, which claimed the highest rate of incarceration in colonial Africa, corporal punishment inflicted on African men, discursively infantilized as "boys," was legally institutionalized in 1897.[63] An entire repertoire of ominous devices, the *kiboko*, the *sjambok*, and the cat-o'-nine tails became fearsome symbols of colonial punishment, designed to inflict pain on the body rather than rehabilitate the soul.

Colonial prisons thus appropriated and disseminated a basic culture of confinement. But their regimes of physical punishment and forced labor exceeded the norms of European incarceration, while their collective living arrangements and the billeting of prisoners in makeshift huts and barracks pioneered elements of mass confinement that would be replicated by twentieth-century dictators, who treated conquered populations in analogous ways to colonial masses devoid of rights. Though European prisons and workhouses imposed inhuman living conditions and assembled new tactics of discipline, surveillance, and rehabilitation, and while contemporaries recognized class warfare as a low-intensity guerrilla conflict that demanded indiscriminate and sometimes extrajudicial measures, the military conquest of Africa, Asia, and the Americas opened alarming new possibilities. It is to the imperial world that we now turn.

Notes

1 E.P. Thompson, *The Making of the English Working Class* (New York: Vintage, 1966), 219.

2 Michel Foucault, *Discipline & Punish: Birth of the Prison*, trans. Alan Sheridan (New York: Pantheon Books, 1995), 76–77.

3 G.R.W. Baxter, *The Book of the Bastiles: The History of the Working of the New Poor Law* (London: John Stephens, 1841), 386. (Emphasis mine.)

4 Michael Ignatieff, *A Just Measure of Pain: The Penitentiary in the Industrial Revolution, 1750–1850* (New York: Pantheon Books, 1978), 16.

5 Robert Curiel and Bernard Dov Cooperman, *The Venetian Ghetto* (New York: Rizzoli, 1990), 20.

6 Primo Levi, *Survival in Auschwitz*, trans. Stuart Woolf (New York: Touchstone, 1996), 19.

7 E.P. Thompson, *Whigs and Hunters: The Origins of the Black Act* (New York: Pantheon Books, 1975), 211.

8 André Zysberg, "From the Galleys to Hard Labor Camps: Essay on a Long-Lasting Penal Institution," in *The Emergence of Carceral Institutions: Prisons, Galleys and Lunatic Asylums, 1550–1900*, ed. Pieter Spierenburg (Rotterdam: Erasmus Universiteit, 1984), 118–9.

9 "Le Bagne en Guyane," accessed May 21, 2022, https://guyanologie.fr/Bagne.php.

10 Jan Morris cited in Tim Causer, "'The Worst Types of Sub-human Beings'? The Myth and Reality of the Convicts of the Norfolk Island Penal Settlement, 1835–1855," *Islands of History: Proceedings of the 25th Anniversary Conference of Professional Historians Association* (Sydney: Anchor Books, 2011), 3; M.G. Britts, *The Commandants: The Tyrants Who Ruled Norfolk Island* (London: Rigby Publishers, 1980), 158.

11 Tim Causer, "The Norfolk Island Penal Station, the Panopticon, and Alexander Maconochie's and Jeremy Bentham's Theories of Punishment," *Panopticons in Australia* 19 (2021): 21.

12 Barindra Kumar Ghosh, *The Tale of My Exile: Twelve Years in the Andamans* (Pondicherry: Arya Publications, 1922), 31–2.

13 Harriet Deacon, "Patterns of Exclusion on Robben Island, 1654–1992," in *Isolation: Places and Practices of Exclusion*, ed. Carolyn Strange and Alison Bashford (London: Routledge, 2003), 153, 155.

14 Zysberg, "Hard Labor Camps," 83–84, 92.

15 Charles Dickens, *Great Expectations* (London: Chapman and Hall, 1861), 82.

16 Pippa Crerar and Rajeev Syal, "Home Office to Acquire Fleet of Ships to House Asylum-Seekers," *The Guardian*, May 1, 2023, www.theguardian.com/uk-news/2023/may/01/uk-planning-redundant-cruise-ships-house-asylum-seekers.

17 Foucault, *Discipline & Punish*, 219.

18 Marx cited in Enzo Traverso, *The Origins of Nazi Violence*, trans. Janet Lloyd (New York: New Press, 2003), 28.

19 Foucault, *Discipline & Punish*, 116.

20 Charles Dickens, *American Notes for General Circulation* (Paris: Baudry's European Library, 1842), 142.

21 Hilary Marland and Catherine Cox, "Prisoners, Insanity and the Pentonville Model Prison Experiment," *Exploring the History of Prisoner Health*, https://histprisonhealth.com/arts-projects/disorder-contained-a-theatrical-examination-of-madness-prison-and-solitary-confinement/disorder-contained-background-reading/prisoners-insanity-and-the-pentonville-model-prison-experiment/.

22 Quoted in Foucault, *Discipline & Punish*, 109.

23 Foucault, *Discipline & Punish*, 205.

24 *Pennsylvania Journal of Prison Discipline and Philanthropy* 6, no. 2 (1851): 75.

25 Zygmunt Bauman, *Postmodernity and Its Discontents* (New York: New York University Press, 1997), 18.

26 Beate Althammer, "Vagabonds in the German Empire: Mobility, Unemployment and the Transformation of Social Policies (1870–1914)," in *Poverty and Welfare in Modern German History*, ed. Raphael Lutz (New York: Berghahn, 2017), 63.

27 Julie Kimber, "Poor Laws: A Historiography of Vagrancy in Australia," *History Compass* 11, no. 8 (2013): 538, 541.

28 Foucault, *Discipline & Punish*, 297.

29 Baxter, *Book of Bastiles*, 244.

30 Bernard Shaw quoted in *The Cry for Justice: An Anthology of the Literature of Social Protest*, ed. Upton Sinclair (Philadelphia: Winston, 1915), 402.

31 Joel F. Harrington, "Escape from the Great Confinement: The Genealogy of a German Workhouse," *Journal of Modern History* 71, no. 2 (1999): 309.

32 Mary Gibson and Ilaria Poerio, "Modern Europe, 1750–1950," in *A Global History of Convicts and Penal Colonies*, ed. Clare Anderson (London: Bloomsbury, 2020), 343.

33 Markus Wahl, "The Workhouse Dresden-Lebuen After 1945: A Microstudy of Local Continuities in Postwar East Germany," *Journal of Contemporary History* 55, no. 1 (2018): 120–44.

34 Gerard O'Brien, "Workhouse Management in Pre-Famine Ireland," *Proceedings of the Royal Irish Academy* 86, no. 3 (1986): 125; Norman Longmate, *The Workhouse: A Social History* (London: Pimlico, 2003), 101–2.

35 Thompson, *Making of the English Working Class*, 267.

36 Ignatieff, *Just Measure of Pain*, 61–2.

37 Longmate, *Workhouse*, 207.

38 O'Brien, "Workhouse Management," 128; Baxter, *Book of Bastiles*, 583.

39 Baxter, *Book of Bastiles*, 156.

40 Erving Goffman, *Asylums: Essays on the Condition of the Social Situation of Mental Patients and Other Inmates* (New York: Anchor, 1961).

41 Aidan Forth, *Barbed-Wire Imperialism: Britain's Empire of Camps, 1876–1903* (Berkeley: University of California, 2017), 78, 89, 94, 83.

42 Stephen Toth, *Mettray: A History of France's Most Venerated Carceral Institution* (Ithaca: Cornell University Press, 2019), 1.

43 Althammer, "Vagabonds," 62.

44 Edmond Kelly, *The Elimination of the Tramp* (New York: G.P. Putnam's Sons, 1908), 20; Wilson Carlile, *The Continental Outcast: Land Colonies and Poor Law Relief* (T. Fisher Unwin, 1906), 10.

45 Ann Stoler, *Duress: Imperial Durabilities in Our Times* (Durham: Duke University Press, 2016), chap. 3.

46 Kelly, *Elimination of the Tramp*, xviii.

47 *Manchester Evening Chronicle*, cited in Ed Mynott, "Nationalism, Racism and Immigration Control: From Anti-racism to Anti-capitalism," in *From Immigration Controls to Welfare Controls*, ed. Steve Cohen, Beth Humphries, and Ed Mynott (London: Routledge, 2002), 14.

48 William Booth, *In Darkest England and the Way Out* (London: Salvation Army, 1890); Daniel Pick, *Faces of Degeneration: A European Disorder, 1848–1914* (Cambridge: Cambridge University Press, 1989).

49 Barbara Arneil, *Domestic Colonies: The Turn Inward to Colony* (Oxford: Oxford University Press, 2017), 70.

50 Carl Schmidt, *The Concept of the Political*, trans. George Schwab (Chicago: University of Chicago Press, 2007).

51 "To Check the Survival of the Unfit: A New Scheme by the Rev. Osborn Jay ... for Sending the Submerged to a Penal Settlement," *The London*, March 12, 1896.

52 William Harbutt Dawson, *The Vagrancy Problem: The Case for Measures of Restraint for Tramps, Loafers, and Unemployables* (London: P.S. King & Son, 1910), 62.

53 Arneil, *Colonies*, 56–66.

54 Toth, *Mettray*, 195.

55 Althammer, "Vagabonds," 69, 71.

56 Arneil, *Colonies*, 69.

57 Gibson and Poerio, "Modern Europe," 347.

58 George Orwell, *Burmese Days* (1934; Boston: Mariner Books, 1974), 18.

59 Peter Zinoman, *The Colonial Bastille: A History of Imprisonment in Vietnam, 1862–1940* (Berkeley: University of California Press, 2001), 29.

60 Frank Dikötter, "The Promise of Repentance: The Prison in Modern China," in *Cultures of Confinement: A History of the Prison in Africa, Asia, and Latin America*, ed. Frank Dikötter and Ian Brown (Ithaca: Cornell University Press, 2007), 297.

61 Anthony Gorman, "Regulation, Reform and Resistance in the Middle Eastern Prison," in Dikötter and Brown, *Cultures of Confinement*, 118–21.

62 Florence Bernault, "The Politics of Enclosure in Colonial and Pre-colonial Africa," in *A History of Prison and Confinement in Africa*, ed. Florence Bernault (Portsmouth, NH: Heinemann, 2003), 16.

63 Paul Ocobock, "Spare the Rod, Spoil the Colony: Corporal Punishment, Colonial Violence, and Generational Authority in Kenya, 1897–1952," *International Journal of African Historical Studies* 45, no. 1 (2012): 37, 33, 29–30.

2 | Colonial Compartments: Slave Plantations and Native Reservations

As Western nations developed the rudiments of democracy at home, they pursued conquest overseas. The growth of national identity in the nineteenth century was premised, in part, on an encounter with racial and cultural difference – with others who could be excluded from the community and consigned, very often, to camps. Colonies were authoritarian environments where populations marked as racially and culturally inferior lacked basic civil rights, and where the rule of law did not prevail – or else where it unduly favored the interests of conquerors. At times, empires were lawless spaces in which settlers could run riot. Enthralled by wide-open living spaces (invariably already occupied by native populations), the quest for romantic adventure often generated a bloodletting inconceivable in Europe. Yet empires, according to the political theorist Hannah Arendt, were also venues that assembled many features of modern statecraft. Projecting power at a distance over vast territories and unfamiliar populations, Western states developed bureaucratic and organizational tactics – many of them codified in manuals and official publications – necessary to extract labor and resources, to conquer and occupy land, and to organize bodies over space. And as venues for what Arendt called "administrative massacres," violence and confinement in overseas colonies became matters of policy.[1]

Above all, empires were fertile grounds for the development of racism. As early as the sixteenth century, Europeans pondered the humanity (or perceived lack thereof) of the Indigenous peoples they encountered in Africa and the Americas. Enlightenment philosophers like John Locke (1632–1704) and classical liberals like Alexis de Tocqueville (1805–59) distinguished between nomadic tribes who inhabited or moved through land and settled Europeans who "improved" and therefore rightfully occupied it through the imposition of fenced, geometric plots. "Civilizing missions"

that introduced natives to the discipline of sedentary labor, along with genocidal campaigns to erase the Indigenous presence entirely, were dual legacies of such thinking. Meanwhile, the intensification of transatlantic slavery
in the eighteenth century presaged the development of hardening forms
of biological racism – the idea that dark skin was a marker of intellectual
and biological deficiency rather than cultural or environmental difference.
Such ideas facilitated ethnic cleansing, forced migrations, and the violent
exploitation of native populations. To the extent that "inferior races" were
permitted to survive, they would do so in segregated plantations or native
reservations, providing labor when useful, and swept physically from the
path of progress when necessary.

A World Divided into Compartments

Colonial societies were "world[s] divided into compartments."[2] Such were
the words of Frantz Fanon (1925–61), a Caribbean-born psychiatrist and
Algerian independence activist. Fanon's statement refers, in part, to the
mental walls constructed by imperial governance: the psychic barriers
internalized by imperial rulers and subjects alike that designate some human
beings as different from and inferior to others. But mental enclosures had
material manifestations. Upon founding Kaapstad (Cape Town) on the
southern coast of Africa in 1660, the Dutch colonist Jan van Riebeeck
planted a "bitter almond" hedge (*Brabejum stellatifolium*) to demarcate
colonial society from the "wilds" of Africa; intertwined branches covered
in thorns, coupled with wooden fences and rudimentary watchtowers, disrupted Khoikhoi grazing routes and ultimately secured the nascent colony –
initially little more than a military encampment – from native reprisals. And
as the colony's labor demands grew, a nearby slave lodge detained Africans
behind stone walls. Thus began the opening chapter in a long history of
native detention and dispossession that would ultimately develop into one
of world history's most destructive systems of racial segregation – that of
apartheid South Africa (chap. 7).

Van Riebeeck's almond hedge was hardly unique. In the colony of New
Amsterdam (now New York City), Peter Stuyvesant erected a wall in 1652
(along what is now Wall Street, still a privileged site of settler power) to
keep Indigenous people out. And in the East Indies, natives required
passes to enter the Dutch colonial city of Batavia (now Jakarta, Indonesia),
while Chinese merchants inhabited a street gated at both ends, in imitation of Amsterdam's Jew Street. In the empire, ancient practices of social

segregation, like medieval ghettos, found new applications that continued into modern times. As the Netherlands' greatest imperial rival, Britain also built walls. Inaugurating a string of "plantations" starting in Ireland and spreading west to America, English settlers planted trees or hedges, establishing roots in the soil and symbolically branding land as private property to be cultivated and enclosed. In early modern Ireland, a "ditch, raised some ten or twelve feet from the ground, with a hedge of thorn on the outer side" segregated "civilized Britons" from the "wild ... barbarous and most filthy Irish."[3] Such was the Irish pale (from the Latin *palus*, a stake or fence). To live beyond it was, literally, to be "beyond the pale." Imperial Russia's "pale of settlement" likewise excluded social undesirables, Jews in particular, from residing in the Russian and Christian heartland. Such practices had ancient roots: Hadrian's wall demarcated "civilized" Roman England from Scottish "savagery," while Chinese fortifications, built with unfree labor, compartmentalized Han China from "barbarian" tribes. Yet as European powers embraced a new, modern age of empire, fences and walls proliferated exponentially.

When British settlers encountered Indigenous peoples in the New World, they brought Old World prejudices with them. As Hugh Peter of Massachusetts explained in 1646, "the wild Irish and the Indians do not much differ." And as in Ireland, walls emerged as symbols of civilization that would divide a privileged European polity from an Indigenous hinterland. An exclusive "city on a hill" required fortification, and Mayflower pilgrims built their first stone wall in the winter of 1620. Responding to Powhatan attacks, meanwhile, Virginia colonists razed villages and crops, driving natives from the Chesapeake peninsula. A six-mile pale fortified with blockhouses soon emerged as mutual interdependence gave way to violent encounters and genocidal rhetoric: "Extirpate this execrable race," the army officer and colonial governor Jeffrey Amherst demanded in 1763.[4] Elihu Yale, the former governor of Connecticut (and founder, like Amherst, of an elite New England college), exported segregationist practices still further overseas. As president of the East India Company's Fort St. George in the late seventeenth century, he built a mud and later stone wall to divide the city of Chennai into "black town" and "white town."[5]

In Spanish America, where colonists debated whether "New World" natives were "natural-born slaves" or full human beings, colonization likewise oscillated between the competing demands of humane intervention, economic exploitation, and religious (and increasingly racial) prejudice. Decades after Columbus's initial contact, the Spanish Empire forcibly

concentrated South America's Indigenous population into monitored settlements or *reducciones* (reductions). In the process, colonists burned native
settlements to the ground and forcibly relocated 1.5 million to fenced
barrios like the walled El Cercado quarter of Lima, Peru, or to "new villages" administered by the Catholic Church. Jesuit missionaries genuinely
believed Christian conversion would save souls. But the billeting of natives
in geometric barracks, built according to uniform templates, also facilitated
the work of counting, taxation, and control. And diseases spread rapidly
among concentrated converts, portending demographic catastrophe and the
destruction of Indigenous cultural and economic networks.[6]

Though religion motivated imperial conquest, so did economic gain –
from silver, gold, cotton, sugar, rubber, and later oil. In Karl Marx's words,
"the discovery of gold and silver in America [and] the extirpation, enslavement, and entombment in mines of the aboriginal population" signaled
"the rosy dawn of the era of capitalist production."[7] To this end, *reducciones*
served as convenient depots for billeting, organizing, and extracting native
labor. Elsewhere, densely populated native villages were picked clean of
human life as military generals conscripted Indigenous peoples into forced
and later tributary labor in mines and plantations. Conditions were horrendous. One Spaniard witnessed a "murderous journey" of 7,000 natives who
marched 100 miles to the silver mines of Potosí (in modern-day Bolivia)
where they worked "twelve hours a day, going down ... to where night
is perpetual ... and the air thick and ill-smelling." As long as the supply
of brute labor appeared unending, it was cheaper to work natives to death
and then replace them than it was to feed and care for them. Missionaries
believed the discipline of sedentary labor was a "civilizing" force, but in
the silver-mining regions of Peru, life was expendable. *Reducciones*, accordingly, resembled slave labor camps more than spiritual sanctuaries. The life
expectancy, the historian David Stannard comments, was "not much more
than three or four months – about the same as that of someone working at
slave labor in the synthetic rubber manufacturing plant at Auschwitz in the
1940s."[8] As later chapters make plain, the racial and ideological motives
and cold calculation of Nazi death camps were objectively different from
Spanish silver mines, as were the industrial methods employed, but the subjective experience of toiling inmates was not entirely dissimilar.

Contemporaries like Bartolomé de Las Casas, a Franciscan friar and
"Defender of the Indians," would bear witness to the atrocities. With Biblical
metaphor, his *Short Account of the Destruction of the Indies* (1552) described
Spanish overseers as "devils in human form" who had "dispatched ... four

or five million souls to the depths of hell."⁹ Responding to domestic and international criticism, the Spanish Crown passed laws to limit the enslavement of captured Indigenous people. But exploitation continued. And while Las Casas defended Indigenous Americans, his proposed solution – to replace native labor with that of enslaved Africans – was no improvement. Indeed, the collection of Indigenous populations in gridiron labor compounds presaged the more systemic enslavement of African captives.

Mobile Citadels

An Anglo-American reverence for "liberty" was constituted in conjunction with coercive systems of racialized slavery. As America's Indigenous population perished from famine, disease, and war, a transatlantic trade triangle converted African bodies into capitalist commodities. In the process, slave traders established many of the carceral and organizational structures that would define the modern world – and underpin future camps. As historian Sidney Mintz comments, sugar plantations in the Caribbean and American South were "absolutely unprecedented social, economic, and political institution[s]"¹⁰ – ones that set a template for the management of concentrated bodies for centuries to come.

The Americas, in large part, were originally settled and developed by criminal convicts, who worked as indentured servants (chap. 1). After release, however, some established their own plantations, which they populated with enslaved Africans. Between 1700 and 1869, ships from Spain, Portugal, France, and especially Britain collected a human cargo of more than 12 million in exchange for textiles, ironware, and the very firearms and ammunition used to round up slaves in the first place. Often, African chiefs sold criminals or POWs to European merchants, though some captives were victims of organized slave hunts in which concentrated military attacks swept interior settlements, rounding up civilians and confining them with chains, ropes, and wooden yokes before transporting them, sometimes hundreds of miles, in caravans and forced marches. When they arrived at coastal prisons, the abolitionist Thomas Clarkson (1760–1846) observed, slaves underwent processing: counted, stripped naked, marched in chains, and then "branded upon the breast with a hot iron" – dehumanizing marks of identification that survivors would carry for the rest of their lives."¹¹

The slave ship was, in many ways, a floating camp. Like naval hulks in Europe (chap. 1), these carceral spaces applied the logistics of military planning to detain human bodies in unspeakable concentrations. Though

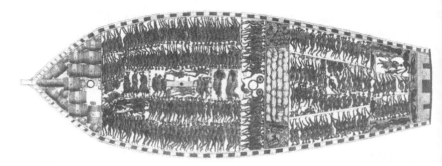

FIGURE 2.1 Human bodies, transported like cargo, on the Nantes-based transatlantic slaver the *Marie Séraphique* (1764–73). (Source: Musée de Nantes.)

shipwrights often built "by eye," standardized blueprints over the course of the eighteenth and nineteenth centuries codified the emerging sciences of mass confinement. And as "moveable fortress[es] or citadel[s]," they helped diffuse a general uniformity of design across the Atlantic world. Technologies of both transportation and incarceration, armed slave ships (like the ironically named *Liberty*) were "military installation[s] ... from which the crew guarded and controlled the enslaved people on board." Sailors doubled as prison sentries: fastening chains; supervising visits to the main deck, which came to resemble "a closely guarded prison yard"; and erecting a "fencelike assemblage of ropes to prevent slaves from jumping overboard."[12] Suicide was a final, desperate act of resistance, and a common occurrence to be prevented or (when unsuccessful) punished. In this way, slave captains claimed absolute powers not only over life but over death.

Medical surveillance complemented military coercion. Yet sanitary measures like spraying captives with disinfectant (a practice adopted from cattle ranching), mandatory inoculations, and "dancing" above deck (a demeaning form of exercise) rarely prevented smallpox, dysentery, or other diseases. Onboard medical officers conducted regular inspections and quarantined the sick on longboats, but mortality on the "Middle Passage" exceeded 12 percent. Given the "pestilent atmosphere," the British physician and planter David Collins remarked in 1803, it was a "wonder that so many [did] survive." "Slaves," he added, were "debarred the free use of their limbs, oppressed with chains, harassed by seasickness ... stinted in provisions, and poisoned with corrupted water."[13] And while economies of scale generated ever larger ships over the course of the eighteenth century, captives hardly benefited. Each unit of human cargo received a mere three square feet of space and was unable to stand up – the below-deck was only four feet high.

Those who survived the voyage faced humiliating inspections. Eclipsing the indignities of the workhouse (chap. 1), captives were stripped of clothing, their hair shaved, and their skin rubbed with palm oil to disguise cuts and bruises from the journey, though "emaciated objects" in "too deplorable a state to be exhibited" were segregated from the others.[14] Dehumanization is often a prerequisite for violence; in the case of transatlantic slavery, racial tropes seduced purchasers into believing they were trading animals rather than human beings. As Mary Prince (1788–1833), an enslaved woman from Bermuda, testified, strange men examined and handled her "in the same manner that a butcher would a calf or a lamb."[15] Families were also separated. Driven by economic incentive rather than human sentiment, planters and wholesalers purchased captives "without any consideration whether the wife is separated from her husband, or the mother from her son," and "if relations, when they find themselves about to be parted should cling together," Clarkson commented, "the lash instantly severs them from their embraces."[16] The slave pens of the Caribbean and Brazil thus offered precedents for the dehumanization experienced by prisoners in twentieth-century concentration camps – whether in Stalin's Soviet Union (chap. 4), Nazi Germany (chap. 5), or colonial Africa (chaps. 3 and 7). In the eighteenth and nineteenth centuries, though, survivors looked to Biblical allusions, like the exodus of the Jews from Israel, to frame narratives of oppression and deliverance.[17]

Following the trauma of family separation, a period of acculturation initiated plantation slaves into new lives of discipline and labor. The process of "seasoning" helped "break in" new arrivals (much like the practice of breaking horses) by conditioning them, biologically, to the climate and disease environments of the New World. Seasoning also introduced the "socially dead" to a new social order: older, seasoned slaves supervised newcomers, introducing them to the routines of labor and obedience that defined chattel slavery (survivors of twentieth-century camps would recount similar periods of physical and psychological adjustment). Often, seasoning took place on the plantation itself, though in some cases, purpose-built dormitories or "seasoning camps," as they were known, acculturated slaves before they were auctioned. Whatever the case, the experience was traumatic and often deadly – designed to obliterate old identities, break wills, and sever bonds with the past. One third of Africans arriving in the Caribbean died in their first year from disease, overwork, or suicide.

Slave Villages

The segregation of slave labor was not inevitable. Indeed, the Roman Empire, ancient China, and the Indigenous societies of western Africa considered slaves valued members of the household bound to their masters by ties of physical and emotional intimacy. But the intensification of transatlantic slavery in the late eighteenth century inaugurated unprecedented forms of confinement and coercion, particularly in Brazil and the Caribbean, where it attained its most systematic form. Biological racism opened an affective chasm between European "masters" and African "slaves," generating new forms of coercion. The colonial administrator Edward Long described "negroes" in 1774 as "bestial," "stupid," and "void of genius" – an irony given the skill Africans brought with them in the cultivation of rice and sugarcane – while the planter James Ramsay felt the "Orangutan not inferior in intellect to many of the Negroe race." An "Orangutan husband," he added "would be no dishonour to a Hottentot female."[18] Whereas previously, enslaved workers lived in their masters' houses, exploitative labor at large sugar and cotton plantations – and the system of racial supremacy that increasingly compartmentalized Africans as separate and inferior – relocated them, by the late eighteenth century, to distinct, segregated compounds.

When he toured the American South in 1852, the urban planner Frederick Law Olmsted remarked upon the "dozen rude looking log-cabins" typically scattered around large cotton plantations[19]; had he visited the sugar islands of the Caribbean, he would have found substantial "slave villages" billeting many hundreds. As institutions of private enterprise rather than of centralized state planning, plantations varied by owner and colony. By the end of the eighteenth century, however, influential "how-to" manuals assembled developing guidelines for the arrangement of plantation housing and labor. By codifying emerging forms of organizational expertise, such documents are important sources in the history of camps.

Preoccupied with the specter of insurrection following Haiti's 1791 slave revolt, a persistent anxiety among the planter class, Pierre Joseph Labourie's influential guidebook *The Coffee Planter of Saint Domingo* (1798) outlined "principle[s] of government" for the management of "negroes and cattle." To "keep [slaves] in subjection [and] chastisement," he recommended they be housed in communal dormitories divided into individual cells.[20] Preferred arrangements in Latin America consisted of enclosed barracks surrounding a central square, in imitation of a military camp. An observer

 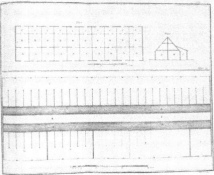

FIGURE 2.2 Roehampton, Jamaica (*left*), billeted slave laborers in a segregated compound typical of large sugar plantations. P.J. Labourie in Santo Domingo drew up a blueprint for a slave barracks (*right*). Despite the development of rich creole cultures, the compound was hardly a home. (Source: slaveryimages.org; P.J. Labourie, *The Coffee Planter of Saint Domingo*.)

in Brazil described "barracks ... built in the form of a square, the outer wall being much higher than the inner wall," with a large gate at the entrance and a "powerful lamp which lights up the whole place."[21] In British North America, however, rows of wattle-and-daub cabins, erected by inmates themselves, proved more common. Individual huts permitted a semblance of family life, but they were typically wretched habitations with dirt floors and hard planks for beds, though enterprising captives made mattresses of dried plantain leaves. Whatever the case, preferred technical arrangements emphasized discipline and surveillance. Barracks were to be placed "within the eye, ear, and command of the master," Labourie instructed, though far enough from the "big house" that the master would "be removed from the ... offensive exhalations" emitted by perspiring African bodies. Slave barracks should likewise "be secured as not to admit [their inmates] going out in the night," and be located away from nearby roads to prevent travel or communication with inmates at neighboring plantations.[22]

Violence results from dehumanization but also from physical, cultural, and experiential distance. By the turn of the eighteenth century, compounds physically and symbolically removed enslaved people from their masters' homes, and from the comity of humankind. Just as missiles and drones depersonalized death in the twentieth century – in modern war, killers may never see their victims – segregated compounds facilitated a new brand of violence that depended less on the enmity of individual masters than on the delegation of responsibility. As slave laborers transformed from trusted helpmates into interchangeable units of production, the planter became a manager who coordinated production from afar. The further removed an authority is from the violence they organize, the more desensitized they become. In application of this general rule – one that recurs throughout the history of mass confinement – the worst living conditions, harshest labor, and highest mortality often prevailed on plantations owned by absentee landlords who lived in Europe and delegated violence from a distance. And while the history of slavery abounds with cruel masters, on large plantations the lash was wielded not by planters themselves but by overseers and "drivers" – enslaved people who had risen to positions of prominence.

The cruelty of the plantation, then, depended on a bureaucratic system. At the very moment that rigid time discipline and factory organization proliferated across industrial Europe (chap. 1), the plantation at Worthy Park, Jamaica, organized a workforce of 446 into a system of gangs according to an elaborate specialization and division of labor. "The bell and whip of the driver" awakened inmates "one hour before daylight," while schedules and ledger books monitored labor output.[23] "Working and living together in gangs of hundreds [in] huge sugar-factories," Caribbean slaves (and also those in Brazil and Spanish America) "were closer to a modern proletariat than any group of workers in existence at the time," the historian C.L.R. James remarked.[24] Such institutions represented a new scale of organization. White overseers and a "slave elite" with paraprofessional occupations directed unskilled labor in the cane fields, while industrial workers conducted repetitive and dangerous tasks in the boiling house and mill.

As demand for sugar, coffee, and cotton surged in the salons of London and Lisbon, cat-o'-nine tails, designed to maximize pain, coerced workers overseas. "Terror" and "the gross operation of fear" were necessary to force obedience and punish insubordination, a planter manual maintained; here violence emerges not from the bloodlust of the sadist but as a principle of good governance – much as the workhouse and prison were favored institutions of Enlightenment rationality. With surgical precision, planters calibrated violence to stimulate harder work. In order to reduce mortality (and hence save investment), however, medical officials like David Collins, author of the guidebook *Practical Rules for the Management of Negro Slaves* (1803), recommended "freshly knotted whips" soaked in disinfectant. Any well-managed plantation, he advised, should also have a hospital with multiple infectious disease wards.[25] Maintaining the health and biopolitical welfare of plantation inmates was essential to production. The lives of the enslaved were valuable, but only as instruments of economic production.

Sundays offered the one respite from compound life: inmates could sleep until daybreak. Upon rising, however, they were required to clean their huts and barracks, which overseers inspected. They then "repair[ed] to prayers on the [drying] platforms, where all the tools [were] produced for the examination of the master."[26] Like forced-labor camps in the twentieth century, slave plantations reduced their inmates to what the political theorist Giorgio Agamben calls "bare life," stripped of the rights and autonomy that clothe the human being. Though plantations resembled prisons, their inmates had committed no crime. And in contrast to metropolitan prisons, "rehabilitation," outside the production of docile workers, was incompatible with slavery's racial and economic logic.

The New Slaveries

Though enslaved populations were nominally "emancipated" over the course of the nineteenth century, their captivity continued. Traders in West Africa concealed captives in fenced compounds (or *barracons*) to escape the surveillance of abolitionist patrols, while missionaries supervised survivors in naval hulks and semi-enclosed "villages of liberty." Corporate profit, however, continued to coerce Black bodies. This was especially true for labor-intensive industries and regions that had not fully transitioned to a free market, like the American South, which scholars have compared to colonial societies in Africa (or alternately to what the political sociologist Barrington Moore deemed the "Prussian road to modernity," characterized by unfree labor and political authoritarianism).[27] Despite the Emancipation Proclamation (1863), Jim Crow legislation following the US Civil War (1861–65, chap. 3) systematically stripped Black Americans of civil rights, rendering them practically stateless "non-citizens" who existed in a captive, semicolonial relationship. Exploiting a constitutional loophole (the Thirteenth Amendment, which permitted slavery to continue as punishment for a crime), debt bondage coupled with the selective application of vagrancy and loitering laws facilitated racial profiling, arbitrary arrest, and the discriminatory sentencing of tens of thousands of formerly enslaved Black Americans, who worked on many of the same plantations as their ancestors. Though some convictions were legitimate, many were fabricated or embellished; like the "Black Acts" of industrial Europe, the application of justice guaranteed the interests of a (white) ruling elite. In early-twentieth-century Mississippi, for example, the convict population, disproportionately young and Black, grew at ten times the rate of the general population. The goal, according to the critic Michelle Alexander, was to "reestablish a system of control that would ensure a low-paid, submissive labor force."[28] Prisons, in effect, replaced the plantation.

While indentured convicts and African captives built America's original infrastructure, penal slavery remained central to the postwar economy and its labor-intensive agriculture. Opened in 1901, prisons like Mississippi's Parchman Farm, a sprawling industrial and agricultural complex consisting of 13 discrete "camps" (as wardens called them) had all the hallmarks of a gigantic plantation. Long, single-story barracks commonly called "cages" resembled colonial prisons in Africa and South Asia more than Benthamite panopticons. Parchman's isolated location prevented escapes, while a maximum-security unit comprised a guard tower, fences, and gates, along with a solitary confinement wing and a gas chamber for executions. By day, the imprisoned and formerly enslaved worked in lumber and brickyards, providing material to build new barracks – camp construction itself often depended on further arrests. But the late-nineteenth-century prison industry was also hugely profitable. In states like Alabama, the "leasing out" of unpaid convicts, at submarket rates, to private plantations and corporations generated substantial profit. In such cases, the physical penitentiary became "virtually synonymous with the various private enterprises in which convicts labored": inmates lived onsite at cotton plantations or else slept in tents at lumber and railroad camps.[29] Like slavery, too, production was premised on violence. Parchman employed armed guards, drawn from the most violent offenders, the "trusty-shooters," who were housed separately to reward collaboration.[30]

In the Caribbean, too, the formerly enslaved remained on plantations as "apprentices," while emancipation witnessed a period of prison and workhouse expansion in the late nineteenth century. In Jamaica, public works officials, many of them local planters, subjected those arrested for vagrancy or petty theft to "slavery by another name," forcing penal gangs to work on sugar cane plantations.[31] Driven by the demand for captive labor, French and Portuguese penal colonies experienced a similar renaissance. Yet labor shortages persisted, particularly as freed captives formed autonomous maroon communities in highland interiors. In this context, Caribbean officials transported half a million indentured "coolies" from South Asia between 1838 and 1917, housing them on sugar plantations and closed residential compounds for the duration of their contract. Revived systems of indenture and encampment thus reproduced the infrastructure of slavery and the Middle Passage.

The demands of colonial capitalism also mobilized unfree labor in Africa in the final decades of the nineteenth century. French authorities contracted convicts to private entrepreneurs in Senegal, who operated temporary work camps attached to road sites, mines, and salt marshes. Native prisons in Algeria were likewise "little more than slave labor camps," one critic contends.[32] In the rubber districts of French, German, and Belgian West Africa, likewise, systems of *corvée* (taxation via labor) permitted governments and private companies to impress forced labor at will. Described by modern critics as a "Gulag labor camp of shocking brutality,"[33] the Congo Free State, with a mortality of 10 million, was the most egregious example. Here, concessionary companies anticipated practices of extermination through labor surpassed only by the totalitarian regimes of twentieth-century Europe.

Africa's most tightly regulated labor camps, however, were in Cape Colony and the Transvaal in southern Africa, where the discovery of diamonds and later gold transformed Black bodies into liquid capital. As European settlement extended beyond van Riebeeck's almond hedge, the de Beers Company, founded in 1888, established fenced mining compounds to incarcerate native workers. Though ostensibly voluntary, 3-to-18-month labor contracts were often signed under duress. Crackdowns against strikes and unions, and the criminalization of native mobility via coercive pass laws, likewise ensured a steady flow of convict labor – a system described by one colonial policeman as "nothing more or less than a kind of slave trade."[34] Inspired by Brazilian slave lodges, though exhibiting significant advances in the tactics of surveillance, the Bultfontein compound (figure 2.3) had a formidable military appearance. A large panoptic square surrounded by cramped living quarters arranged in a single row, along with a ten-foot corrugated iron fence, a single gate as an entrance, and a tower outlook constituted an inviolable barrier: inmates could only enter the mines via enclosed underground tunnels.

Fears that workers would smuggle diamonds, uniquely small and valuable products, prompted additional security infrastructure like wire mesh above the compound, while full cavity searches reflected a surveillance regime that exceeded other nineteenth-century slave-labor arrangements. At the end of a contract, inmates were detained, completely naked, for five to ten days' observation and forced to defecate over meshed pit latrines in order to monitor their digestive systems and detect swallowed stones. Reducing inmates to an "assemblage of orifices," the compound objectified and scrutinized African bodies in much the same way as the mineral-rich soil they were tasked with

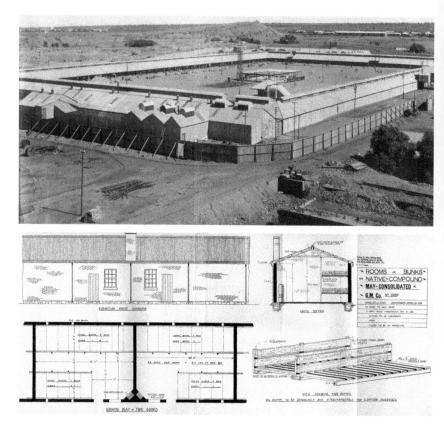

FIGURE 2.3 Opened in 1889, the Bultfontein compound in Kimberley, Southern Africa, was carefully planned by professional engineers skilled in the extraction of both natural resources and native labor. Colonial officers with experience in the army, police, and on native reservations patrolled the complex. (Source: McGregor Museum, Kimberley, South Africa; Kimberley Africana Library.)

extracting.[35] Diamonds recovered in this way would grace the fingers of fashionable European brides. Historians have compared living conditions to the Soviet Gulag, where prisoners mined gold at the infamous Kolyma complex (chap. 4), though more locally, de Beers inspired the development of gold mining compounds near Johannesburg along with concentration camps during the South African War (chap. 3). For their part, Africans commemorated their latest journey into bondage, a vertical Middle Passage 3,000 feet into the ground, with song: "At home I was secure / But now I am on this side / I am in a place of danger / Where I may lose my life at any time."[36]

HUMANITARIAN RELIEF

Serious famines in India in the 1870s and 1890s created a social and political crisis, and a new pretext for encampment. Ten million died from starvation, while displaced "criminal classes" – "intolerable pests," the "scum of the community" and "social parasites," as officials called them – camped on city streets and looted government grain stores. In response, the colonial police conducted urban cleansing sweeps, rounding up famine victims and concentrating them in "relief work" camps surrounded by bamboo and bramble fences. Here they lived in canvas tents or wattle-and-daub huts and conducted heavy labor – breaking stones, digging trenches, shifting sand – in return for food. Thus were the vaunted canals and railways of British India constructed.

Though some camps resembled "well-ordered villages" – like planter manuals, government famine codes standardized camp arrangements – living conditions were grim. Surrounded by "an enclosure such as not to be easy to surmount," the camps constituted "practically illegal confinement," officials conceded, and Indians felt the same "repugnance for relief camps which the respectable poor in England have to the Union Workhouse." Surveillance and punishment governed camp life: tin or wooden tickets worn around the neck classified inmates, while "whippings ... judiciously and vigorously applied" enforced daily work quotas. Disease also spread rapidly in crowded confines, and the rations – one pound of grain per day – were wholly inadequate: less than the official ration at Nazi Germany's Buchenwald concentration camp, the historian Mike Davis calculates.[37] Nonetheless, authorities cast famine camps as acts of charity that provided life-saving food in return for edifying labor. How has humanitarian language featured in the history of mass confinement?

Native Concentration

A generation after formally abolishing slavery, European empires presided over vast systems of coerced labor. In the process, camps and compounds emerged as organizational technologies for billeting and controlling forced, mobile, low-paid (or unpaid) workers. At the same time, a new dynamic of settler colonialism, based on the expansion of white settlement and the "freedom of the frontier" rather than the bondage of slavery and indenture, transformed imperial conquest in the nineteenth century.

Settler colonialism involves the elimination of Indigenous people and the occupation of their land rather than simply the exploitation of their labor. Though this dynamic spanned the world, from Australia to Siberia and from Canada to Kenya, it was perhaps most dramatic in the United States. Following a Royal Proclamation in 1763 prohibiting settlement west of the Appalachian Mountains, the American Revolutionary War (1776–83) was fought, in part, to protect the property (including the slaves) of white Americans and their right to occupy "Indian" land. Following independence, the pursuit of a transcontinental land empire and the celebration of white frontier settlers were touchstones of American nationalism. The myth of manifest destiny and the "divine right" of the white settler provided ideological foundations for the forced removal of Indigenous populations and their concentration on reservations.

With echoes of Spanish colonization in previous centuries, civilizing missions sought to assimilate native peoples. Missionaries preached Christianity, while some Indigenous nations, like the Cherokee, established cotton plantations and became slave owners in their own right – important markers of civilization in the Anglo-American tradition. As the Euro-American population boomed, however, a new generation in the 1830s embraced hardened racial outlooks. No longer were "savagery" and "barbarism" – whether of native Africans or Americans – the products of religious and environmental differences alone; rather, they stemmed from innate biological deficiencies. Commentators in the 1860s, like the German anthropologist Theodor Waitz, offered an early taste of social Darwinism when they argued that "the right of the White American to destroy the red man" was "predestined by nature."[38] As the ideological foundation of the plantation economy, racism directed toward enslaved Africans could easily be transferred to Indigenous groups, especially in the American South. Here, the presence of sizable Indigenous nations on large tracts of fertile land – ratified by treaties – represented a growing economic threat to white settler expansion.

In 1828, President Andrew Jackson was elected with overwhelming support in the US South. Promising open land for his white populist base, he vowed to remove and forcibly concentrate 100,000 Cherokee, Creek, Seminole, Chickasaw, and Choctaw – once known as the "five civilized tribes" but now members of a "problem race" – to designated reservations west of the Mississippi. "The whole Cherokee nation ought to be scourged," he proclaimed.[39] Despite its dubious legality and challenges from the

Supreme Court, Jackson's 1830 Indian Removal Act provided foundations for the ethnic cleansing of America's Indigenous population. Legal pressure and the threat of military violence in the early 1830s compelled many tribes to travel to unsettled land in present-day Oklahoma. By 1838, all that remained were 16,000 Cherokee holdouts. Beginning on May 26, 1838, 7,000 federal and state militia troops rounded up civilians at New Echota, the Cherokee capital. Some soldiers expressed disdain for the operation: "future generations," Private John Burnett wrote in his memoirs, "will read and condemn the act and I do hope posterity will remember that private soldiers like myself ... were forced ... to execute the orders of our superiors" (posterity would indeed confront the moral dilemma posed by soldiers "just following orders").[40] The result was tragic: "families at dinner were startled by the sudden glean of bayonets" as "squads of troops ... search[ed] out with rifle and bayonet every small cabin." And as they marched west, survivors "turn[ed] for one last look" to see "their homes in flames, fired by the lawless rabble that followed on the heels of the soldiers to loot and pillage."[41]

The captives were transported first to 33 military collection points and then to a network of 11 internment camps, where they were detained for six months as preparations ensued for their deportation to "Indian Territory." Surrounded by blockhouses and wooden stockades, the camps boasted a substantial security apparatus. Responsible for forced removal and representing the interests of land-hungry settlers, however, the US government had little incentive to keep inmates alive. Some soldiers even commented "they would not be happy until all Cherokee were dead," though commanding officers placed a brake on genocidal impulses with orders to treat inmates "with kindness and humanity."[42] Nonetheless, authorities dedicated little forethought to housing, labor, or sanitation, while inmates remember hunger, exposure, and neglect. In this, President Jackson's camps provided an object lesson in the management of concentrated spaces, one that would be forgotten and relearned throughout the twentieth century: without proper medical facilities and clean water supply, epidemic diseases like measles, typhus, dysentery, and cholera killed between 2,000 and 4,000 inmates.

Cherokee camps were not tightly ordered disciplinary spaces but makeshift installations. In this, they reflected the weak, incompletely bureaucratized structures of the frontier society that generated them. As waystations of deportation rather than final destinations, they were necessarily temporary, and after several months, surviving inmates faced further deportations. Loaded like cattle into wagons or else forced to march on foot (arrangements to transport them via riverboat fell through), they embarked in 1838 on a deadly 800-mile trek now known as the "Trail of Tears." The deportees were ill-equipped for the grueling journey, as survivors recount, and many perished during one of the Midwest's coldest winters on record.

While the Cherokee settled on remote reservations, the pattern of deportation shifted west. In the Apache Wars (1849–86), state militias responded to insurgent raids by pushing natives into the Sonoran Desert. Resisting what they considered a settler invasion, the Dakota Sioux also turned to guerrilla combat against white settlements, killing hundreds. The governor of Minnesota demanded revenge: "Indians ... must be exterminated or driven forever beyond the borders of the State," he proclaimed. In 1862, 307 Dakota POWs were sentenced to death in summary trials lasting only five minutes, while an act of collective punishment deported another 1,600 women and children. Many endured harrowing marches through hostile towns where "streets [were] crowded with an angry and excited populace cursing, shouting ... [and] armed with guns, knives, clubs, and stones." Settlers attacked and robbed the Dakota and in one case "an enraged white woman," motivated by racism and revenge (perhaps her own child had been killed?), "rush[ed] up to one of the wagons and snatch[ed] a nursing babe from its mother's breasts and dash[ed] it violently upon the ground." Others were packed onto trains or boats, an ordeal the missionary John Williamson described as "nearly as bad as the Middle Passage." The destination was a "fenced camp of tepees" outside the military outpost of Fort Snelling, Minnesota (figure 3.1). To this day, elders in the Dakota community refer to their forced relocation as a "death march" and draw conscious parallels with the Holocaust and the Bataan Death March in World War II, when 70,000 Filipino and American soldiers endured a 63-mile trek to a Japanese prison camp.[43] More immediately, military actions against native fighters, lauded for their skill and cunning but derided as uncivilized for their lack of uniforms or European-style command structure, inspired future networks of civilian concentration camps, including those of the South African War, where colonial armies faced a similar dynamic of guerrilla war (chap. 3).

Humanitarian Protection?

Despite boasts about collecting Cherokee scalps, Andrew Jackson and his lieutenants deployed a humane but condescending language – a key tactic, as future chapters suggest, of justifying mass confinement in democratic countries. Removal, then, was often depicted as an act of paternal kindness rather than of ethnic cleansing. Reservations, accordingly, offered refuge from the same vigilante violence Jackson had committed and encouraged. "Your father has provided a country large enough for all of you where your white brother will not trouble you," he proclaimed.[44] Yet while some native communities embraced reservations as spaces in which self-government and cultural expression could continue secure from settler assaults, they were often sites of punishment and institutionalized neglect. In retaliation for the Battle of Little Big Horn (1876), Dakota Sioux were confined to reservations as POWs, while in western Canada pass systems and vagrancy laws functioned as counterinsurgency measures, limiting mobility, segregating natives from European communities, and converting reserves, at times, into what the Canadian historian James Daschuk describes as "centers of incarceration." Barriers against Indigenous land ownership and commerce further concentrated natives into ever shrinking spaces, as did the policy of only distributing food (an entitlement negotiated by treaty) on reserves – a tactic of spatial control that mimicked contemporary relief camps for "famine wanderers" in India. Crowding and malnutrition spread deadly diseases, and when they came, rations fell short of those distributed to state prisoners in Siberia.[45]

Elsewhere, reservations functioned as depots of cheap labor. In California, where gold rush settlement extirpated remaining native communities in the 1850s, reservations concentrated survivors in tiny tracts of marginal land where federal troops monitored their movement but provided little protection from settler incursions. Desperate for food (promised federal rations were either inadequate or never materialized), residents of the Klamath and Round Valley reservations had no option but to find work on settler farms, where "locals worked hundreds of … Indians to death, treating them as slaves who were no more than disposable laborers." Today, the Tolowa Nation remembers their reservation (anachronistically, perhaps) as the "Klamath concentration camp."[46]

As the frontier closed and forced emigration opened living room for white settlement, humanitarian efforts to "civilize" and "assimilate" expedited the erasure of native society. In the nineteenth century's final decades, residential schools and large industrial complexes replaced small missionary outposts. Opened in 1879, the Carlisle Indian Industrial School in Pennsylvania occupied a former military barracks, and its superintendent, Lieutenant Richard Pratt, instituted disciplinary regimens adopted from the army and from his experience with POWs at St. Augustine, Florida. As a model institution, it offered a blueprint for state-sanctioned residential boarding schools, often run by church organizations, across Canada, Australia, and the United States. In contrast to the temporary internment and deportation camps on the Trail of Tears, life was "heavily regimented, with little deviation allowed from a rigid schedule for sleeping, rising, praying, studying, and working." The development of a bureaucratic surveillance state was thus a byproduct of efforts to more tightly monitor concentrated natives. Upon entry, students received new names, new clothes, and new identities, and as part of their initiation, wardens cut the children's hair, thereby severing connections to their culture and their past. The goal, according to Pratt, was to "kill the Indian" but "save the man." Such routines resembled those of European workhouses (chap. 1), though racial rather than class animus prevailed. The belief that "abstract ideas develop slowly in the Indian child" meant that residential schools, described by the Canadian Truth and Reconciliation Committee in 2015 as sites of "institutionalized child labor," were more successful at enforcing unskilled field work than in educating their pupils.[47] Indeed, "calling them schools," the Canadian minister of Indigenous Services suggests, "is probably a euphemism. These were labor camps."[48]

Transnational Connections

The dynamic of settler expansion and native concentration was hardly unique to North America. Like the American West, Japan's far north and Russia's far east witnessed familiar cycles of settler violence, epidemic disease, and encroachment on native land. The Aboriginals of southern Africa likewise found themselves confined to segregated reserves – what would later become the homelands and "Bantustans" of apartheid (chap. 7). And in Algeria, the racially segregated casbah confined Arabs while an extensive campaign of spatial and social reconstruction in the countryside followed what the French traveler Alexis de Toqueville deemed an American model. It is "essential to group together these people who are everywhere and nowhere," the colonial officer Charles Richard wrote in 1846. By "agglomerating" and thus "put[ting] them within our grasp," the Indigenous population would "bend to our domination," he believed.[49] Demarcated "colonies," developed by the Indigenous Affairs Office, grouped scattered populations into barracks-like structures surrounded by "a wide ditch shielded by cactus," where Algerian natives performed agricultural work or provided cheap labor for the military.[50] Such was the world divided into compartments described by Frantz Fanon.

Australia offered the most explicit counterpart to the Americas. Frontier violence killed roughly 10,000 Aboriginal people in Queensland between 1824 and 1908 as language like "dispersal" and "customary chastisement" masked what the historian Jürgen Zimmerer describes as "mobile death squads aimed at eradicating Aborigines."[51] In the same year (1830) that

US President Jackson passed the Indian Removal Act, the settlers of Van Diemen's Land (present-day Tasmania) organized the "black line," a large-scale quasi-military operation in which 2,000 men, 550 of them soldiers, formed a connected human chain, 300 miles long, and systematically scoured the island from north to south in an anti-guerrilla action. This was part of the "Black War" (1825–32), a series of skirmishes led by roving parties of European settlers and convicts appointed under martial law to drive out Tasmania's remaining Aboriginal people. Though only a few were captured, survivors, already weakened by disease, were relocated to the Wybalenna settlement at Flinders Island, and later to Oyster Cove, a former penitentiary.

As in America, humanitarian language framed Australian actions – settlements would "protect" Aboriginal Australians from alcohol, prostitution, and frontier violence while introducing them to Christianity, settled farming, and "habits of industry." Nonetheless, inadequate housing, rations, and clothing on the remote, windswept archipelago caused lethal respiratory illnesses like influenza, tuberculosis, and pneumonia. Damp, poorly ventilated barracks were unsuitable to the "violent and cold winters," impure water spread disease, and flour and salt-meat rations were inadequate, despite efforts by inmates to supplement them with hunting (farming was largely impossible owing to poor soil). Out of nearly 400 original inmates, only 47 survived. Infant mortality was high, and surviving children were relocated to an orphanage in the colony's capital, Hobart, or else placed under "supervised" employment. Government ministers (in contrast to individual settlers) rarely expressed genocidal intent, but a general impression that "this race of human beings will soon become extinct altogether" fostered apathy and inaction. Extinction, in other words, was "the will of Providence."[52]

Tasmania's island settlements offered a geographical precedent for off-shore detention camps administered by Australia today (chap. 8), though more immediately they influenced Aboriginal policy on the Australian mainland. Despite strict work regimes and monastic lifestyles of prayer and toil, some settlements offered benign sanctuaries from settler violence. Lured by the provision of food, Aboriginals sought refuge at the Loddon River compound on their own volition, while at Coranderrk the Kulin people helped select their settlement site on a traditional camping ground. Nonetheless, a 2008 government of Australia report concluded, the pattern of "removal, concentration, and segregation protected settler interests" while "confin[ing] and constantly monitor[ing] how Aboriginal people lived and how they could be controlled." With immense discretionary powers, governments stripped Aboriginal people of basic human rights and punished those who disobeyed regulations with beatings, incarceration, and "forced relocation to ... punishment areas."[53]

Apart from clearing land for settlers, native compounds also facilitated racial segregation in urban settings. In 1913, for example, Australia's Northern Territorial police concentrated Larrakia and Wadjiginy people – whom residents in the town of Darwin viewed as moral and sanitary nuisances – in the Kahlin compound. Surrounded by wire fences, the inmates, housed at night in locked dormitories, were contracted out as manual laborers and cheap domestic servants. As a key provider of labor, then, Kahlin transformed into a work camp – its residents quite literally built the city of Darwin. The "new slaveries" thus continued in another guise. And while sanitary measures – fear of "infectious disease" and the "indescribable ... filth and dirt" of native bodies – motivated segregation, continued removals produced severe overcrowding. When John McEwen, the new federal minister for Indigenous affairs, toured the facility in 1937, he commented there were "many stock breeders who would not dream of crowding their [animals] in the way these half-caste children are huddled."[54]

Though normally associated with white settler colonies, colonial governments also detained Indigenous populations in Africa, Asia, and Latin America. Codified by nineteenth-century anthropology, the stock figure of the nomadic and "uncivilized" Aboriginal, distinct from tax-paying peasants, emerged as a threat to social and political order. Starting in the 1830s, and thus converging with American and Australian developments, officials in British India took action to settle nomadic groups in "guarded villages" and "schools of industry," segregating them from settled farmers in the process. Informed by the emerging "science" of eugenics, efforts intensified after legislation in 1871 classified tribes like the Bawarias, Minas, and Sanorias as "criminal" by virtue of their heredity, empowering police to corral them into monitored settlements. In the judgment of the Salvation Army "general" Frederick Booth-Tucker, "criminal tribe camps" resembled American measures "adopted with great success in dealing with the Red Indians" and in weaning them "from their evil and lawless habits." They also, of course, resembled measures taken against Europe's "habitual criminals," who were also recast as genetically defective (chap. 1). Like workhouses and labor colonies, criminal tribe settlements enforced "hard but honest industry," supposedly for the benefit of inmates, though security concerns were paramount. As Booth-Tucker likened tribal raids on agricultural villages to "a guerrilla war, which defies the combined efforts of an army of 150,000 ... to repress," the "stout barbed-wire fences" and thorn hedges at Bitragunta (figure 2.4) anticipated camps erected in future colonial

FIGURE 2.4 Children behind a wire fence at the Kahlin compound in Australia (*left*) and a detained child at the Bitragunta "criminal tribes" settlement in India (*right*). (Source: AIATSIS; Madras Government Press.)

counterinsurgencies (chaps. 3 and 7). Conversely, the settlement, still in existence after colonial independence, reminded a 1947 investigative committee of "a Nazi concentration camp" – the "children being bred behind barbed wire as though they are very dangerous animals was a very tragic sight."[55]

Conclusion

As laboratories of violence, European empires assembled many of the essential ingredients of future camps: ideologies of racism, authoritarian power, and the divine right of white settlers generated new logistical and disciplinary technologies. The forced relocation and internment of Africans in plantations, and of Aboriginals in settlements and reservations, established patterns of forced labor and ethnic cleansing that are familiar to the historian of twentieth-century violence. Frontier wars in America and Australia, meanwhile, initiated practices of anti-guerrilla warfare and military detention that would motivate future episodes of encampment in Africa, Asia, and eventually in Europe.

Notes

1 Hannah Arendt, *The Origins of Totalitarianism* (New York: Harcourt, 1968), 221.

2 Frantz Fanon, *Wretched of the Earth*, trans. Richard Philcox (New York: Grove Press, 1963), 37.

3 Peter Spring, *Great Walls and Linear Barriers* (Barnsley: Pen & Sword, 2015), clvii.

4 Amherst quoted in Noble David Cook, *Born to Die: Disease and the New World Conquest, 1492–1650* (Cambridge: Cambridge University Press, 1998), 214.

5 Carl Nightingale, *Segregation: A Global History of Divided Cities* (Chicago: University of Chicago Press, 2012), 62.

6 Nightingale, *Segregation*, 50.

7 Karl Marx, *Capital: A Critical Analysis of Capitalist Production*, vol. 2, trans. Samuel Moore and Edward Aveling (London: Swan Sonnenschein, Lowrey & Co, 1887), 775.

8 David Stannard, *American Holocaust: The Conquest of the New World* (Oxford: Oxford University Press, 1992), 90, 89.

9 Bartolomé de Las Casas, *A Short Account of the Destruction of the Indies*, ed. and trans. Nigel Griffin (Toronto: Penguin, 1992), 97.

10 Sidney Mintz, "Foreword," *Sugar and Society in the Caribbean: An Economic History of Cuban Agriculture* by Ramiro Guerra y Sanchez (New Haven: Yale University Press, 1964), xiv.

11 Thomas Clarkson, *An Essay on the Slavery and Commerce of the Human Species* (Georgetown: David Barrow, 1816), 92.

12 Markus Rediker, *The Slave Ship: A Human History* (New York: Penguin, 2008), 65, 55, 70–71.

13 Dr. Collins, *Practical Rules for the Management and Medical Treatment of Negro Slaves in the Sugar Colonies* (London: J. Barfield, 1803), 53–5.

14 Collins, *Practical Rules*, 56.

15 Mary Prince quoted in Kitty Millet, *The Victims of Slavery, Colonization and the Holocaust: A Comparative History of Persecution* (London: Bloomsbury, 2017), 53.

16 Clarkson, *Essay on Slavery*, 100.

17 Adam Potkay, "Olaudah Equiano and the Art of Spiritual Autobiography," *Eighteenth-Century Studies* 27, no. 4 (1994): 677–92.

18 Edward Long, *The History of Jamaica* (London: T. Lowndes, 1774), 476; J. Ramsay quoted in John Wilson Ramey, "*The Coffee Planter of Saint Domingo:* A Technical Manual for the Caribbean Slave Owner," *Technical Communication Quarterly* 23, no. 2 (2014): 157.

19 John Michael Vlach, *Back of the Big House: The Architecture of Plantation Slavery* (Chapel Hill: University of North Carolina Press, 1993), 153.

20 P.J. Laborie, *The Coffee Planter of Saint Domingo* (London: T. Cadwell and W. Davies, 1798), 157.

21 T.C. Kitto quoted in Robert Turrell, *Capital and Labour on the Kimberley Diamond Fields, 1871–1890* (Cambridge: Cambridge University Press, 1987), 98.

22 Laborie, *Coffee Planter*, 73.

23 Ramey, "Technical Manual," 155.

24 C.L.R. James, *The Black Jacobins: Touissant L'Ouverture and the San Domingo Revolution* (New York: Vintage, 1989), 85–6.

25 Collins, *Practical Rules*, 197.

26 Laborie, *Coffee Planter*, 178.

27 Barrington Moore did not actually coin the phrase, but it is widely associated with his argument in *Social Origins of Dictatorship and Democracy* (Boston: Beacon, 1967); see also Alex Lichtenstein, *Twice the Work of Free Labor: The Political Economy of Convict Labor in the New South* (New York: Verso, 1996), 6–7.

28 Michelle Alexander, *The New Jim Crow: Mass Incarceration in the Age of Colorblindness* (New York: New Press, 2010), 34–5, 37.

29 Lichtenstein, *Twice the Work*, 3.

30 David Oshinsky, *"Worse than Slavery": Parchman Farm and the Ordeal of Jim Crow Justice* (New York: Simon & Schuster, 1997), 143–50.

31 Henrice Altink, "Slavery by Another Name: Apprenticed Women in Jamaican Workhouses in the Period 1834–81," *Social History* 26, no. 1 (2001): 40–59.

32 Anthony Gorman, "Regulation, Reform and Resistance in the Middle Eastern Prison," in *Cultures of Confinement: A History of the Prison in Africa, Asia, and Latin America*, ed. Frank Dikötter and Ian Brown (Ithaca: Cornell University Press, 2007), 122.

33 Peter Bate, dir., *White King, Red Rubber, Black Death* (New York: ArtMattan Productions, 2004).

34 Alan Jeeves, *Migrant Labour in South Africa's Mining Economy: The Struggle for the Gold Mines' Labour Supply, 1890–1920* (Montreal: McGill-Queen's University Press, 1985), 189.

35 Zandi Sherman, "Infrastructure and the Ontological Question of Race," *e-flux Architecture*, September 2021, https://www.e-flux.com/architecture/coloniality-infrastructure/411239/infrastructures-and-the-ontological-question-of-race/.

36 Frederick Johnstone, "Rand and Kolyma: Afro-Siberian Hamlet," *South African Sociological Review* 1, no. 2 (1989): 9.

37 Aidan Forth, *Barbed-Wire Imperialism: Britain's Empire of Camps, 1876–1903* (Berkeley: University of California, 2017), 51–2, 102, 61, 57, 105; Mike Davis, *Late Victorian Holocausts: El Niño Famines and the Making of the Third World* (New York: Verso, 2002), 38.

38 Theodor Waitz, *Introduction to Anthropology*, ed. and trans. Frederick Collingwood (London: Longman, Green, Longman & Roberts, 1863), 351.

39 Jackson quoted in Stannard, *American Holocaust*, 121.

40 Burnett quoted in Stephen Huggins, *America's Use of Terror: From Colonial Times to the A-bomb* (Lawrence: University Press of Kansas, 2019), 62.

41 Patrick Wolfe, "Structure and Event: Settler Colonialism, Time, and the Question of Genocide," in *Empire, Colony, Genocide: Conquest, Occupation and Subaltern Resistance in World History*, ed. A. Dirk Moses (New York: Berghahn, 2008), 107.

42 "Cherokee Removal Forts," accessed May 29, 2020, http://www.aboutnorthgeorgia.com/ang/Cherokee_Removal_Forts.

43 Angela Wilson, "Decolonizing the 1862 Death Marches," *American Indian Quarterly* 28, no. 1&2 (1994): 190, 200, 195, 202.

44 Daniel Feller et al., eds., *The Papers of Andrew Jackson, Volume 7: 1829* (Knoxville: University of Tennessee Press, 2007), 112.

45 James Daschuk, *Clearing the Plains: Disease, Politics of Starvation, and the Loss of Indigenous Life* (Regina: University of Regina Press, 2019), xxii, 118.

46 Benjamin Madley, *An American Genocide: The United States and the California Indian Catastrophe* (New Haven: Yale University Press, 2007), 261.

47 *Canada's Residential Schools: The History, Part 1, Origins to 1939, Final Report of the Truth and Reconciliation Commission of Canada, Volume 1* (Montreal: McGill-Queen's University Press, 2015), 72, 78, 138–9.

48 "'These Were Labour Camps': Minister Miller," *CTV News*, June 2, 2021, https://www.ctvnews.ca/video?clipId=2213997.

49 Benjamin Claude Brower, "Regroupment Camps and Shantytowns in Late-Colonial Algeria," *Dossier: L'inévitable prison* 20 (2019): 93–106.

50 Pierre Bourdieu and Abdelmalek Sayad, *The Uprooting: The Crisis of Traditional Agriculture in Algeria*, ed. Paul A. Silverstein, trans. Susan Emanuel (Cambridge: Polity, 2018), 13.

51 Jürgen Zimmerer, "Colonialism and the Holocaust: Towards an Archaeology of Genocide," in *Genocide and Settler Society: Frontier Violence and Stolen Indigenous Children in Australian History*, ed. A. Dirk Moses (New York: Berghahn, 2004), 64.

52 Benjamin Madley, "From Terror to Genocide: Britain's Tasmanian Penal Colony and Australia's History Wars," *Journal of British Studies* 47, no. 1 (2008): 101–2.

53 Celmara Pocock, *"From Segregation to Assimilation": A Thematic Study of Policies and Practices in Australia, 1800–1970* (Canberra: Department of Environment, Water, Heritage and the Arts, 2008), 121, 60, 61.

54 *Kahlin Compound: Background Historical Information* (Darwin: Heritage Branch, Northern Territory Department of Natural Resources, Environment, the Arts and Sport, 2009), 4–5, 10–11; Pocock, *Segregation to Assimilation*, 139.

55 Forth, *Barbed-Wire Imperialism*, 34–7.

3 | Military Captivity: Soldiers and Civilians in Modern War

The nineteenth century, according to Eurocentric narratives, was an era of progress and humanity. Yet from a global perspective, it was anything but. Mass detention and the forced relocation of Indigenous populations in America foreshadowed the proliferating "small wars" of European empire. According to developing doctrines of counterinsurgency, European generals detained colonial people, from Cuba to southern Africa, in enclosures contemporaries called "concentration camps." At the same time, changes in Europe's political culture – the development of nationalism, democracy, and popular representation – led to vast "people's armies" and the advent of total war. Mass conscription along with the logistical mobilization of arms, transport, and other resources resulted in larger militaries and larger conflicts: the French Revolutionary and Napoleonic Wars (1789–1815), the American Civil War (1861–65), and ultimately, World Wars I (1914–18) and II (1939–45). In the process, modern militaries drilled and disciplined soldiers, in both Europe and the empire, as the coercion of the army camp complemented the coercion of the plantation (chap. 2).

Colonial insurgencies and modern total war developed in tandem. Indeed, violent overseas conquests in the nineteenth century were training grounds for soldiers, European and colonial, facing off on the Western Front. In both cases, war devastated combatants and noncombatants alike, compromising efforts like the Hague Convention (1899) to restrict and codify military combat. Yet according to the racial ideologies of empire, the principles of "civilized" warfare did not apply to the "uncivilized," as imperial armies unleashed indiscriminate slaughter against entire peoples, clearing landscapes of their human content. If colonial war eschewed distinctions between soldier and civilian, so did the national mobilization of World Wars I and II, as civilians became fair military targets. Though the

65

reasons were different, the results were similar: mass violence against civilians and their eventual concentration in camps.

Nations in Arms

The political culture of the European Enlightenment and French Revolution (1789–99) dramatically changed the nature of human violence. In a new era of nationalism, people were no longer subjects of kings or local lords, but citizens of an imagined community – a nation – endowed with natural rights and common identities. Nationalism embraced citizens as equal members, but excluded those who did not belong: migrants, foreigners, traitors. French revolutionaries like Maximilien Robespierre (1758–94) fought foreign and civil wars in the name of peace and justice but executed thousands of suspected counterrevolutionaries in the process. The guillotine emerged as a rational technology of administrative slaughter – and a necessary means to achieve apparently utopian ends. Amid domestic insurrections and foreign wars, islands and military hulks also detained suspects throughout the 1790s, including royalists and refractory priests. And while French revolutionaries did not preside over a formal system of camps, they considered the possibility. In 1796, for example, the proto-communist Gracchus Babeuf proposed a network of detention sites as an emergency measure to restore order, reform political deviants, and protect republican values.[1]

As legacies of the French Revolution, democracy and popular representation augured great human progress – but even greater violence. Patriots fighting for abstract ideals like freedom and identity were arguably more motivated than early modern conscripts fighting for tyrants or tax privileges. And as the stakes of conflict rose, so did the bloodshed. War, its propagandists maintained, was no longer fought simply to gain territory or vanquish rivals, but to achieve more noble goals: peace, a new era, an earthly utopia. As citizens dedicated to a national cause, modern populations, both French and foreign, actively contributed ideological support and economic resources to battle – and they were more likely than their predecessors to resist invaders. Both exemplary and systematic, collective reprisals against guerrilla fighters and their civilian supporters could thus be justified with the colonial language of civilization. Thus would Russian "barbarians" and Spanish "bandits," many of whom resembled Arabs and Africans in French imperial minds, be "liberated." Wars also expanded in scope. Spanning from Moscow to Madrid, and from Egypt to India, the Napoleonic Wars (1799–1815) signaled a new scale to human conflict. France mobilized 3 million citizen-soldiers; Russia 2.1 million; and the British army (not including its navy) grew from 40,000 in 1793 to a quarter million by 1813. In all, some 3 million people, 5 percent of Europe's population, died.[2]

The new citizen-soldiers needed to be drilled. Though they date back to ancient Rome, military camps proliferated as technologies *par excellence* for converting raw bodies of men into disciplined armies. The rectilinear huts and barracks of the Boulogne camp in northern France, erected in 1803, billeted 60,000 soldiers in serried rows, introducing them to regimented discipline. Residential confinement fostered group solidarity, transforming fragmented amateurs into disciplined machines. Camp life was "structured to the extreme," one historian remarks; "soldiers were merely a fragment of space, a piece in the line. They had to unlearn their individuality ... in order to take their place in the column and rank." With precise movements across space and with roll calls and bugle horns regulating time, camps disciplined inmates, much like workhouses, prisons, and the armaments factories that supplied materiel to mass armies. Camp discipline won wars, but crowded conditions resulted in epidemic diseases and mental illness, as soldiers became seasoned to their new camp surroundings. Death from "nostalgia and putrid fever" were not uncommon.[3]

Over time, military camps became larger, more permanent installations, and they proliferated across the Western world – from Aldershot to Philadelphia, and from Potsdam to Terezín. As technologies of confinement, they reflected significant advances in logistical organization, offering templates that could be applied to enemy combatants. In previous generations, hostile powers either executed POWs, released them on prisoner exchanges, or paroled them on the gentlemanly understanding they would not take up arms again. But in the total wars of the modern era, such arrangements were hardly feasible. Fighting for principles rather than mercenary pay, and loyal to their national army rather than generic soldiers' codes, captured combatants could no longer be trusted. And when Enlightenment or humanitarian sentiment forestalled their execution, they were encamped. Opened in 1797, the world's first purpose-built POW camp at Norman Cross, England, set precedents for the institutionalization of purpose-built camps for captured soldiers in future wars. Although shackles and a dungeon (the "Black Hole") awaited those who violated rules, prisoners, dressed in yellow uniforms with gray caps, enjoyed wholesome rations, a library, and craft workshops. The camp also pioneered routines of medical inspection, keeping inmates in good health.[4] But lessons were soon forgotten: military camps during the Crimean War (1853–56), two generations later, are best remembered for devastating typhus and cholera epidemics, which killed more soldiers than active combat – and for women like Florence Nightingale, the pioneering nurse and social reformer, who developed professional standards of care among concentrated populations.

Never a More Appalling Site: The American Civil War

Enlightenment ideals and unwritten honor codes sometimes governed military conduct. But not always. The American Civil War (1861–65) was an ominous portent. The stakes of the conflict – the triumph of freedom over slavery, and the resultant collapse of southern plantation economies – motivated citizen-soldiers in new ways. Union (Northern) and Confederate (Southern) generals ordered the devastation of homes, crops, and businesses not as incidental byproducts but as central strategies of war. Though federal armies had long practiced indiscriminate violence against native populations, Union General Philip Sheridan's destruction of the Shenandoah Valley and William Tecumseh Sherman's "march to the sea" offered early applications of "scorched-earth warfare" against white civilians. The purpose, Sheridan communicated in a letter to the Prussian army, was to cause "inhabitants so much suffering that they must [demand] peace."[5] Noble ends – the abolition of slavery – justified ignoble means: death, destruction, and the arbitrary imprisonment of civilians. In Loudon County, Virginia, Union General Ulysses Grant detained all male civilians "as prisoners of war, not as citizen prisoners," on the preemptive logic they would become soldiers "the moment the rebel army gets hold of them."[6] Not even women were immune. In New Orleans, General Butler detained hostile Confederate women by controversially applying laws originally intended for prostitutes.

A system of prisoner transfer, the Dix-Hill Cartel, initially facilitated the exchange of captured soldiers. But when Confederate generals refused to treat Black prisoners as equal to whites, the system collapsed, presaging an expansive network of POW camps, some purpose-built, some occupying former training camps or prisons. In total, 195,000 Union and 215,000 Confederate soldiers – enormous numbers in a country of 30 million – faced captivity. Camp Douglas, in suburban Chicago, billeted inmates in well-constructed army barracks. By contrast, the notorious Andersonville camp in Confederate Georgia was nothing but an empty swamp. Though surrounded by stockade walls, pack hounds, and guard towers, prisoners had to erect their own shelter with sacking and sticks. For water they dug into the bare ground. Rations, if they arrived, were stale. By August 1864, Andersonville concentrated 33,000 prisoners in a space intended for 9,000. In desperation, inmates excavated tunnels to escape. But anyone crossing the "dead line," a 15-foot perimeter around the stockade, was shot. Others, hoping to depart the hellish landscape before them, hid among corpses, which were piled onto wagons and removed from camp. Thirty percent died, with a peak of one hundred per day. Those who survived were walking skeletons, covered with filth.

A longer process of mental and psychological breakdown often preceded physical death. Inmates described themselves acting like "idiots" and becoming "peevish and childish."[7] Friendship and solidarity broke down in crowded confines: armed with axes and knives, a gang of prisoners, "the Raiders," robbed and murdered fellow inmates. "Thieving was the order of the day," Private S.O. Lord complained: "when we lay down at night, we would tie our cup and spoon to our arms … None but an old prisoner can realize the value of a cup and spoon." Andersonville thus anticipated a much-repeated theme in the history of mass confinement: placing inmates in a perverse struggle to survive, camps turned men into beasts. A privileged group, atop an internal hierarchy, survived through brute strength and ruthless organization. Those on the bottom gave up the will to live – in Andersonville, they simply laid down in the marsh to die. Private Northrup described "one poor boy," who "cried all night and wished to die and suffer no longer; he is an awful object … his body a mere frame; his hair has fallen out from his head … I never saw a sight more appalling." And then the awful thought occurred: "he is a man, somebody's darling boy, dead, and yet breathing."[8] Eighty years later, the Auschwitz survivor Primo Levi described similar scenes: though still physiologically alive, inmates were psychologically and spiritually dead.

Though Andersonville foreshadowed dehumanizing conditions in Nazi concentration camps, Confederate authorities did not intend to kill inmates. The camp commandant, Henry Wirz, described by his poetic prosecutor as more "demon than a man," was executed for war crimes.[9] But the truth was more banal. At his trial, Wirz complained he was being punished simply for obeying orders. More than individual cruelty, Andersonville resulted from bureaucratic systems – and their tragic failures. In other words, "problems of modern supply and transportation … overwhelmed the capabilities of military administration." Wirz petitioned his superiors for food and medical supplies, but they simply never arrived. In the history of concentration camps, neglect and incompetence were often more lethal than the "savage orgies" of which Wirz stood accused. Death from dysentery and typhus was the rule, willful genocide the exception. In this sense, at least, the historian Robert Davis is correct to argue that "Andersonville can be said to mark the beginning of the modern concentration camp."[10]

Apart from POWs, the Civil War entailed mass population displacements. Fleeing invasion and occupation, Americans on both sides transformed into a nation of nomads. The only nineteenth-century conflict to wreak greater havoc was China's Taiping Rebellion (1850–64), in which 200,000 refugees flooded into cities like Shanghai and Hong Kong, where they slept in the rough or erected timber frame huts, as no formal campsites were built to receive them. In America, wealthy refugees fled to Europe and Canada; others camped in wagons or sheltered in farms or city tenements. Fleeing the Confederate South, meanwhile, escaped slaves, known as "contraband," congregated in northern towns and at Union army bases. But while their cause elicited sympathy, emaciated, destitute "negroes" squatting on city streets were rarely welcomed by white townsmen. Fears of racial contamination and wartime labor shortages led, instead, to the concentration of Black refugees in suburban "contraband camps," where they dug ditches, hauled equipment, and performed agricultural labor. For 12–15 percent of America's total Black population, some 474,000 people, the first taste of freedom was, ironically, the log cabins and army surplus tents of a refugee camp. Though they were safe spaces from slavery and provided schools and paid work, contraband camps nonetheless controlled and spatially segregated a population that national leaders deemed undesirable and out of place. Having escaped the plantation, evaded slave hunters, and hidden in Underground safe houses, Black Americans traded one form of confinement for another.[11] White refugees, significantly, received rations but were never segregated in demarcated encampments.

As technologies of both racism and humanitarian relief, contraband camps anticipated ambiguities in the future of refugee management (chap. 8). Amid unprecedented violence, the Civil War also generated a legal regime designed to curb modern warfare's many depredations. Signed by President Lincoln, the Lieber Code (1863) mandated the humane treatment of POWs and enemy civilians, offering a reference for the 1899 and 1907 Hague Conventions. Forbidding the execution of captured soldiers, these codes laid legal foundations for the sprawling POW camps of modern war, whereby imprisonment was preferable to death. But military law had limits. Apart from weak enforcement, international conventions favored the interests of their signatories – of occupying armies and powerful imperial states rather than civilians resisting invasion. Significant to the global history of camps, international law criminalized guerrilla warfare (conducted by small irregular bands of nonuniformed fighters, including Indigenous insurgents in the American West) and permitted the imprisonment or even execution of civilians resisting occupation. The more nineteenth-century legislation helped constrain war, the more it consolidated the power of Western armies and justified reprisals against those whose resistance did not adhere to the selective customs of "civilized" combat. This was especially true for colonial populations, both in America, where the Confederacy refused to apply the Lieber Code to Black captives, and in the looming conquest of Africa.

The Scramble for Africa

The late-nineteenth-century "scramble for Africa," much like the "scramble for America," was a violent affair. Though total war in Europe and America dissolved boundaries between soldiers and civilians, such categories made little sense in Africa, where European armies denied civilian status to the supposedly "uncivilized." Colonial "small wars," from the Ashanti rebellions in Ghana (1823–1900) to the Mahdist uprising in Sudan (1881–99), treated entire populations of men, women, and children as indiscriminately subhuman.

The biggest of all "small wars," the South African (or Anglo-Boer) War (1899–1902), saw Britain expand into the Transvaal and Orange Free States, two independent republics populated by Boer (or Afrikaner) ranchers, the descendants of seventeenth-century Dutch settlers, along with Sotho, Tswana, and other African tribes. Although the conflict commenced, with great fanfare, as a "white man's war," Black Africans fought on both sides. And as British military frustrations mounted, racial depictions framed operations. As the war degenerated into an "uncivilized" guerrilla conflict, the language of social Darwinism transformed the Boers, discursively, from virile Anglo-Saxons into what the British general Herbert Kitchener described as "Afrikander savages with only a thin white veneer." They were a "half caste race," the poet Rudyard Kipling added, who had "gone native" after centuries on the "dark continent." For Major F.C. Fuller, a future luminary of the British Fascist Party, there "appeared something intensely animal about these people," while voices in the tabloid press even recommended the Boers be "exterminated" with "the same ruthlessness that they slay a plague-infected rat." Others compared Afrikaners to Native Americans who, as seminomadic "wanderers," had supposedly failed to settle the land. Their habitations, British commentators observed, presented "none of the usual signs of a neighborhood; no fertile and cultivated land surrounds [them]; no trees or parks or pleasure grounds are near [them]." And while Boers had maintained strict racial boundaries ever since van Riebeeck planted his bitter almond hedge (chap. 2), cultural depictions increasingly cast them as a colonial race. Tainted by a strong "infusion of the negro," they would endure practices of forced removal and concentration previously reserved for "savages."[12]

As racial camaraderie disintegrated, violence intensified. With superior firepower, Britain achieved rapid victory in conventional pitched battles. But it struggled to pacify lingering resistance by canny guerrillas like Christiaan de Wet and their Black attendants, whose intimate knowledge of the landscape allowed them to ambush railway lines and supply depots before vanishing into the wilderness. Meant to restrict military violence, the conventions of "civilized war" – face-to-face encounters between formal armies on demarcated battlefields – instead gave Britain *carte blanche* to punish insurgents who engaged in "uncivilized" (though militarily effective) resistance. The Boers' treachery and cunning, their mobility and stealth, their capacity for camouflage – to cite common British tropes – elicited comparisons with local Zulu and Xhosa warriors, as well as Indigenous tribes in America: "the Boer was a man of ambushes [and] the trickeries of war as formerly was the Sioux Indian," the military observer Adalbert Sternberg noted. Hoping to anticipate Boer tactics, meanwhile, Field Marshall Frederick Sleigh Roberts recruited as his chief scout a Minnesotan man, Frederick Burnham, who was raised on a Dakota Sioux reservation and had worked as an "Indian tracker" during the Apache Wars.[13]

Far from the "gentleman's war" some had anticipated, the South African conflict soon resembled "Indian skirmishes" in the American West. Similar representations yielded similar solutions. Studying the "desultory warfare of United States troops against the nomad Red Indians," the military theorist Charles Callwell warned that "irregular war" demanded measures that "may shock the humanitarian."[14] The American Civil War also loomed large. A British government memo warned that "American precedents," if rigorously applied, would "undoubtedly lead to the wiping out of the Boer nationality."[15] But Roberts, channeling Sheridan, was adamant: "unless the people are generally made to suffer ... the war will never end." Facing partisan fighters, whom Britain racialized as semicolonial savages, in a war many Afrikaners conceived as a fight for national survival, British generals combined elements of both colonial and total war. The conflict built on scorched-earth and counterinsurgency tactics on the American plains, and it anticipated civilian internment practiced in the world wars of the twentieth century.

FIGURE 3.1 If native reservations in America provided "militarily useful spaces for concentrating and monitoring native fighters,"[16] so did the fortified towns and subsequent camps of South Africa. The internment camp at Fort Snelling, Minnesota (*above*), which detained Dakota warriors and their families, was militarily analogous to Barberton, South Africa (*below*). (Source: Minnesota Historical Society; British Library of Economics and Political Science.)

Cuba also set a precedent. Just a few years previously, the Spanish Empire had faced guerrilla rebels fighting a War of Independence (1895–98). In response, General Valeriano Weyler had pillaged the island's food supplies and relocated – or *reconcentrated*, in his words – Cuba's rural population into fortified towns, evacuating and thus pacifying the countryside. British commentators condemned "Weylerian barbarity" even as they embraced "stern reconcentration" as a solution in South Africa.[17] And while farm burnings compelled civilians to find shelter in nearby towns, British forces

FIGURE 3.2 Civilians rounded up and relocated in Cuba (*left*) and a sensationalized image of the same dynamic in South Africa (*right*). Until the Anglo-Boer War, operations in Cuba were unprecedented in scale, intensity, and efficiency, placing them "closer to the camps of the twentieth century," the historian Andreas Stucki writes. Both conflicts also drew from deeper trajectories. If the Boers resembled Sioux Indians, Weyler's *pueblos reconcentrados* reenacted the forced urbanization of natives in *reducciones* – a history to which Cubans were no strangers. (Source: W.A. Rogers, *Harper's Pictorial History of the War with Spain* [New York: Harper, 1899], 137; Jean Veber, *L'Assiete au Beurre*, September 28, 1901.)

compartmentalized South Africa into a geometric matrix of fortified block-houses connected with barbed wire – a technology recently invented in the American West to herd cattle and occupy Indian land. Recalling the violent Cherokee removals of the 1830s, flying columns then combed each grid, burning villages, searching houses for contraband, and rounding up scattered populations, both Boer and Black, who endured forced marches to garrison towns where they were concentrated, monitored, and immobilized. It was like trapping "wild animals" in a cage, Kitchener proclaimed.[18]

A global network of POW camps, from Cape Colony to St. Helena, and from Bermuda to Ahmednagar, India (which recycled corrugated-iron huts from famine relief camps), interned Boer men caught with arms. Eager to avoid the specter of Andersonville, however, British POW camps complied with the Hague Convention by providing rations and accommodation comparable to those allotted to British soldiers. But civilians, including large numbers of women and children, denied the status of POWs, were another matter. At one point, General Kitchener considered banishing the entire civilian population to "some island or country ... Fiji for instance, or ... Madagascar," though logistical barriers forestalled such permanent solutions – Madagascar would not be South Africa's Oklahoma. Instead, the army left it to civil administrators, whom it deemed better equipped to manage women, children, and elderly men, to feed, accommodate, and control them in occupied towns. From here, the development of camps was rapid but haphazard: facing hunger, disease, and social unrest, including riots and looting, district commissioners erected rows of surplus army tents to shelter those driven from their farms. Such was the genesis of the first "refugee concentrated camps," as they were called.[19]

WHAT'S IN A NAME?

Today, "concentration camps" are indelibly associated with Nazi violence. But the term has deeper and more varied historical roots. Nineteenth-century commentators used the noun "camp" and the verb "concentrate" to describe the collection of slave laborers, Indigenous populations, and other displaced or marginal groups into crowded enclosures. But the ubiquitous "concentration camp" did not formally enter European languages until 1900 during the South African War. Initially, the term simply described the physical concentration of a target population into a circumscribed space. Speaking to the ambiguities of this neologism, officials in South Africa referred to such enclosures as both "concentration camps" and "refugee camps."

During World War I, "internment camp" and "concentration camp" were likewise interchangeable terms. And even after the war, European officials used the term "concentration camp" to describe both the Ottoman Empire's murderous collection points during the Armenian genocide (below) and the shelters Allied powers erected to protect refugees fleeing the violence (chap. 8). From the beginning, the terms were contested. While some inmates, fleeing scorched-earth operations, did indeed seek refuge on their own volition, others denied they were "refugees." The "enemy hunted us round like dogs," one woman complained, but "sought to hide their infamy by saying that we were refugees."[20] It was not, however, until World War II that the terms "refugee camp," "concentration camp," and "internment camp" were definitively differentiated.

> Language is never fixed, and definitions are never final: they respond to change, to history. How might the meaning of "concentration camp" change in the twenty-first century? What historical developments and institutions might "concentration camp" describe in the future? And how helpful might it be, either politically or intellectually, to continue using the term?

Surveillance, Classification, Control

In Cuba, emaciated *reconcentrados* erected makeshift lean-tos or huddled on city streets, where starvation and disease killed a third of the population between 1896 and 1898. Much like native reservations or Victorian industrial cities, concentration presaged epidemics. Britain, however, made significant advances in the management of captive populations – particularly when large numbers of women and children of European ancestry were involved – by providing shelter, rations, and medical care in a dedicated system of camps. Though their record was hardly better than in Cuba – 20 percent mortality, largely from epidemics and childhood diseases, which British officials blamed on the "criminal neglect" of Boer mothers – South African concentration camps suggested an ironically "humane," albeit far from adequate, alternative to wanton neglect.

Tidy rows of army tents (figure 3.1) depicted by aerial photographs belied chaos on the ground as officials experimented with new systems of social and military control. Some camps lacked fences and allowed regular visits to nearby towns, while others, like Vredefort Road, were "real prisons" with "entanglements all around ... and fences and sentries ... at the entrances." In some cases, capable superintendents erected hospitals, while in others, measles, smallpox, and typhoid killed thousands. Over time, however, British camps developed institutional structure as medical and military experts cemented lessons in discipline and sanitation. At new purpose-built enclosures like Amalinda Bluff, the careful disposition of buildings along with stringent rules and regulations rendered inmates "easier to manage than any English crowd," the British high commissioner Alfred Milner boasted. And such arrangements reduced camp mortality to rates that compared favorably with nearby seaside towns.[21]

The macro-social management of encamped populations depended on the developing bureaucratic capacities of modern states and professional militaries, along with inspiration from Victorian prisons and workhouses. Colonial secretary Joseph Chamberlain (1836–1914), the ultimate authority for camp management, was himself a former Poor Law guardian. Britain also recruited officials from colonial India with analogous experience at plague segregation and famine relief camps, while nearby de Beers compounds and Cape Town's slave lodge (chap. 2) offered lessons in the control of concentrated colonials – including native Africans, who were also swept up in British patrols and ultimately encamped. Much like contrabands in the American Civil War, congregations of destitute "negroes" unsettled white town dwellers, while the "lessons of Indian famine camps ... taught the advisability of keeping natives employed." In a spatial manifestation of the colonial strategy of "divide and rule," officials thereby segregated Black inmates in a separate camp system that enforced a work-or-starve policy. "We have to work hard all day long," one inmate complained, "but the only food we can get is mealies [corn porridge]." Largely self-sufficient, native camps also grew grain for the army and drafted inmates to military contract work. What they did not do was provide education or fair wages. Concentrating inmates of European lineage, officials conceived Boer camps as "tools of modernization" that would teach British history and the English language while endowing inmates with the hygienic habits and industrial skills necessary to thrive in the modern world. But they feared that a similar education for Black Africans, destined for lives of unskilled labor, would "unsettle the ... present system of control."[22] Native camps, then, were preludes to a series of betrayals that laid the groundwork for twentieth-century apartheid.

In addition to racial segregation, officials quickly realized that camps were useful tools for gathering information that rendered enemy internees "legible" to the colonial state. Dividing the population according to political status, Britain released those deemed loyal, fed "bona fide refugees" with superior rations (1,939 versus 1,747 calories a day), and confined "political undesirables" in punishment cells. Covered with wire mesh, much like de Beers' Kimberley compound, the "Bird Cage" in Bloemfontein enforced eight hours of work a day for all "singing birds" – inmates with anti-British attitudes – while the "showyard" camp in Winburg concentrated "undesirables" in diminutive livestock sheds. Coupled with hunger, disease, and the prolonged discomfort of leaky tents and barren barracks, such experiences inflicted lasting trauma. "May we see to it that the defenseless and innocent are respected and protected. And that such inhuman institutions as Concentration Camps are never resorted to again," the dissident inmate

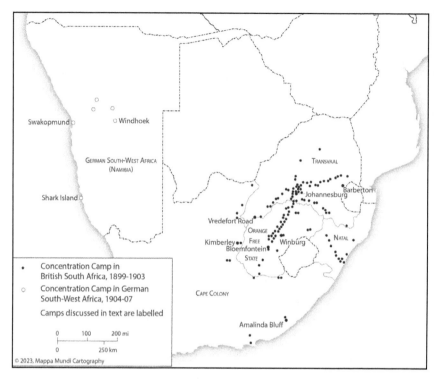

MAP 3.1 Camps of colonial southern Africa, 1899–1907.

Elizabeth Neethling wrote in an early iteration of the camp memoir – a genre that would burgeon in the twentieth century.[23] Her warnings went unheeded.

Concentration Zones and *Konzentrationslager*

South African concentration camps and Cuban *pueblos reconcentrados* became major media spectacles. The *Chicago Tribune* published articles about the "horrors of Boer concentration camps," Paris's *Le Temps* spoke of the courageous perseverance of inmates, while German periodicals ran articles like "What can we learn from the Boer War?"[24] The Russian Communist Leon Trotsky read about camps in the press, as did the Chinese Nationalist Sun Yat Sen. As a result, the term and concept "concentration camp" and its European cognates – *camp de concentration*, *Konzentrationslager*, and *konslager* – circulated throughout the world's languages. But while reactions to civilian concentration were largely negative – an example of what not to do – other powers soon established their own camp systems.

An expansionist empire in its own right, the United States remained critical of European imperialism and particularly of Spanish reconcentration. But if Americans described Weyler as a latter-day conquistador, the Spanish general retorted that he had only followed Sherman's and Sheridan's tactics. And he (accurately) predicted that America would do the same in similar circumstances. While Cuba achieved nominal independence in 1898 – apart from the US army camp at Guantanamo Bay (chap. 7), which remained an extralegal enclave for decades to come – US forces annexed the Philippines, a Spanish colony, in a broader imperial conflict. The Pacific Ocean, then, proved no barrier to America's insatiable dynamic of westward expansion. Marking the rise of a new imperial nation, the future British prime minister Winston Churchill gave a speech in New York City defending Boer War concentration camps, while Rudyard Kipling counseled America to "take up the white man's burden, to serve your captives' need." History repeated – but in more ways than one. Demanding independence, Filipino insurgents resisted American occupation with guerrilla tactics self-consciously inspired by the Boers – indeed, a small Filipino contingent had even fought on the Boer side during the South African War. In response, US forces deported civilians and suspected guerrillas to fenced "concentration zones" as opposition congressmen accused their military of "adopt[ing] the very tactics of Weyler in Cuba and of Kitchener in South Africa."[25] America drew from domestic precedents as well. Many US soldiers were veterans of the Civil War and of skirmishes with Native Americans; Filipino tribes, they commented, were "identically the same … as the Indians of our country" and "must be subdued in … the same way."[26]

Germany also erected colonial *Konzentrationslager*. Following rapid and violent wars of national unification in the 1860s, the Kaiserreich emerged as a world power eager to pursue imperial expansion. As 5 million Germans settled in the United States, others looked to Africa, where the German geographer Friedrich Ratzel (1844–1904) popularized the concept *Lebensraum*. The racial health of a virile and vigorous people, like the Germans, demanded "living space," he argued. To this end, the colony of South-West Africa (present-day Namibia) served as "Germany's California." Its first governor, Heinrich Göring, implemented a system of racial segregation inspired, in part, by the inequities of the American South and pursued frontier conflicts with the Indigenous Herero and Nama peoples.[27] Citing the United States and Australia as examples, Ratzel was explicit: *Lebensraum* demanded the violent removal of weaker Indigenous races, whose destiny, predetermined by the laws of nature, was to perish.

The German military was a formidable force. Though it admired General Sherman's tactics in the American South, which it applied in the Franco-Prussian War (1870–1) and in quelling the Boxer Rebellion in China (1900), the Kaiser's military stood out for its results-oriented emphasis on instrumental rationality: soldiers would obey commands, however morally dubious, to achieve victory by any means. When Herero and Nama warriors attacked German settlers intruding on their land, the Kaiserreich's military and political culture reflexively demanded "absolute destruction." At the decisive Battle of Waterberg (1904), colonial *Schutztruppen* overwhelmed Herero forces with belt-loading machine guns – a demonstration of the immense disparities of power that often foreground genocide. Instead of then negotiating peace, however, Commander Lothar von Trotha (1848–1920) issued an "extermination order" to shoot all survivors. In desperation, 60,000 Herero men, women, and children fled into the Kalahari Desert, where they died from starvation and thirst.[28]

In contrast to other powers, then, the *Schutztruppe* did not use camps as components of anti-guerrilla war. Instead, it drove the Indigenous population into exile and death. Six months after the Herero's military defeat, however, the German chancellor Bernhard von Bülow reversed Trotha's genocidal order on the grounds that it had depleted the nascent colony's labor supply. He thus ordered the military to establish camps to provide "asylums where Herero who had participated in the war … could find quarter and refuge." Cleansing patrols swept the desert, while railway cattle cars deported survivors to six main camps connected to cities and military forts.[29] Like their British counterparts, then, German camps claimed a dubious humanitarian mandate.

Far from being safe havens, however, colonial *Konzentrationslager* were carceral sites of suffering and neglect. In a climate of racial animus, the colony's military was uninterested, at best, in sustaining native lives – a contrast to the Boers, who enjoyed a quasi-European status and aroused the attention and empathy of the Western world. Already weakened by months of emaciation and exile, Nama and Herero survivors were placed behind double rows of barbed wire and billeted in pathetic semicircular structures consisting of sacking and planks (figure 5.1). Daily rations – 500 grams of rice, half that for women and children – only prolonged starvation. And tellingly, German authorities referred to inmates not as refugees but as POWs (albeit ones denied the legal protections of the Hague Convention). Armed sentries and corporal punishment governed the camps accordingly: "I have never seen an overseer without a *sambok* [a club], whip, or truncheon," one witness observed, and sexual violence was commonplace: bare-chested Herero women were subjects of the erotic gaze of German guards.[30]

HUMANITARIAN BACKLASH

Turn-of-the-century Africa is important not only for the violence it endured, but for the development of humanitarian traditions protesting concentration camps. The British philanthropist Emily Hobhouse (1860–1926) became a powerful critic of camps in South Africa. Focusing on the shocking plight of Boer women and children, she described inmates as "more or less prisoners" who died like flies of starvation, exposure, and disease. When Hobhouse returned to Britain in 1901, she spoke at dozens of public events and lectures. The government would yield only to fear, she believed, "the fear of public opinion."[31] Although conservative publications like the *Daily Mail* dismissed Hobhouse as a "hysterical" woman, large segments of the British public sympathized. In the words of the colonial secretary Joseph Chamberlain, "concentration camps had undoubtedly roused deep feeling" and "many good people [were] distressed" as a result. Although Hobhouse had a racial blind spot for Black African camps (which she never visited) and was naïve in praising conditions at World War I German internment camps (which she toured in 1914), her campaign prompted an official commission of prominent women – an important milestone in the history of female public activism – to investigate camp conditions and recommend reforms. Death from epidemic disease dropped dramatically once their proposals were implemented.[32]

Colonial camps also aroused criticism in Germany. Social Democrats like August Bebel condemned Germany's treatment of Indigenous peoples as "not only barbaric, but bestial."[33] The German-Jewish dissident Otto Eltzbacher similarly deemed colonial *Konzentrationslager* an "offence against justice and humanity."[34] Yet protests fell largely on deaf ears. The power and prestige of the Kaiser's military kept it insulated from domestic scrutiny, while weak civilian institutions – South-West Africa lacked a civilian high commissioner, for example – meant that public opinion was a less reliable brake on military extremism than it was elsewhere. The importance of a free press and lively civil society – along with the democratic recognition that opposition to government is both legitimate and patriotic – emerge as important lessons in the early history of camps. German colonial camps, some historians argue, were unique not because German soldiers were especially cruel, but because Germany's constitution silenced dissent. Germany had its own Emily Hobhouses, but it was inconceivable that German humanitarians – let alone women – could publicly criticize the military or recommend reforms.[35] How might twentieth-century history have developed had Germany's hyper-masculine military culture allowed more space for civil dissent and for female input?

More than their British, American, and Spanish counterparts, German *Konzentrationslager* were venues of forced labor, corporal punishment, and death. From early morning until late at night, inmates at Swakopmund "had to work under the clubs of raw overseers," a missionary recorded. And despite lip service to the civilizing virtues of work, the real purpose of inmate labor was to build roads, buildings, and railways for the fledgling settler colony: just as the people of Kahlin built the city of Darwin in Australia (chap. 2), camp labor was directly linked to the town of Swakopmund's economy.[36] Camps were also major suppliers to private industry: in a system that resembled "the cooperation that developed [in World War II] between the SS and [the] arms industry," the historian Jonas Kreienbaum observes, the Woermann Shipping line and Lenz and Koppel railway company employed so many inmates that they opened their own subcamps.[37] At times, however, punishment and brutality eclipsed economic rationality: dead bodies could not work. With mortality approaching 50 percent – and at the notorious Shark Island camp, 75 percent – *Konzentrationslager* represented "a continuation of annihilation by other means," the historian Isabel Hull contends.[38] They thus anticipated the combination of forced labor and annihilation of the Third Reich (chap. 5), albeit in a far less systematic or premeditated form.

Life for colonial Africans, then, was not a human right but an economic function. Herero prisoners, even more than transatlantic slaves, survived only so long as they retained a productive value. Responding to critics, German politicians noted that Britain had invented concentration camps in South Africa. This was not the last time Germany would justify its camps via reference to British precedents. But while the comparison had merit, the

German military's disposition toward stringent punishment differentiated its culture of encampment from more liberal approaches in Britain, America, and France. And this predilection for brutality would reemerge in World War I. As global violence shifted to Europe, the unfortunate detainee Wim Hopford recognized the difference. "Twice interned," first as a Boer prisoner in South Africa and then, in 1914, as a British subject in Germany, Hopford found life at the Ruhleben internment camp, outside Berlin, to be harsher than in South Africa: "Prussian militarism" made "violent blows" routine.[39]

Enemy Aliens

World War I (1914–18) was both a rupture and a pivot. Unprecedented in scale and scope, the Great War intensified dynamics of total war that had developed throughout the nineteenth century. No longer was killing a feat of chivalric courage but of "cold, alien, hostile machine[s]," of "serialized death, [and] indirect killing."[40] Professional command structures displaced the psychological burden of killing from individual soldiers to automatic weapons and anonymous bureaucracies, while the logic of instrumental rationality enshrined military necessity and national security over civil liberties and human rights. No longer heroic warriors, soldiers resembled proletarian factory workers, obeying orders to dispense a depersonalized death. And like a boomerang, the conflict imported violent practices from Africa and America to the heart of Europe. If camps had thrived in the martial and authoritarian climate of empire, emergency decrees placed Europe under a similar state of legal exception. Meanwhile, the dual forces of nationalism and democracy, invented during the French Revolution, inducted civilians into war as never before. In such conditions, internment camps, for civilians and POWs, proliferated.

Total war blurs distinctions between soldiers and civilians, but it also forces citizens to draw clear boundaries between "us" and "them," "friend" and "enemy." Ethnic nationalism, spawned in the nineteenth century, generated enmity alongside colonial racism; indeed, the two phenomena were linked. As Europeans celebrated the outbreak of war, nationalist hysteria exacerbated xenophobic fears – already evident in prewar legislation excluding "aliens" (chap. 1) – about outsiders, immigrants, and foreigners, while national governments fortified their frontiers. Jingoistic media racialized the enemy: Germans became "hordes" and "huns" similar to the "semi-savage peoples of central Africa";[41] Ottomans were untrustworthy "Orientals"; Russians and Slavs were backward and inferior; and German media conflated the British, French, and later Americans with the "negro" and "cannibal" soldiers that populated their armies, both on the Western Front and overseas. Meanwhile, German nationals interned on Rottnest Island in the Indian Ocean witnessed the white Australian policy "reimagined to exclude not only Asians and coloureds but all non-members of the 'British race.'"[42] Discourses of public health likewise framed foreigners as disease carriers, while locals approached refugees, along with criminal deviants, prostitutes, and vagrants, with renewed suspicion. Thus did the logic of wartime internment intersect with that of the workhouse. And as war drew social boundaries, it militarized national borders, introducing police surveillance and mobility restrictions with the passport regime we know today (though pass systems had long curtailed colonial mobility). The hardened borders of the modern world thus offered a broader context for proliferating barbed-wire camps detaining internal and external outsiders.

The Great War mobilized a staggering 60 million soldiers, of whom 9 million were captured and detained within world history's largest network of POW camps. The logic was nothing new, but the scale dwarfed statistics from the Anglo-Boer and American Civil Wars. And while early camps were largely improvised, the war's duration, and the increasing state capacity it entailed, fostered planned, purpose-built enclosures, along with international agencies, like the International Committee of the Red Cross, to inspect conditions according to recognized standards. The iconic "Nissen Hut," invented by a Canadian mining engineer in 1916, exemplified the material culture of military confinement. Portable, expandable, and easy to transport, the corrugated iron skin, supported by steel ribs and wooden purlins, could be erected in a mere four hours. Formally patented and mass produced according to generic designs, 100,000 huts billeted soldiers, POWs, and, later, refugees, asylum-seekers, and migrant workers (chap. 8). Though economical and convenient for state authorities, however, inmates found them drafty, uncomfortable, and institutional.

Enemy civilians also faced mass confinement. World War I marked a definitive end to earlier cultures of military captivity, already eroded by colonial warfare, that restricted internment to soldiers. If Boer guerrillas in South Africa blurred distinctions between combatant and civilian, World War I incorporated entire civilian societies into a giant global battlefield. As wartime hardships heightened ethnic suspicion, German waiters in London, Ottoman traders in India, and Serbians in Austria-Hungary were detained as suspect collectivities, not for their actions as individuals but for their ethnic

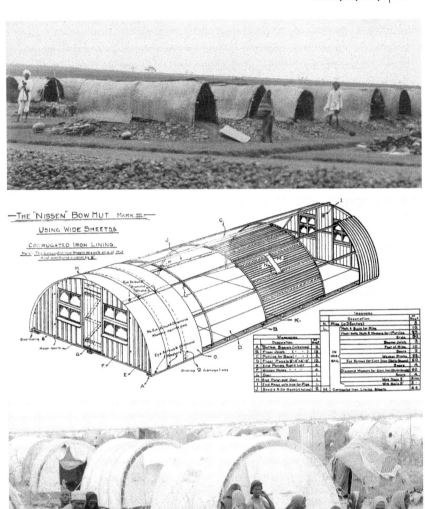

FIGURE 3.3 The basic design of the "Nissen Hut," patented in 1916 (*middle*), resembled cylindrical huts in nineteenth-century famine camps (*above*, chaps. 2 and 8) and inspired collapsible tents at modern refugee camps like Dadaab, Kenya (*below*, chap. 8). (Source: British Library; National Archives of the United Kingdom; hikrcn/Shutterstock.)

identity. As swarms of imagined spies and foreign saboteurs infused a guilt-by-association paranoia common in moments of uncertainty and war, camps also detained internal others and suspect minorities, along with refugees fleeing warzones or deported from enemy states – ethnic Germans from Russia, Ukrainians from Austria-Hungary, and above all, Jews, who were singled out for expulsion by both sides. Germany, Austria, France, and Italy revoked the status of naturalized citizens of enemy origin, rendering them effectively stateless and thus doubly liable to encampment, while Britain interned Irish rebels and their supporters. And as war exacerbated social tensions, countries like France detained left-wing agitators and common criminals alongside enemy aliens – an entanglement of military detention, political imprisonment, and criminal punishment that would later be replicated by concentration camps in World War II. In the multinational Austro-Hungarian Empire, meanwhile, ethnic tensions generated hastily erected "guarded villages" to intern citizens of Serbian and Italian origin. Suffering from hunger and disease, inmates at a camp in Ljubljana were "like living skeletons,"[43] suspended between life and death, while Italian inmates referred to another enclosure as a *campo della morte* – a "death camp."[44]

Civilian internment camps were preemptive and collective institutions: regardless of military realities, civilians were interned as potential agents of the enemy's war effort. Such actions violated democratic norms, but they also reflected populist politics. Following the 1915 sinking of the RMS *Lusitania* by a U-boat, for example, anti-German riots in London and popular xenophobic publications like the *Daily Mail* compelled government action. Herbert Kitchener, the Boer War general and new secretary of war, expressed the popular will when he ordered the internment of Germans resident in Britain, ostensibly for their own protection from vigilantes, but also, clearly, to retaliate against German war crimes. Fearing that the internment of women and children would "savor too much of concentration camps in the Boer War," however, Britain restricted the policy to men, a dubious dispensation that separated families and left wives and children in dire economic straits.[45]

In total more than 800,000 civilians across Europe and the world became inmates during World War I in institutions known, interchangeably, as "internment camps" and "concentration camps." The scale and global reach dwarfed previous internments, and in contrast to one-sided colonial conflicts, in which only occupying imperial powers erected camps, all major belligerents concentrated civilians. Britain's largest facility, Knockaloe on the Isle of Man, accommodated enemy aliens in circular bell tents familiar from the Boer War, as did work camps in Siberia, desert outposts in French

Algeria, and army installations in South Africa. Camps at Mauthausen, Austria, and Ruhleben near Berlin likewise interned Allied citizens, including Wim Hopford, the hapless Boer-turned-Briton. And in a significant moment of globalization, camps spread to every corner of the world: Japan introduced mass confinement to Asia with the Bandō POW camp, Britain interned civilians from German East Africa at Ahmednagar, India, in facilities recycled, once again, from famine relief and Boer POW camps. French Indochina erected bamboo camps raised 1.8 meters off the jungle floor, while Ukrainian migrants in Canada, interned as citizens of the Austro-Hungarian Empire, built the infrastructure of Banff National Park. Even independent Siam, whose tiny expeditionary force fought on the Western Front, interned enemy aliens in camps administered by British India.

Despite processes of standardization, conditions varied from camp to camp, often in response to the politics of gender, race, and class or to the priorities of disparate military cultures. With the notable exception of Russia, where many died in hostile Siberian environments, Allied powers mostly conformed to international standards. Applying sanitary lessons from the South African War, officials prevented widespread mortality in British camps, while Lofthouse Park in northern England accommodated upper-class Germans in a former amusement park. Gentlemanly norms prevailed as inmates enjoyed theater performances and university lectures. And though internees suffered from boredom and anxiety, diagnosed in 1919 as "barbed-wire disease," they rarely faced physical danger. In contrast, Red Cross inspectors observed special brutality at German and Austro-Hungarian camps, including punitive rations, isolation in dungeons, and the dreaded *Anbinden*, a torture device that tied victims by the back of their hands to a wooden post so that their feet could not touch the ground. Loss of consciousness and ruptured tendons soon followed. According to Red Cross officials in Austria-Hungary, ethnic Serbs, blamed collectively for the assassination that first triggered the war, faced special hardship: they "reached the concentration camps haggard, bare-foot, and hungry" but found "no installations ready," only "bare fields surrounded with barbed wire." Women faced their own privations. At Thalerhof, also in Austria-Hungary, female detainees had to strip naked and bathe in front of the whole camp; officers, who traveled from Graz to see the spectacle, "made the unfortunate women pose before their cameras." Organized into labor battalions and identified with red armbands, meanwhile, women in German-occupied Belgium were treated like common prostitutes and forced to undergo compulsory gynecological exams.[46] With consequences for the future, such practices proved increasingly common in a military culture that celebrated masculine strength and traditional gender norms – and that already veered toward extremes.

Forced labor, prohibited by the 1907 Hague Convention, defined camp life for civilians and POWs alike. Allied governments recruited labor corps from China (3 million in total), Africa (1.25 million), and India (563,000, including convicts) to dig trenches and haul supplies. Unable to mobilize colonial workers and outmatched in economic and human resources, however, Russia forced German and Austrian POWs to labor on the Murmansk railway where 25,000 out of 70,000 died – a precedent for the Soviet Gulag (chap. 4). Indeed, the extensive Krasnoyarsk camp in Siberia, visited by Josef Stalin in 1916, offered a potential prototype for prison labor in the Soviet Union. Yet Russians were also victims. As captive labor became increasingly central to Germany's war economy, East Europeans, including large numbers of Jews and Slavs, faced horrendous conditions. The belief that "dirty and uncivilized" Russians were "accustomed to iron coercion in their homeland" lowered standards accordingly.[47] Detained at "distribution centers" and "industrial laborers' lodgings" – names chosen, perhaps, to avoid the increasingly pejorative term "concentration camp"[48] – noncombatants worked side-by-side with POWs draining swamps and fulfilling daily quotas at coal and iron mines. Here, familiar patterns reemerged. Apologists depicted work as a civilizing enterprise, or else a necessary means to an end. Yet brutal conditions and gratuitous violence from military guards proved counterproductive to fulfilling labor demands. Camps in Germany's occupied east, the *Ober Ost*, were sites of hunger, disease, and death that "acclimatiz[ed] the European mind," the historian Peter Pastor argues, "to the existence of concentration camps."[49]

Ethnic Hatreds

Total war also exacerbated tensions in the Ottoman Empire, an ally of Germany and Austria-Hungary, where ethnic tension motivated World War I's largest genocide. As military defeat and wartime hardships brought the Ottoman Empire to the brink of collapse, internal others became targets for elimination as a new generation of revolutionary Young Turk nationalists shattered earlier ethnic equilibriums. Despite longstanding traditions of multicultural toleration, Christian minorities, including Greeks, Assyrians, and, above all, Armenians, who constituted the empire's leading professional and mercantile class, faced suspicion of being pro-Russian saboteurs.

In the Caucasus mountains, some Armenians had indeed sided with Russian forces, which had traditionally protected Christians in the region. As natives of the country, familiar with the landscape, they acted as scouts in small semi-guerrilla bands. A pattern of indiscriminate violence, targeting an ethnic collectivity rather than guilty individuals, soon followed. As if parroting Sherman and Roberts, though in more explicitly violent terms, the Turkish governor Djevdet Bey (1878–1955) threatened to "kill every Christian man, woman, and child … if the rebels fire a single shot."[50] In this context, Ottoman regiments engaged in scorched-earth warfare as they pillaged Armenian villages and organized mass deportations from the Anatolian heartland.

Like the Kalahari in South-West Africa, the Arabian desert was a tool of genocide. In a Mesopotamian reenactment of the Trail of Tears, forced marches pushed Armenian civilians south toward the arid Syrian steppe. On the way, militia shootings and drownings claimed the lives of thousands of deportees, as did modern refinements like poison gas and morphine injections in the city of Trebizond. Camps, on the outskirts of towns, were not permanent destinations but transit points, directing and concentrating the dead and dying as they fled deeper into the desert. With shelter consisting of shoddy sacks and tents, and lacking food and water, conditions were horrendous. Inmates used corpses as pillows; mothers sold their children for crusts of bread; girls were trafficked as sex slaves; and local Arabs and Bedouins looted the camps at night. Appointing inmates themselves as guards, the camps also set moral traps, forcing Armenians to collaborate in their own destruction. Meanwhile, typhus and cholera added another chapter to the intertwined history of encampment and epidemics. The aim, according to the historian Raymond Kevorkian, was "to eliminate the deportees by creating health conditions of the kind that bred disaster."[51] Though outbreaks of disease at earlier camps, from Andersonville to Africa, had killed thousands, the organized and premeditated nature of the Armenian genocide suggests that camps may well have been conscious, if ad hoc, implements of biological warfare. More direct measures also emerged. At de Zor, authorities concentrated survivors in desert caves – a stone-walled captivity – and burned them alive. As primitive preludes to Nazi gas chambers, this "final solution" illustrated the horrifying potential of modern war and ethno-nationalist hatred.

In total, more than a million Armenians were murdered or expelled; today, their mass graves compete for space with the victims of ISIL and the Vladimir Putin-aligned regime of Bashar al-Assad in Syria. Those who survived, however, found themselves concentrated in a different type of camp as Allied armies and international relief committees erected humanitarian shelters, which they referred to, interchangeably, as "refugee camps" and "concentration camps" (chap. 8). The genocide thus indicated the linguistic ambiguity of early-twentieth-century camp terminology along with the varied applications, both murderous and humane, that camps fulfilled.

Conclusion

In the twentieth century, nationalism gradually replaced imperialism as the normative principle of geopolitical organization. In the nineteenth century, however, they were coequal forces that partitioned the world and concentrated ethnic and racial others behind barbed wire. Imperial "small wars" were themselves big news, propagated on a global stage by national media. By the outbreak of World War I, the concentration of potentially dangerous populations was a familiar practice. The Great War, then, did not invent anything new. But its mass scale facilitated the global proliferation of camps along with refinements in sanitary, disciplinary, architectural, and economic logistics. Camp memoirs aroused growing awareness of the subjective hardships inmates faced, while international agencies like the Red Cross established uniform standards. By 1918 camps had developed into sophisticated systems of mass confinement, enforcing discipline, surveillance, and forced labor for suspect, uncivilized, or otherwise displaced or undesirable groups. Essential features of modern states across the ideological spectrum, camps also operated according to varying national styles. Already detectable in the nineteenth century, these would have legacies in the future, as fallout from World War I generated authoritarian and revolutionary regimes in Germany and the Soviet Union.

Notes

1 Joël Kotek and Pierre Rigoulot, *Le Siècle des Camps: detention, concentration, extermination, cent ans de mal radical* (Paris: JC Lattes, 2000), 24.

2 Philip Dwyer, "Violence and the Revolutionary and Napoleonic Wars: Massacre, Conquest and the Imperial Enterprise," *Journal of Genocide Research* 15, no. 2 (2013): 117–31.

3 Francois Houdecek, "Training and Teaching of Conscripts during the Boulogne Camp," *Napoleonica. La Revue* 2, no. 32 (2018): 86–96.

4 Harold Mytum and Naomi Hall, "Norman Cross: Designing and Operating an Eighteenth-Century British Prisoner of War Camp," in *Prisoners of War: Archaeology, Memory, and Heritage of 19th- and 20th-Century Mass Internment*, ed. Harold Mytum and Gilly Carr (New York: Springer, 2013), 75–91.

5 Carl Degler, "The American Civil War and the German Wars of Unification: The Problem of Comparison," in *On the Road to Total War: The American Civil War and*

the German Wars of Unification, 1861–1871, ed. Stig Forster and Jorg Nagler (Cambridge: Cambridge University Press, 1997), 68.

6 John Y. Simon, ed., *The Papers of Ulysses S. Grant, Volume 12: August 16–November 15, 1864* (Carbondale: Southern Illinois University Press, 1984), 15.

7 Robert S. Davis, "Escape from Andersonville: A Study in Isolation and Imprisonment," *Journal of Military History* 67, no. 4 (2003): 1068.

8 "The Prison Camp at Andersonville," accessed July 5, 2021, https://www.nps.gov /parkhistory/online_books/civil_war_series/5/sec1.htm.

9 John Fabian Witt, *Lincoln's Code: The Laws of War in American History* (New York: Free Press, 2012), 301.

10 Davis, "Escape from Andersonville," 1067, 1065–66.

11 Chandra Manning, *Troubled Refuge: Struggling for Freedom in the Civil War* (New York: Vintage, 2016).

12 Aidan Forth, *Barbed-Wire Imperialism: Britain's Empire of Camps, 1876–1903* (Berkeley: University of California, 2017), 137–8, 141.

13 Forth, *Barbed-Wire Imperialism*, 134.

14 Charles Callwell, *Small Wars: Their Principles and Practice* (London: HMSO, 1906), 22, 40.

15 Aidan Forth and Jonas Kreienbaum, "A Shared Malady: Concentration Camps in the British, Spanish, American and German Empires," *Journal of Modern European History* 14, no. 2 (2016): 248.

16 Laleh Khalili, *Time in the Shadows: Confinement in Counterinsurgencies* (Stanford: Stanford University Press, 2013), 18.

17 Forth and Kreienbaum, "Shared Malady," 249.

18 Forth, *Barbed-Wire Imperialism*, 143.

19 Forth, *Barbed-Wire Imperialism*, 164, 152.

20 Emily Hobhouse, *War without Glamour or, Women's War Experiences Written by Themselves, 1899–1902* (Bloemfontein: Nasionale Pers, 1924), 34.

21 Forth, *Barbed-Wire Imperialism*, 164, 207–8.

22 Forth, *Barbed-Wire Imperialism*, 173–4.

23 Forth, *Barbed-Wire Imperialism*, 166, 212.

24 Forth and Kreienbaum, "Shared Malady," 257.

25 Forth and Kreienbaum, "Shared Malady," 259.

26 Iain Smith and Andreas Stucki, "The Colonial Development of Concentration Camps (1868–1902)," *Journal of Imperial and Commonwealth History* 39, no. 3 (2011): 419.

27 David Olusoga and Casper W. Erichsen, *The Kaiser's Holocaust: Germany's Forgotten Genocide and the Colonial Roots of Nazism* (London: Faber and Faber, 2010), 108–11.

28 Isabel Hull, *Absolute Destruction: Military Culture and the Practices of War in Imperial Germany* (Ithaca: Cornell University Press, 2005).

29 Forth and Kreienbaum, "Shared Malady," 261–62.

30 Hull, *Absolute Destruction*, 76.

31 Jennifer Hobhouse Balme, ed., *To Love One's Enemies: The Work and Life of Emily Hobhouse Compiled from Letters and Writings, Newspaper Cuttings and Official Documents* (Cobble Hill, BC: Hobhouse Trust, 1994), 93, 665, 224.

32 Forth, *Barbed-Wire Imperialism*, 181.

33 Jonas Kreienbaum, *A Sad Fiasco: Colonial Concentration Camps in Southern Africa, 1900–1908*, trans. Elizabeth Janik (New York: Berghahn, 2019), 47.

34 Jeremy Sarkin-Hughes, *Colonial Genocide and Reparations Claims in the 21st Century: The Socio-Legal Context of Claims under International Law by the Herero Against Germany for Genocide in Namibia, 1904–1908* (London: Praeger, 2009), 119.

35 Hull, *Absolute Destruction*, 187–93.

36 Olusoga and Erichsen, *Kaiser's Holocaust*, 163–4.

37 Kreienbaum, *Sad Fiasco*, 232.

38 Hull, *Absolute Destruction*, 90.

39 Wim Hopford, *Twice Interned: Transvaal 1901–02, Germany 1914–18* (London: John Murray, 1919).

40 Enzo Traverso, *The Origins of Nazi Violence*, trans. Janet Lloyd (New York: New Press, 2003), 83, 44–45.

41 Traverso, *Origins of Nazi Violence*, 92.

42 Matthew Stibbe, "Enemy Aliens and Internment," in *International Encyclopedia of the First World War*, October 2014, https://encyclopedia.1914-1918-online.net/article/enemy_aliens_and_internment.

43 Traverso, *Origins of Nazi Violence*, 87.

44 Alan Kramer, *Dynamic of Destruction: Culture and Mass Killing in the First World War* (Oxford: Oxford University Press, 2007), 59.

45 Forth, *Barbed-Wire Imperialism*, 220.

46 Matthew Stibbe, "Civilian Internment and Civilian Internees in Europe," *Immigrants and Minorities* 26, no. 1–2 (2008): 63.

47 Oxana Nagornaja, "United by Barbed Wire: Russian POWs in Germany, National Stereotypes, and International Relations, 1914–22," *Kritika* 10, no. 3 (2009): 480.

48 Jens Thiel and Christian Westerhoff, "Forced Labour," *International Encyclopedia of the First World War*, October 2014, https://encyclopedia.1914-1918-online.net/article/forced_labour.

49 Peter Pastor quoted in Alon Rachmaninov, *POWs and the Great War: Captivity on the Eastern Front* (Oxford: Berg, 2002), 80–2.

50 Henry Morgenthau, *Ambassador Morgenthau's Story: A Personal Account of the Armenian Genocide* (New York: Cosimo, 2010), 205.

51 Raymond Kevorkian, *The Armenian Genocide: A Complete History* (London: I.B. Tauris, 2011), 663.

4 | The Soviet Gulag: Revolution, Labor, and Punishment

The "Gulag archipelago," as the Soviet dissident and Nobel Prize-winning author Alexandr Solzhenitsyn (1918–2008) called it, was the incarnation of a war-torn revolutionary state. The Soviet Union arose, brutalized, from the ashes of World War I and a protracted civil war (1917–23). As military modalities continued into peacetime, a counterinsurgency against unruly peasants and political suspects detained millions. With sanitary and industrial metaphors, Solzhenitsyn described the Gulag, a Soviet acronym for *Glavnoye Upravleniye Lagerey* (Main Administration of Corrective Labor Camps), as a "sewage disposal system" that "purified" the body politic by excising undesirables. "Organs of state" swept up "parasites" and "unwanted matter" before flushing them "bodily down the sewer hatches."[1] "Class enemies" (in an inversion of previous norms, this meant wealthy capitalists) and political prisoners (accused, often wrongfully, of espionage or sabotage) were detained in a collective, extrajudicial manner and denied rights to due process or free speech. Meanwhile, a creeping xenophobia, the currency of dictators the world over, targeted ethnic minorities, enemy aliens, and POWs during World War II. Yet vagabonds, drunkards, and "hooligans," petty thieves and violent criminals, sentenced by criminal courts, were the camps' largest constituency. For such inmates, the vast but silent majority, the Gulag enforced patterns of discipline and punishment that predated and outlasted the Soviet regime.

The memoirs of "politicals" – the history professor Evgenia Ginzburg (1904–77), the German émigré Margarete Buber-Neumann (1901–89), along with Michael Solomon, Jacques Rossi, Varlam Shalamov, and above all, Solzhenitsyn – are literary classics. But they do not encapsulate the Gulag in its entirety. Implements of political and ideological terror, Soviet camps were also products of contingency and chaos, criminal punishment, and internal colonization. Indeed, Gulag memoirs showcase the experience of literate intellectuals but neglect the waves of nonpolitical offenders who comprised the majority of inmates in a diverse system of mass confinement. Though deadly arctic camps occupied the extreme end of a diverse carceral spectrum, "special settlements" and "corrective labor colonies," neglected until recently by historians, afforded prisoners relative degrees of freedom, with porous boundaries rarely demarcated by wire. Nonetheless, the Gulag enforced draconian punishment and labor in a system that concentrated arbitrary power in an authoritarian state; of some 20 million inmates, at least 2 million died. And in an irony not lost on its victims, the apparent quest to free humanity from the fetters of capitalism incarcerated Soviet subjects on unprecedented scales. Though it condemned Western imperialism, the Soviet Empire treated its own population like colonial subjects, devoid of rights. "[We were] the scum of the earth," one prisoner recounts, in echoes of Frantz Fanon.[2] As such, the Soviet era constituted a prolonged occupation characterized by levels of repression and military violence that matched and, in many cases, surpassed the colonial empires of the nineteenth century. Its legacies were collective trauma and broken lives, separated families and unmarked graves.

Foundations

The Bolshevik Revolution of October 1917 proclaimed a new political order. European Christendom had long considered utopia to be a heavenly, otherworldly endeavor. Yet for the apostles of revolution, a workers' paradise was achievable on earth. Enlightenment political sensibilities – that human agency could match the achievements of the divine – and Karl Marx's powerful critique of industrial capitalism augured a rupture in time, a world turned upside down, in which former masters would become slaves. Camps, accordingly, were instruments to make society anew, to wage war against class enemies, to enforce "obligatory work duty" for wealthy capitalists, and to extend Soviet control to remote peripheries. Yet deeper continuities endured. Tsarist authoritarianism gave way to the dictatorship of the Party; religious icons gave way to Stalin's cult of personality; Russian imperialism gave way to the Soviet Empire; the Okhrana (Nicholas II's secret police) gave way to the NKVD (People's Commissariat for Internal Affairs); and the bonds of serfdom gave way to the slavery of the camp. To achieve their goals, likewise, revolutionaries turned to established repertoires of penal exile and military captivity.

During World War I, Leon Trotsky (1879–1940) was himself detained by British authorities in Canada in what he called a "concentration camp."[3] The Bolshevik leaders Vladimir Lenin (1870–1924) and Józef Stalin (1878–1953) also spent their formative years in Siberian exile under the imperial tsar. Established in 1696 and expanded after 1847, forced labor colonies known as *katorga* punished both political offenders and common criminals – "a class of parasites and beggars," as authorities deemed them.[4] By exiling convicts to remote Siberian outposts like the Sakhalin archipelago, often with the purpose of developing Russia's expanding empire in northeast Asia, such practices resembled the merger of exile and confinement exhibited at the Andamans archipelago in British India and on Devil's Island in French Guiana (chap. 1). And while tsarist Russia was a continental rather than maritime empire, its transportation of political and criminal convicts on trains and ships, over vast landscapes, interior waterways, and arctic seas, resonated with global practices. Indeed, Solzhenitsyn's famous metaphor "the Gulag archipelago" – an image of carceral islands scattered across the Eurasian continent, reimagined as a vast but barren sea – suggests a conceptual compatibility with the practices of imperial Russia and its rivals. Prison trains were "ships of the archipelago," Solzhenitsyn wrote, while exiles in Siberia referred to European Russia as "the mainland."[5]

Despite global synergies, tsarist penal camps displayed moral and administrative shortcomings that would recur under Soviet rule. Nineteenth-century memoirs by Leo Tolstoy (1828–1910) and Fyodor Dostoyevsky (1821–81), literary forerunners to Solzhenitsyn, describe frigid temperatures, endless hunger, and manual labor in mines and lumber camps – deadly worksites that casually degraded human life. As in the Soviet period, poor planning and endemic corruption denied prisoners the rations and clothing to which they were entitled. And in the judgment of historians, convicts and political prisoners on remote Sakhalin faced greater brutality, corruption, and administrative incompetence than their Western counterparts at Mettray (chap. 1) – a model Russian officials studied. Outbreaks of typhoid at crowded transit camps, usually converted stockades or villages of tents and dilapidated huts, proved lethal, while overly ambitious labor assignments resembled later Gulag practices.[6] The construction of the trans-Siberian railway (by convict labor) expedited transport after 1916, but Soviet inmates called their railcars "Stolypin carriages," a term first coined by tsarist political prisoners in 1905 in reference to Nicholas II's prime minister. The tsarist-era Butyrka prison likewise functioned as a Gulag outpost throughout the Soviet period, while Stalin reintroduced the term *katorga* in 1943 to describe the most punishing Gulag camps.

Yet while the tsarist past provided useful carceral repertoires, the Soviet Gulag was harsher, more deadly, and far more expansive. In 1912, 32,000 prisoners resided at Russian penal colonies; in 1953, the Gulag detained more than 5 million across a diverse carceral network. Amid the dislocations of modern war and revolution, Russia's penal archipelago metastasized.

War and Revolution

The new Soviet government, like many regimes, turned to camps as instruments of war. After occupying Petrograd's Winter Palace, the revolutionary Bolshevik party found itself besieged by a "White Army" of monarchists, liberals, social democrats, and 13 foreign armies – an existential crisis that inaugurated a long tradition of Soviet anxiety about enemies of the state. Apart from tsarist penal colonies, the Bolsheviks also inherited an existing system of recently (and, given their labor utility, reluctantly) vacated POW camps (like Krasnoyarsk, chap. 3) from World War I, what the historian Bettina Greiner calls "a Gulag before the Gulag."[7] Instead of being dismantled at war's end, these camps, which subjected approximately 2 million enemy troops to forced labor, were absorbed by Soviet authorities. Amid civil war and social dislocation, one form of detention flowed into another.

In the countryside, forced conscription and the requisition of food and materiel triggered peasant uprisings and guerrilla resistance. In Tambov, southeast of Moscow, the pacification of anti-Bolshevik insurgents resulted in familiar carceral and anti-partisan measures (see chaps. 2 and 3). To suppress what it called "banditry," the Red Army interned some 50,000 "hostages," mostly women and children, in what Leon Trotsky called *konslager*, Russian for concentration camp. "Throughout the province," Solzhenitsyn writes, "camps were set up for the families of peasants who had taken part in the revolts. Tracts of open field were enclosed with barbed wire strung on posts."[8] As a counterinsurgency measure, the concentration of peasants in Tambov and elsewhere resembled the colonial camps of Cuba, South Africa, and the Philippines (chap. 3). Yet Soviet camps also operated according to a paranoid politics inherited from past cycles of revolutionary bloodletting. To consolidate a "dictatorship of the proletariat," and to defend the revolution from its enemies, the Bolsheviks demanded eternal vigilance and a necessarily violent purge. Facing threats both foreign and domestic, Lenin echoed Robespierre's 1793 "Law of Suspects" (chap. 3) when he established revolutionary tribunals to arrest bankers, merchants, speculators, landowners, and foreign spies – all representatives of the "old regime" – along with Christian priests and, in central Asia, Muslim clerics. A cult of revolutionaries soon replaced an orthodox pantheon of saints.

Yet as high priests of Marxist-Leninism, the Bolsheviks reserved their greatest disdain for apostates, especially other communist groups like the Mensheviks and Social Revolutionaries (SRs), who had opposed the 1917 October coup. The merciless dictates of revolutionary justice and ideological conformity liquidated thousands. Others were imprisoned in churches and gymnasiums, prisons, former POW camps, and Romanov dungeons. And as arrests expanded, purpose-built enclosures soon emerged to accommodate the Bolsheviks' victims. There were 21 registered concentration camps by the end of 1919 and 107 by 1920.[9] The most famous, reserved for prominent political prisoners, repurposed an abandoned monastery on the windswept Solovetsky Islands in the White Sea. A continental empire of camps was thus prefaced by detention on an actual archipelago.

NORMALIZATION

When he visited the Solovetsky Islands in 1929, the respected Soviet writer Maxim Gorky (1868–1936) dashed prisoners' hopes when he concluded "Camps ... were absolutely necessary ... [O]nly by this road would the state achieve in the fastest possible time one of its aims: to get rid of prisons." The moral imprimatur of a celebrated writer was essential in justifying Soviet concentration camps, turning them into enduring institutions. What Gorky witnessed, however, was a charade, a Soviet "Potemkin Village." Camp authorities, in preparation, had organized a carefully curated show: soldiers dressed as well-fed compliant prisoners, while authorities distributed plentiful food and assembled piles of luxury items at the camp store. For the occasional outside inspector, it was possible to "make Solovki look like a wonderland" – just as Nazi authorities would later deceive Red Cross observers at Theresienstadt concentration camp with choreographed soccer tournaments and wholesome meals at canteens built in preparation for the inspection. The sanction of foreign powers was also crucial. Beguiled by the Soviet Union's economic miracle amid America's Great Depression, the American journalist Walter Duranty described the Gulag as "equivalent to the 'concentration camps' which the European countries established for enemy aliens during the World War." And to "make an omelet," Duranty famously added, "it is necessary to break some eggs." Meanwhile, the American vice president Henry Wallace, impressed by the "can-do" attitude he witnessed at Kolyma labor camps, compared them to Depression-era make-work sites established by the Tennessee Valley Authority.[10] Though such observers were victims of Soviet disinformation, the global history of camps enabled them to assimilate what they saw into the prevailing norms of modern statecraft.

Does the relative global acceptance of Soviet camps in the late 1920s contain any moral lessons for today? And can we recognize similarities between different camp systems while avoiding false equivalencies?

Class Warfare

The Civil War officially ended in 1923. Yet wartime measures endured. Some historians describe the Soviet Union as the first regime to establish permanent concentration camps in a peacetime setting. It may, however, be more useful to consider the entire Soviet period as one extended state of exception governed by the paradigm of civil war and military violence. Born in a state of siege, the Soviet Union never stabilized. Following the death of Lenin and the deposition of Trotsky, Stalin reinvigorated the revolution with a series of Five-Year Plans (1928 onwards) that renewed armed struggle against potential enemies. In an effort to transcend history and annihilate tradition – in this, the Bolsheviks practiced, *in extremis*, the same goals as French Revolutionaries – Stalin hoped to achieve 100 years of social and industrial progress in five years, or even, according to ambitious zealots, in four: the slogan "$2 + 2 = 5$," parodied by the English novelist George Orwell, aptly captures the Soviet offense against reality.

Following a relative truce in the 1920s, new offensives transformed Soviet society in the 1930s. Class "warfare" was conducted as a military campaign. Like an occupying army, Soviet forces invaded the countryside, scouring it for "class enemies" and "social parasites," confiscating private property, and concentrating farmers, often at gunpoint, in collective farms or *kolkhozes*, where they were forced to fulfill mandatory labor and grain quotas. A blitzkrieg of modernization thus forcibly transformed "primitive" peasant societies into industrialized workers – and it did so more dramatically and more violently than nineteenth-century enclosure or the concomitant consolidation of colonial holdings. As Stalin commented, the imperial powers of western Europe had funded industrialization through the "merciless exploitation" of colonial peoples. The Soviet Union, however, had no (overseas) colonies "to plunder."[11] Instead, it squeezed its own peasantry, envisioned as subjects to be exploited rather than citizens to be empowered, in order to mobilize industrial wealth to the cities. Collectivization was thus "an act of virtual war," the historian Lynne Viola comments, a prolonged counterinsurgency that approached the Soviet countryside like "a foreign country to be invaded, occupied, and conquered."[12]

This violent advance by the Red Army and secret police, however, encountered mass uprisings and guerrilla opposition. Ukrainian partisans and Islamic militants like the Basmachi movement of Turkestan actively resisted, while grain riots and peasant revolts accompanied the forced liquidation of village communities and economies. To pacify the country, preemptive arrests herded hundreds of thousands of "counterrevolutionaries" and their suspected supporters, including entire families, into makeshift prisons and eventually into camps and monitored villages. Yet if such tactics were rough and brutal counterparts to the colonial camps of Cuba and South Africa, or the "strategic hamlets" and "new villages" erected by Western powers to corral Communist insurgents and their families in Malaya and Vietnam (chap. 7), such practices became engrained as normative rather than exceptional measures of Soviet power. In 1930, a system of temporary wartime camps became a permanent network of mass detention, overseen by a new government department: *Glavnoye Upravleniye Lagerey*, or Gulag.

As collectivization continued, Stalin's revolutionary campaign targeted an ever-widening array of "enemies." The main victims were wealthy, market-oriented peasants, or *kulaks*. Semicolonial relations between city and village had long cast Russia's peasantry as exotic and uncivilized; mired in tradition and superstition, they were an alien and unwanted presence in a rapidly modernizing state. Grafted onto existing prejudices, the kulak, as both primitive "other" and exploitative capitalist, was a doubly egregious specter. Propaganda images casting them as ape-like oppressors, vampires, or bloodsuckers made the message clear: kulaks were inhuman, they were beasts to be detained or destroyed.[13] Between 1930 and 1931, 1.8 million kulaks flowed into the Gulag, massively expanding what until then had been a relatively modest population of 100,000. For Solzhenitsyn, the liquidation of the kulaks was "the *first* such experiment" (he failed to consider earlier colonial precedents) in which an entire category of people, including women and children, were detained collectively, not for what they had done, but for who they were. Substituting class for racial enemies, he adds, this experiment was "subsequently repeated by Hitler with the Jews."[14]

Though "kulak" was originally an economic category describing acquisitive landholding peasants, local Soviet agents expanded the classification dramatically. Soon, anyone resisting Soviet rule became a class enemy or "kulak terrorist," including large numbers of Ukrainians and Poles, who suffered in disproportionate numbers, and whom the NKVD associated with foreign (and mostly imaginary) conspiracies. As the 1930s progressed, the Gulag transformed into an enduring technology of mass repression, one that operated in the world of imaginary plots and paranoid conspiracies rather than real insurgencies. Everywhere they looked, Party officials discovered "wrecker agronomists who ... had worked honestly all their lives but who now purposely sowed weeds in Russian fields"[15] – gardening metaphors accompanied associations between kulaks and parasites – or who vandalized machinery or concealed grain for private use (though many, desperate and starving, had done just that).

The revolutionary "plot mentality" reached its climax during the "Great Terror" (1936–8), which saw the arrest of intellectuals, Bolshevik Party members, and Red Army officers, who confessed to trumped-up charges of sabotage, espionage, and anti-Soviet activity under article 58 of the criminal code. Absurdist elements abounded. At a district party conference, secret police arrested the first person to sit down, exhausted, after an 11-minute ovation honoring Stalin.[16] A seven-minute trial sent the memoirist Evgenia Ginzburg to the infamous Kolyma complex on largely fabricated charges. Margarete Buber-Neumann, herself a Communist refugee from Nazi Germany, was also swept up in the '37 wave, accused of heretical proclivities. Ostensibly based on scientific planning, the Soviet Union degenerated into a twentieth-century witch hunt that surpassed the violence of medieval Inquisitions. Even the NKVD commissar Nikolai Yezhov, who first conducted the Terror, was arrested in 1938 after falling from Stalin's favor. In this way, the revolution devoured its children. Those who survived did so in camps.

Ethnic Enemies

Political prisoners, with their vivid Gulag memoirs, dominate popular memory. Yet they were outnumbered by other victims. Bolshevism claimed to be a cosmopolitan, antinationalist, and antiracist movement. "Workers of the *world* unite!" Marx implored. Yet despite invocations to multinational toleration, the Soviet Union, in the late 1930s, became "a land of unequalled national persecutions." In a retreat from Trotskyite internationalism, Russian chauvinism, xenophobic paranoia, and imperial racism – previously masked by the materialist categories of class – framed operations against suspect minorities, who were 20 times more likely to be arrested in the 1937 purge than other Soviet citizens. As the historian Timothy Snyder writes, "the most persecuted European national minority in the second half of the 1930s was not the four hundred thousand ... German Jews ... but the six hundred thousand ... Soviet Poles." Depicted as terrorists and "fascist-insurgents" and associated with foreign governments, 111,091 Polish men were executed in 1937; their families faced exile in special settlements and Gulag camps.[17]

Actions against minorities intensified during World War II. Consolidating power in the Far East, Stalin transported ethnic Koreans *en masse* to Gulag facilities in central Asia and deported ethnic Chinese to Xinjiang Province in China. In Europe, meanwhile, the Gulag detained half a million Estonians, Lithuanians, Latvians, Moldovans, Belarusians, Ukrainians, and Poles from Russian borderlands and from occupied territories, while Soviet forces also arrested 1.5 million ethnic Finns and Volga Germans as part of a pacification campaign following the Nazi invasion of 1941. Muslim minorities like Chechens, Ingush, Karachai, Kalmuks, Balkarians, and Tartars, accused of collaborating with German invaders, were also ethnically cleansed from Crimea and the Caucasus. Though Soviet officials feared such groups would conduct pro-German partisan activities, operations targeted suspect collectivities rather than guilty individuals. "The determining factor," Solzhenitsyn maintained, "was *blood*."[18]

Xenophobic purges extended to Soviet citizens themselves, when Stalin's forces arrested captured Russian POWs – men like the titular character of Solzhenitsyn's best-selling, semi-autobiographical novel, *One Day in the Life of Ivan Denisovich* (1962) – for fear they had been recruited as foreign agents. In a satire of Stalin's isolationist turn, Captain Buinovsky, a character in the novel, was arrested for receiving a gift from a British admiral, a wartime ally but suspect nonetheless. Ethnic violence reached its climax, however, in 1953, shortly before Stalin's death, with the intended mass internment of Soviet Jews on spurious charges of espionage. Fears of a secret Jewish conspiracy echoed Nazi propaganda as well as racist pogroms in early-twentieth-century Russia. Whether as a starting point or an end, antisemitism was an endemic feature of European dictatorships.

Common Criminals

The Gulag's largest demographic, however, were common criminals arrested under article 35 of the criminal code. As it waged war against its enemies, real and imagined, foreign and domestic, the Soviet state struggled to maintain law and order. Indeed, the Gulag was, at base, a system of criminal punishment. While Stalin's war against the countryside helped consolidate his iron rule, it dramatically uprooted rural society. Moreover, it was an economic failure. Liquidating the most productive farmers of Russia and Ukraine caused a predictable humanitarian disaster. Collectivization's most immediate result was agricultural decline and a devastating famine – the Holodomor of 1932–3, which killed nearly 7 million in Ukraine and Kazakhstan. Survivors fled to towns and cities as refugees, camping at railway stations, begging for food, and often committing crime, as did homeless children orphaned by the arrest of their parents. Fugitive kulaks even formed armed gangs to defend their property or engage in hit-and-run sabotage operations. As Solzhenitsyn comments, "the country-wide poverty and shortages of the period when the government, all institutions, and the laws themselves were being reorganized, could serve only to increase greatly the number of thefts, robberies, assaults [and] bribes."[19] If industrialization and urbanization in nineteenth-century Europe presaged social dislocation and a concomitant system of prisons and workhouses, the forced and abrupt nature of the process in Stalin's Soviet Union caused even greater turmoil – and even greater mass confinement.

Though Bolsheviks regarded "habitual criminals" as potential class allies, the victims of capitalist exploitation, Stalin nonetheless pursued a "merciless suppression of attempts at anarchy on the part of drunkards [and] hooligans."[20] Starting in 1927, preemptive "cleansing sweeps" purged large cities of vagrants, prostitutes, and drug addicts. By the 1930s, violent felons and enormous numbers of petty thieves, sentenced to short terms, made up 60 percent of Gulag inmates – a proportion that continued to grow amid pervasive postwar homelessness, alcoholism, and the passage of draconian antitheft laws in 1948.[21] Distinct criminal subcultures, like the *urki* and *vory*, with their own customs, rituals, tattoos, and dialects, also populated the camps. The linguist and Gulag inmate Dmirtri Likhachov felt they resembled "primitive" colonial people, while Evgenia Ginzburg described such groups as "half-naked, tattooed, ape-like hordes" governed by the "law of the jungle."[22] Others likened them to "gorillas" with "Mongolian faces," or to the Apache, a French criminal subculture whose fearsome reputation reminded some of Native American insurgents.[23] Against organized banditry, the Gulag performed an analogous role to the criminal tribe camps of British India (chap. 2), rounding up populations with the uncivilized and identifiable marks of criminality. For others, the Gulag transformed into a system of mass penal exile that imposed harsh punishments according to dubious standards of evidence, often for trivial offenses committed in the context of hardship and privation.

Despite the many millions detained, criminal prisoners remain a silent majority, whose experience can be only imperfectly reconstructed from the sometimes-unsympathetic accounts of intellectuals. Ginzburg deplored the "ferocious obscenities" and "wild laughter" with which a "mongrel horde set about terrorizing and bullying" other inmates,[24] while Buber-Neumann felt camp life only encouraged criminals to commit further violence. Through brute force and impressive organizational skills, criminal and asocial elements "occup[ied] all the minor posts in the camps and they lead what might even be called a social life," she noted. In this way, criminals attained power and prestige – better rations, favored barracks, and even a release from heavy labor – denied to them on the outside. Encouraged by the guards, criminals also regarded political prisoners with contempt. Like the "notorious *Kapos* in Nazi concentration camps" (chap. 5), Buber-Neumann concluded, they were "often more cruel and brutal than the real authorities." Like the Bolshevik Revolution more generally, then, camps inversed prevailing social hierarchies. Lured by the power and protection criminal gangs afforded, young inmates committed thefts or assaults to gain respect; even for the educated Buber-Neumann, the first lesson in camp life was how to steal soap.[25] Much like the American prison system, the Gulag was arguably more successful at producing criminals than reforming them.

Camps, Colonies, and Settlements

Soviet camps were as varied as the populations they detained. Like many carceral systems, a complex hierarchy of punishment and detention filtered inmates according to their perceived threat. "Corrective labor" or *katorga* camps, the harshest and most deadly, concentrated prisoners with sentences over three years – a category that included "politicals" like Ginzburg and Buber-Neumann alongside hardened criminals. Above all, the menacing and often murderous complex at Kolyma in the far east stood out as the pole of cold and cruelty. Yet it was exceptional rather than typical. Smaller, less remote, but more numerous, "corrective labor colonies" incarcerated petty criminals and others sentenced to shorter terms. Meanwhile, "special settlements" in central Asia and Siberia interned kulaks and suspect ethnicities, reviving traditional practices of banishment and exile. Formally part of the Gulag apparatus, they "occupied a space halfway between freedom and the concentration camp," the historian Steven Barnes remarks, or a "gray zone," as Cynthia Ruder calls it, where "the Gulag and non-Gulag world overlapped." As such, they challenge stereotypes. A "high palisade crowned by barbed wire" surrounded some camps, but others were unfenced. To Buber-Neumann's surprise, prisoners at her corrective labor facility could move freely within half a mile of the camp perimeter, while some inmates, like nomadic tribesmen herding cattle, had permission to roam the steppe for many miles. Inmates at the vast Dmitlag camps (population 198,000) on the Moscow-Volga canal could interact with locals in relatively unrestricted ways, as could Gulag inmates working at armaments factories during World War II. They thus inhabited a world "without ... barbed wire, or barracks, and frequently without guard."[26] Remote Siberian complexes, similarly, had few fences: they were so isolated that escapees had nowhere to go – though guards had orders to shoot anyone leaving without permission.

Camp conditions were often horrendous. Human life was clearly expendable, and mortality in Kolyma's "Arctic death camps," as the historian Robert Conquest called them, approached 25 percent. Across the archipelago, one in ten inmates, at least 2 million in total, died between 1929 and 1953, though the Soviet practice of releasing prisoners on the verge of death in order to artificially suppress numbers meant the real rate was higher.[27] Nonetheless, the Gulag was not explicitly genocidal, and its death rate never approached the 60 percent mortality of Nazi concentration camps, the 90 percent mortality at Auschwitz (chap. 5), or even the 25 to 50 percent of inmates killed by epidemic diseases at colonial camps in southern Africa (chap. 3). Inmates recount summary executions, institutionalized brutality, and sexual violence by guards and other inmates. Women like Ginzburg and Buber-Neumann, at the bottom of both political and gendered hierarchies, were especially vulnerable. But most deaths resulted from neglect rather than willful extermination, as poor sanitation and nutrition spread epidemic diseases like malaria, measles, typhus, and tuberculosis, especially among the elderly and young. This was particularly true at special settlements, which repeated a common folly in the global history of camps: though authorities deported kulaks with alacrity, they gave little thought to how they might be accommodated at their destination. At Nazino on the river

Ob, inmates were left to fend for themselves without food or shelter; half of them died of starvation and disease, while others turned to cannibalism. Noted for their powers of totalitarian organization, Soviet authorities were remarkably poor planners. As a German, Buber-Neumann was shocked by the administrative chaos at her camp in Kazakhstan, a stark contrast to "Prussian discipline" at home.

Despite harsh conditions – one inmate remembered waking up to find his head frozen to his bunkbed, another recalled a bowl of amputated frost-bitten fingers in the infirmary[28] – most inmates had a legitimate chance of survival. A "revolving door" saw the release of between 20 percent and 40 percent of prisoners every year, particularly petty criminals in the labor colonies. Yet release did not mean freedom. As Stalin assembled an authoritarian police state, the concentration camp became an organizing motif for society writ large – the "epitome of the regime that wrought it," the former inmate Jacques Rossi writes.[29] A system of internal passports (a tsarist inheritance) monitored Soviet citizens both inside and outside the camps. And many former prisoners remained in exile, often in satellite towns, which exhibited a Gulag aesthetic of uniform housing blocks that Siberia retains today. Indeed, cities like Magnitogorsk, the "Pittsburgh of the Urals," even started their life as Gulag outposts. And like Darwin in Australia (chap. 2), or Swakopmund in German South-West Africa (chap. 3), camp labor built the town of Vorkuta.

Once "released," meanwhile, inmates often found employment as guards and officials in the same camps that had imprisoned them. This "enormous zone of half freedom," the historian Oleg Khlevniuk comments, illustrates the "indeterminate … boundaries between [the] Gulag" and what he calls the "non-Gulag."[30] On the "outside," collective farms were themselves camps of sorts, with coerced labor and minimal comforts but extensive surveillance. Anyone escaping risked imprisonment and social stigma. The Gulag, then, was only "the most extreme variant of captivity in a continuum of incarcerated geographies."[31] Whether on the collective farm, the state-run factory, or in the Gulag proper, Soviet citizens faced starvation, violence, and death. In 1939, Gulag rations actually exceeded those of peasants and industrial workers outside. And the NKVD limited mobility for the population at large: indeed, many "criminals" were sentenced simply for violating internal passport regulations. As such, the metaphor of the Gulag archipelago – of isolated islands of confinement – is perhaps problematic: with porous boundaries, the Gulag and non-Gulag often merged into each other.

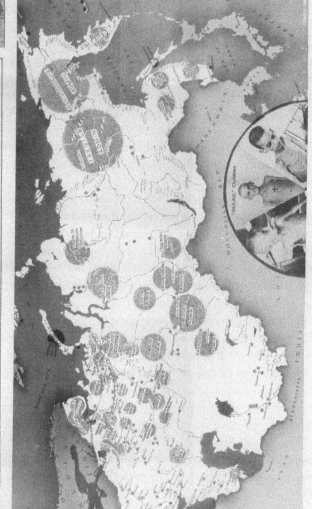

FIGURE 4.1 Cold War-era American publications identified forced labor in the Gulag with histories of slavery. This 1947 map of Gulag camps in the Soviet Union indicates the archipelago's rough spatial distribution. (Source: Cornell University Library.)

Slave Labor

The Gulag, in essence, was a system of forced labor. For Buber-Neumann, who considered herself a field slave tending sunflowers in Kazakhstan, the Soviet secret police force was "a great slave trust." "Wherever labor is needed," she continued, "it sends its prisoners. They fell timber in Central Siberia ... work in heavy industries in the Urals ... mine gold in Kolyma ... [and] build towns in the far east."[32] Others harvested cotton at plantations in Uzbekistan or built railways and canals in the taiga. And wherever they labored, the memoirist Varlam Shalamov recalls, inmates were "harnessed to ... Egyptian yoke[s] like slaves."[33]

Following imprisonment and summary trials, inmates embarked on journeys that approached the horrors of the Middle Passage, both on repurposed passenger trains and dilapidated vessels, which carried more than 3 million across the icy waters of the Arctic Ocean and Sea of Okhotsk. The voyages reminded the exiled Menshevik historians David Dallin and Boris Nicolaevsky of "the ships, a century back, which carried cargoes of Black slaves from the Ivory Coast to the American ports of Charleston and New Orleans."[34] On her two-week crossing to Kolyma, Ginzburg described prisoners "packed in [their] hundreds so tightly [they] could not breathe, [they] sat or lay on the dirty floor or on one another spreading [their] legs to make room for the person in front."[35] For Shalamov, the journey symbolized a definitive break from the comity of mankind, a transition from "our first life" to "our second life."[36] But for others, it meant death. When fire broke out on the transport ship the *SS Dzhurma*, prisoners locked in bolted hatches were burned and boiled alive.

For those who survived, a "regular slave market" awaited. Overseers demanded "the *merchandise* be displayed alive and bare-skinned for them to inspect" so they could ensure "last-leggers and invalids didn't get shoved off on them." Officials "felt men's muscles, opened their mouths to check their teeth and looked at eyes, head, and shoulders," the Kolyma survivor Michael Solomon confirms: "it was like watching a slave market scene in some remote equatorial village two centuries ago."[37] And since the "natives [prisoners] on the islands [camps] kept dying," Solzhenitsyn added, the labor supply needed to be continually replenished.[38]

Though Russia's engagement with transatlantic slavery was minimal, the coercion of state socialism sometimes converged with that of colonial capitalism. The Gulag drew from homegrown repertoires as well. "Serfs!" Solzhenitsyn observed, "this comparison occurred to many when they had the time to think about it." Though Russia emancipated its serfs in 1861 amid

FIGURE 4.2 Extramural Jim Crow "chain gangs" in America, which billeted inmates in convict-leasing camps (*left*); inmates of the Soviet Gulag (*right*). Historians have connected slavery, and the continued use of unfree prison labor, to an underdeveloped free market economy in the American South. As collectivization dismantled the free market, penal labor in the Soviet Union flourished. (Source: World History Archive/Alamy; Getty Images.)

a transnational conjuncture that also witnessed the abolition of American plantation slavery, the Gulag reflected deeper continuities. Like the estate owner of tsarist Russia, Solzhenitsyn continued, the camp commandant punished with the lash and "could take any slave to be his lackey, cook, barber, or jester" or "any slave woman as a housekeeper [or] concubine."[39] Yet analogies with serfdom and slavery were not exact. Gulag inmates were Soviet citizens rather than racialized captives. And while serfs enjoyed religious holidays, owned livestock, and "had full bellies," the Gulag imposed cavity searches, separated families, and transformed inmates into famished and sickly skeletons.[40] More than beasts of burden, inmates were enemies to be punished, and Gulag labor, the historian Golfo Alexopolous argues, was punitive and destructive by design.[41] Total war also enhanced the Gulag's disciplinary rigor. Apart from nineteenth-century convict labor, Russia organized World War I POWs into work battalions commanded by brigadiers to build railways and other infrastructure (chap. 3). Gulag inmates, similarly, were "soldiers" in an "army" conscripted in the battle to build socialism, a 1937 propaganda film proclaimed.[42] Conversely, they were cannon fodder.

Economy and Reform

Historians debate the extent to which the demand for cheap labor drove the Gulag's expansion. Though authorities initially struggled to find useful occupations for inmates – many ended up shifting stones from one pile to another – camps eventually operated as labor recruitment centers for large-scale construction projects. Apart from back-breaking labor in mines, fields, and factories, imprisoned engineers constructed aircraft and nuclear reactors, while others secured administrative posts as nurses and doctors or accountants and secretaries. Many camps were located in strategic proximity to resources, and they proved especially important to timber, gold, and nickel production, as well as to key sectors like construction and military equipment. On the other hand, Gulag labor only comprised 2 percent of the total workforce, and penal laborers were only 50–60 percent as productive as civilian workers.[43] As such, the expense of constructing, guarding, and administering camps cost the state more than it received back, while poor working conditions compounded the inefficiencies of a state-planned economy. Camps lacked equipment and expertise, and emaciated prisoners struggled to achieve unrealistic quotas. At only 11 feet deep, the White Sea Canal, constructed by Gulag labor, could not be navigated by seagoing vessels. Likewise, the Salekhard–Igarka Railway in the far north was abandoned in 1953 at a cost of 42 billion rubles and countless inmate lives. Despite a revolutionary attitude that "anything was possible," permafrost made laying tracks impossible, while chaos and improvisation on the ground compromised the modernist aspirations of rational planning.

Though rarely profitable, Gulag labor, at least on paper, had a redemptive function. Work defined the proletariat as a class, and for Marx humanity was best realized through cooperative effort. Throughout the Gulag's history, though especially in the Soviet Union's early, idealistic phase, authorities voiced the rhetoric of "work therapy" and "corrective labor." As the historian Steven Barnes writes of Karaganda, Buber-Neumann's camp, "instruction in collective agricultural labor" would "reeducate tens of thousands of former lawbreakers."[44] Socialization in collective labor columns, which lived, worked, slept, and ate together, would provide ideological training, reforging inmates into loyal Soviet workers. Like the reformed prisons of nineteenth-century Europe, then, Gulag authorities articulated a broader ethos of discipline and punishment: humanity was malleable, politics could reshape society, and confinement would permit inner reformation. Like workhouses and Benthamite prisons, Gulag camps were putatively transformative technologies that would "cure" the dangerous and diseased or else excise them, through isolation or death, from the social body. Communal living and a greater economic reliance on forced labor, however, distinguished Communist reeducation camps from the individual cellular prisons of many Western societies.

Yet if Gulag authorities saw themselves as engineers reforging human materiel, how did inmates see it? Posters published by the Gulag's Culture and Education department announced that "work redeems guilt" and "through work we shall return to society."[45] In a mirror image of Soviet society outside, authorities promoted the virtues of Stakhanovite "shock work" (the ambitious overperformance of quotas) and collective solidarity. Some inmates mouthed the language of redemption, internalizing the values of the system that repressed them. At Dmitlag on the Moscow-Volga canal, a Roma woman, Polya Chetverikova, hoped camp life would help her family "forget the nomadic life" and become "honest worker[s]."[46] Another inmate, writing in a camp newspaper, celebrated the "advantages of [the] Socialist organization of labor," while an elderly survivor boasted, in 2004, that she had worked "hard and well" and was thereby rewarded with the Medal for Valiant Labor.[47] Yet for others, particularly political prisoners for whom the prospect of reform was as farcical as their initial arrest, socialist discourses of education and reform were as empty as the "civilizing mission" Western powers used to justify colonial exploitation overseas.

BLACK MARKETS

Collectivization aimed to replace private trading with state planning. Yet the complete suppression of capitalism proved impossible, the historian Stephen Kotkin notes. Ultimately, authorities had no choice but to tolerate illegal trading, for without it, basic necessities could not reach the population, and socialist society would collapse as a result. A totally planned economy, then, is perhaps as destructive, and hence as impractical, as a pure free market devoid of any social safety net.[48]

What was true outside the camps was also true inside. Even in an environment where everything was controlled, human ingenuity knew few bounds. Though Ivan Denisovich, the protagonist of Solzhenitsyn's novel, spent his day fulfilling labor quotas at a Gulag factory, he expended much of his energy smuggling contraband and performing informal economic activities like manufacturing a knife, sewing slippers, and running errands in exchange for tobacco, sausages, and extra helpings of soup. In the context of chronic scarcity, everything – spoons, shoes, scraps of metal – had value. They could be stolen and, above all, traded. Cigarettes, in particular, provided a universal currency, from Communist Gulags to Nazi *Konzentrationslager* and American penitentiaries. All prices were local and fluctuated according to supply and demand, but a loaf of bread could fetch three cigarettes; a bottle of vodka, used to bribe guards, was worth two hundred. In this way, a complex shadow economy provided inmates with minor luxuries, which they consumed during precious moments of privacy and rest.

Camp authorities brutally repressed strikes and demonstrations, leaving inmates with "even less chance [of escape] than black slaves of old."[49] Yet black market trading allowed inmates to carve out small pockets of autonomy and social agency outside official command structures. Were such activities quotidian forms of resistance?

Colonial Missions

Whether reclaiming marginal populations or marginal land, the Gulag was part of a broader colonial project. Orientalist rhetoric about exotic Muslim societies accompanied Russian dominion in central Asia, while frontier expansion in Siberia offered a more centrally directed counterpart to American settler colonialism. Soviet leaders inherited the basic challenges and opportunities of the tsarist empire – the occupation of vast, resource-rich, though marginally habitable frontiers, state-led colonization drives, and culturally "backward," economically underdeveloped hinterlands inhabited by less "advanced" ethnic minorities. However inefficient, Gulag camps, like imperial Russia's penal colonies before them, were important tools of colonization. "In much the same way the British crown exiled penal and political prisoners to settle the Australian territories," the historian David Shearer adds, Soviet camps and colonies opened, occupied, and populated new lands.[50]

Rapid industrialization depended on the mass mobilization of human and natural resources. In 1930, Genrikh Yagoda, the deputy chief of Secret Police, voiced a "need to turn the camps into colonization villages."[51] Though Russians had migrated, voluntarily, to Siberia's fertile grain belt since the 1890s, colonization of the far north and "wild east" depended on state coercion. In this way, northern development conformed to common patterns of arctic empire, which also saw the forced relocation, albeit on a much smaller scale, of Canadian Inuit to strategic though barren outposts on Ellesmere Island. To populate the frontier, the Bolshevik official Robert Eikhe (1890–1940) partitioned western Siberia into 13 "police reservations" (*komandatury*), where Gulag authorities administered colonies, camps, and special settlements. As involuntary settlers, deported criminals and kulaks played vital roles in the colonization of occupied land, while camps provided imperial outposts – points of occupation and orientation that claimed Soviet space. Yet "to colonize the North in the fastest of tempos,"[52] as Yagoda put it, mass hardship ensued. Soviet authorities failed to provide shelter or sustenance, and inmates often arrived at their "camp" to find nothing but empty taiga. Slowly, however, survivors, living in tents and huts, constructed permanent barracks and villages. Writing to headquarters, Eikhe pointed to a burgeoning population, the construction of roads and railways, and the development of industrial mining, agriculture, and forestry, as markers of success. A wild and unruly frontier had thus been bound, surveyed, and tamed.

Colonial considerations also framed the development of corrective labor camps in central and northeast Asia. Buber-Neumann recognized a clear contrast between "civilized," metropolitan Moscow and the "exotic" tribal lands of Kazakhstan. In this distinctly colonial and nomadic space, the camp not only offered a fixed population center, the nucleus of the emerging city of Karaganda, but fostered abiding colonial dreams of cultivating the steppe, of turning deserts into gardens. With distant echoes, meanwhile, of nineteenth-century gold rushes in Siberia, Australia, and the American West, Solzhenitsyn described a veritable "gold fever [that] began at the end of 1929."[53] The remote Kolyma gold mines, where Evgenia Ginzburg toiled in an arctic analog of the silver mines of Potosí, or of enclosed mining compounds in South Africa, were ultimate results. Since no rights-bearing citizen would willingly perform such labor – one inmate died for every kilogram of gold extracted – a new state agency, the Dalstroy Development Trust, organized more than 80 Gulag outposts, which coerced inmates much as Caribbean plantations and Congolese jungle camps enforced punishing sugar and rubber quotas. Military concerns complemented economic ones. Kolyma's permanent naval base at the Pacific port of Magadan allayed geopolitical fears of Japanese expansion. As such, camps and forced relocations to the far north were at the vanguard of Soviet colonialism.

The "wild east," of course, was no *tabula rasa*. Long deemed "uncivilized," Siberian tribes, circumpolar cousins of Canada's First Nations, garnered respect among early Bolsheviks, who admired their "primitive communism." So did Muslim nomads in upland Asia. Yet no one was safe from Stalin's collectivizing drives. Though Soviet forces did not target tribal populations specifically, the ambition to achieve 100 years of progress in five proved especially frenzied for "backward tribes" deemed, by one official, to be a thousand years behind.[54] With collectivization in 1929, Bolsheviks reimagined tribal groups as "parasites," whose scattered mobile lifestyle was incompatible with the contained and concentrated space of the collective farm. As in other empires, nomadic populations also proved difficult to tax and surveil: their wandering lifestyle was thus a social and political threat, one soon criminalized by the "Crimes That Constitute Survivals of Tribalism" statute of the Soviet criminal code.

Yet in contrast to capitalist imperialism, which emphasized cultural and racial difference, the categories of class analysis framed Soviet expansion. NKVD agents, accordingly, counted reindeer to classify "tundra kulaks," whom they forcibly deported to settlements and camps, and they likened shamans to superstitious Christian priests. In central Asia, meanwhile, armed militias rounded up nomadic communities and marched them to demarcated "points of settlement" or else rearranged nomadic yurts into geometric rows "like an orderly new village."[55] In this way, they set a template for villagization schemes pursued by modernizing postcolonial states like Tanzania and Ethiopia (chap. 7). Even animals were encamped – the concentration of livestock at fixed sites left nomads with no option but to pitch their tents and settle nearby. The Gulag awaited anyone resisting, or "stealing" livestock they once owned. Part and parcel with more general policies of forced sedentarization, camps and *kolkhozes* thus contributed to a Soviet civilizing mission. Like other empires, however, Moscow struggled to enforce its power in distant peripheries; as long as they paid tributes of fur and fish, some tribes escaped the Gulag, while others crossed the border into China.

By forcibly concentrating nomadic and seminomadic populations, the Soviet Union evacuated and occupied Indigenous lands. Yet the Gulag laborers and collective farmers who replaced them were hardly better off. In contrast to the highly privileged white settler population of America, which viewed the frontier as a space of freedom and empowerment, the Soviet Union practiced a form of internal colonization against its own peasantry, which urban bureaucrats conceived as "the dark masses," a backward other destined like the Indigenous nomads they replaced to be either reformed or annihilated at the altar of progress.[56] And while free markets and individual volition characterized settler colonialism elsewhere, Stalin used force against Soviet citizens themselves, much as Nazi Germany, the Soviet Union's fascist counterpart, would compel ethnic Germans through coercive settlement schemes to occupy newly conquered lands in eastern Europe (chap. 5). As a continental land empire, the Soviet Union, like Nazi Germany, lacked clear legal or territorial distinctions between metropole and colony, between rights-bearing individuals and degraded colonial others. Stalin's empire thus treated its own people as subjects rather than citizens – much as seaborne European empires treated colonial Africans and Asians, or as the United States treated its slaves.

End of the Gulag?

By World War II, the Gulag was a central social and economic institution. It exploited resources in colonial peripheries, punished criminals and political undesirables, and consolidated Stalin's control of vast territories and populations. War against Nazi Germany and imperial Japan, two other powers that would rely heavily on forced-labor camps (chaps. 5 and 6), initiated an ominous phase for prisoners. Well attuned to the mobilization demanded by total war, Gulag labor played a significant role, the historian Wilson Bell argues, in repelling the Nazi invasion.[57] And as Soviet forces faced down Nazi Germany, ideological reform took a back seat to patriotism and collective output – a rapprochement, of sorts, between state and society. Nonetheless, the period 1941–43, with its stringent production schedules and worsening food shortages, was deadly for Gulag inmates, as it was for Soviet society at large. The Red Army, meanwhile, recruited nearly 1 million convicts into the military as expendable penal battalions. Sent to the front, many died, though survivors sometimes secured release.

Wartime turnover opened space in the Gulag for new demographics. As the Soviet Empire expanded west into Poland and the Baltic states, camps reprised their counterinsurgency function by imprisoning hundreds of thousands of enemy partisans and civilians, while waves of arrests conscripted petty criminals into new forced-labor battalions. A postwar network of "filtration camps," meanwhile, screened returning Soviet soldiers. Some were eventually released, though camps imprisoned mass numbers of suspected "spies" along with Ukrainian nationalists and other undesirable groups. Soviet forces occupying eastern Europe after the war also assimilated numerous foreign internment and concentration camps into the archipelago; many inmates at Nazi concentration camps now experienced the Gulag. The prisoner population continued to grow accordingly, both during and after the war. In 1953, when Stalin died, it incarcerated 2.4 million in camps and colonies and resettled another 2.7 million in special settlements.[58] In total, 3 percent of the total population was under state control, turning the Soviet Union into one of world history's most heavily incarcerated societies, rivalled in sheer size only by China (chap. 6) and the United States (see "Prison Industrial Complexes" below), which currently incarcerates 2.3 million, with a further 4.6 million under parole or police surveillance (0.7 percent and 1.4 percent of the total population, respectively).

PRISON INDUSTRIAL COMPLEXES

The Gulag was a "prison industry." Whatever its inefficiencies, prison labor proved important to the Soviet economy, while Soviet bureaucrats had special interests in perpetuating the system. But what of the United States, a proud but beleaguered democracy? America's "military industrial complex," as President Eisenhower called it, emerged to counter Soviet expansion during the Cold War. But as Eisenhower feared, the "garrison state" would be long-lasting and would damage democracy at home. Emerging in the 1970s, a "prison industrial complex" now detains unprecedented numbers. America's constitution, rule of law, and political culture sharply differentiate it from the Soviet Union, where prisoners rarely had legal counsel or means of redress. Yet while waves of prisoners flowed into the Gulag, Jim Crow legislation stripped African Americans of civil rights and incarcerated thousands for trivial offenses like loitering and vagrancy. The racial supremacy that once generated slave plantations now manifests itself in today's criminal justice system. Like Soviet "class warfare," America's protracted "war on drugs" is more than metaphorical – with military-grade weapons, police invade racialized communities, denigrated as foreign and dangerous, while the selective criminalization of certain drugs, prevalent in Black communities, is designed to maintain entrenched racial privileges, critics like Michelle Alexander argue.[59]

Similarities should not be overstated. Stalin's political purges have no counterpart in American history. With better living conditions in American prisons, meanwhile, mortality is less than 1 percent. Nonetheless, the "American Gulag," as critics call it,[60] has assembled a submissive labor force subleased to a "planter-class" of corporations at submarket rates, subsidized, and thus socialized, by the state. Much like the Gulag, the system is economically irrational: expensive facilities, with barbed wire, watchtowers, and armies of wardens, cost taxpayers $182 billion annually. Yet vested interests within the prison industry and political class perpetuate the system. And while American justice, on paper, guarantees a fair trial, legal costs and systemic coercion have resulted in a "plea-to-prison pipeline" where more than 90 percent of sentences are decided without trial, often (as in Ginzburg and Buber-Neumann's cases) in a matter of minutes.[61] And like the Gulag, America's prison industrial complex is self-perpetuating: by excluding those under parole from the economic system, it creates the very criminals it supposedly reforms. Are these comparisons convincing? Disturbing? Misguided?

Following Stalin's death, the Gulag softened and shrank as amnesties released criminals and political prisoners. Yet while the Gulag, as an administrative department, was disbanded in 1960 and the Soviet Union disintegrated in 1991, the islands of the archipelago remained. Even before Vladimir Putin's (1952–) most recent embrace of imperial aggression and Stalinist repression, the geographer Judith Pallot identified compelling similarities between Soviet camps and the carceral geography of contemporary Russia, which likewise transports criminal convicts and political prisoners, under demeaning conditions, to distant correctional colonies. Siberia remains a zone of exile in the popular imagination, while collective punishment and forced labor remain hallmarks of Russian punishment. Indeed, inmates are even detained in repurposed Gulag facilities. And despite a period of "de-Stalinization" in the 1960s and again in the 1980s (facilitated, in part, by the publication of Solzhenitsyn's *Gulag Archipelago*), Russia exhibits a basic authoritarian structure and concomitant disregard for civil rights that has endured multiple regime changes. In the words of the human rights activist Lev Ponomarev, Russia's contemporary prisons constitute a "neo-Gulag" – and a central component of Putin's attempts to rebuild a repressive empire on the Soviet and tsarist model.[62]

The Gulag archipelago has thus witnessed change, has weathered storms and periods of calm, but its bedrock has endured. And while Soviet camps, as a basic model, survived across time, they proliferated globally. Communist countries like China and North Korea followed Soviet blueprints when establishing their own gulags to reform criminals and punish dissent (chap. 6). Rivalry between the Communist East and imperialist West also generated camps in the context of Cold War counterinsurgencies (chap. 7). First, however, we turn to the camps of Stalin's primary geopolitical rival and authoritarian analog, Nazi Germany.

Notes

1 Alexandr Solzhenitsyn, *The Gulag Archipelago: An Experiment in Literary Investigation, I-II*, trans. Thomas P. Whitney (New York: Harper Perennial, 1974), 24–27.

2 Petrov quoted in Frederick Johnstone, "Rand and Kolyma: Afro-Siberian Hamlet," *South African Sociological Review* 1, no. 2 (1989): 22.

3 Leon Trotsky, *My Life* (London: Thornton Butterworth, 1930), 217.

4 Daniel Beer, "Penal Deportation in Siberia and the Limits of State Power, 1801–1881," in *The Soviet Gulag: Evidence, Interpretation and Comparison*, ed. Michael David-Fox (Pittsburgh: University of Pittsburgh Press, 2016), 178.

5 Solzhenitsyn, *Gulag Archipelago I-II*, 489.

6 Sarah Badcock and Judith Pallot, "Russia and the Soviet Union from the Nineteenth to the Twenty-First Century," in *A Global History of Convicts and Penal Colonies*, ed. Clare Anderson (London: Bloomsbury, 2020), 287.

7 Bettina Greiner, "The Gulag: An Incarnation of the State That Created It," in David-Fox, *Soviet Gulag*, 319.

8 Solzhenitsyn, *Gulag Archipelago I-II*, 33.

9 Anne Appelbaum, *Gulag: A History* (New York: Anchor Books, 2004), 9–10.

10 Andrea Pitzer, *One Long Night: A Global History of Concentration Camps* (New York: Little, Brown and Company, 2017), 128–30, 138–9.

11 G.F. Alexandrov et al., *Stalin: A Short Biography* (Moscow: Foreign Languages Publishing House, 1947), chap. 8.

12 Lynne Viola, *The Unknown Gulag: The Lost World of Stalin's Special Settlements* (Oxford: Oxford University Press, 2007), 20, 32.

13 Viola, *The Unknown Gulag*, 6.

14 Solzhenitsyn, *Gulag Archipelago I-II*, 55.

15 Solzhenitsyn, *Gulag Archipelago I-II*, 57.

16 Solzhenitsyn, *Gulag Archipelago I-II*, 70.

17 Timothy Snyder, *Bloodlands: Europe Between Hitler and Stalin* (New York: Basic Books, 2010), 89, 93.

18 Solzhenitsyn, *Gulag Archipelago I-II*, 78.

19 Solzhenitsyn, *Gulag Archipelago I-II*, 33.

20 Solzhenitsyn, *Gulag Archipelago I-II*, 27.

21 Jeffrey Hardy, *The Gulag After Stalin: Redefining Punishment in Khrushchev's Soviet Union, 1953–1964* (Ithaca: Cornell University Press, 2016), 9–12.

22 Federico Varese, "The Society of the *Vory-v-zakone*, 1930s–1950s," *Cahiers du Monde russe* 39, no. 4 (1998): 516; Ginzburg quoted in Robert Conquest, *Kolyma: The Arctic Death Camps* (London: Macmillan, 1978), 30–1.

23 Appelbaum, *Gulag*, 289.

24 Evgenia Ginzburg, *Journey into the Whirlwind*, trans. Paul Stevenson and Max Hayward (New York Harcourt, 1967), 354.

25 Margarete Buber-Neumann, *Under Two Dictators: Prisoner of Stalin and Hitler*, trans. Edward Fitzgerald (London: Pimlico, 2009), 61–2, 74.

26 Steven Barnes, *Death and Redemption: The Gulag and the Shaping of Soviet Society* (Princeton: Princeton University Press, 2011), 22, 44; Cynthia Ruder, *Building Stalinism: The Moscow Canal and the Creation of Soviet Space* (London: I.B. Taurus, 2018), 71.

27 The true death toll is likely more than the 1.5–1.7 million confirmed by official statistics. Golfo Alexopolous, *Illness and Inhumanity in Stalin's Gulag* (New Haven: Yale University Press, 201), 153–4. Official mortality statistics do not include the special settlements, where the death rate is unknown.

28 Appelbaum, *Gulag*, 223; Elinor Lipper, *Eleven Years in Soviet Prison Camps*, trans. Richard and Clara Winston (Washington, DC: Henry Regnery, 1951), 110.

29 Rossi quoted in Oleg Khlevniuk, "The Gulag and the Non-Gulag as One Interrelated Whole," in David-Fox, *Soviet Gulag*, 27.

30 Khlevniuk, "Gulag and Non-Gulag," 28.

31 Greiner, "Gulag," 315.

32 Buber-Neumann, *Two Dictators*, 95.

33 Varlam Shalamov, *Kolyma Tales*, trans. John Glad (New York: Penguin, 1980), 155.

34 Dallin and Nicolaevsky quoted in Johnstone, "Rand and Kolyma," 15.

35 Ginzburg, *Into the Whirlwind*, 267–8.

36 Shalamov, *Kolyma Tales*, 121.

37 Michael Solomon, *Magadan* (London: Auerbach, 1971), 130.

38 Solzhenitsyn, *Gulag Archipelago I-II*, 562.

39 Alexandr Solzhenitsyn, *The Gulag Archipelago: An Experiment in Literary Investigation, III-IV*, trans. Thomas P. Whitney (New York: Harper Perennial, 1974), 149–50.

40 Solzhenitsyn, *Gulag Archipelago III-IV*, 152.

41 Golfo Alexopolous, "Destructive Labor Camps: Rethinking Solzhenitsyn's Play on Words," in David-Fox, *Soviet Gulag*.

42 Ruder, *Building Stalinism*, 60.

43 Mark Harrison, *Accounting for War: Soviet Production, Employment, and the Defence Burden, 1940–1945* (Cambridge: Cambridge University Press, 1996), 98.

44 Barnes, *Death and Redemption*, 33.

45 Barnes, *Death and Redemption*, 59.

46 Ruder, *Building Stalinism*, 78.

47 Barnes, *Death and Redemption*, 60; Dan Stone, *Concentration Camps: A Short History* (Oxford: Oxford University Press, 2017), 76; Jehanne M. Gheith and Katherine R. Jolluck, *Gulag Voices: Oral Histories of Soviet Incarceration and Exile* (New York: Palgrave MacMillan, 2011), 24.

48 Stephen Kotkin, *Magnetic Mountain: Stalinism as a Civilization* (Berkeley: University of California Press, 1997), 239–42.

49 Johnstone, "Rand and Kolyma," 20.

50 David Shearer, "Mastering the Soviet Frontier in the 1930s," in *The Siberian Saga: A History of Russia's Wild East*, ed. Eva-Maria Stolberg (Frankfurt am Main: Peter Lang, 2005), 162.

51 Viola, *Unknown Gulag*, 54–5.

52 Lynne Viola, "The Gulag and Police Colonization in the Soviet Union in the 1930s," in *Stalin's Empire: Imitation and Domination, 1928–1953*, ed. Timothy Snyder and Ray Brandon (Oxford: Oxford University Press, 2014), 34, 29.

53 Solzhenitsyn, *Gulag Archipelago I-II*, 52.

54 Yuri Slezkine, *Arctic Mirrors: Russia and the Small Peoples of the North* (Ithaca: Cornell University Press, 1994), 220.

55 Alun Thomas, *Nomads and Soviet Rule: Central Asia under Lenin and Stalin* (London: I.B. Taurus, 2018), 163.

56 Viola, "Stalin's Empire," 34, 25.

57 Wilson Bell, *Stalin's Gulag at War: Forced Labour, Mass Death, and Victory in the Second World War* (Toronto: University of Toronto Press, 2018).

58 Barnes, *Death and Redemption*, 202.

59 Michelle Alexander, *The New Jim Crow: Mass Incarceration in the Age of Colorblindness* (New York: New Press, 2010), 132–6.

60 Ruth Gilmore, *Golden Gulag: Prisons, Surplus, Crisis, and Opposition in Globalizing California* (Berkeley: University of California Press, 2007).

61 Peter Wagner and Bernadette Rabuy, "Following the Money of Mass Incarceration," *Prison Policy Initiative*, January 25, 2017, https://www.prisonpolicy.org/reports/money.html; Daniel Dosch, "Plea-to-Prison Pipeline: Assessing the Feasibility of Mass Pleas Refusal," *Berkeley Political Review*, October 3, 2019, https://bpr.berkeley.edu/2019/10/03/plea-to-prison-pipeline-assessing-the-feasibility-of-mass-plea-refusal/.

62 Judith Pallot, "The Gulag as the Crucible of Russia's Twenty-First Century System of Punishment," in David-Fox, *Soviet Gulag*.

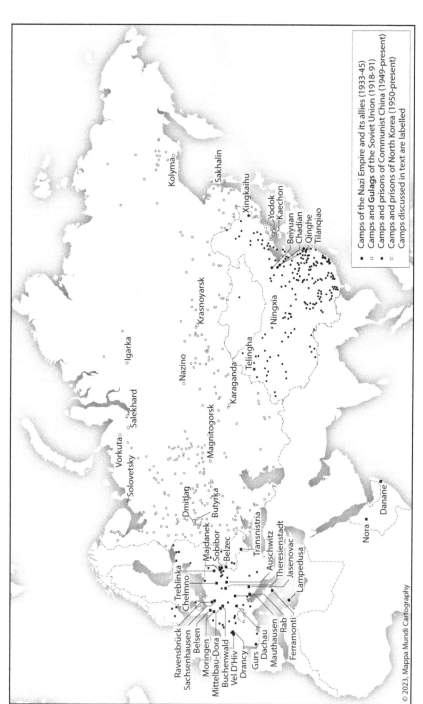

MAP 5.1 Selected camps of totalitarian and revolutionary Eurasia.

Camps of the Nazi Empire and its allies (1933–45)
Camps and **Gulags** of the Soviet Union (1918–91)
Camps and prisons of Communist China (1949–present)
Camps and prisons of North Korea (1950–present)
Camps discussed in text are labelled

Kolyma
Sakhalin
Xingkaihu
Yodok
Kaechon
Beiyuan
Chadian
Qinghe
Tilanqiao
Ningxia
Krasnoyarsk
Telingha
Igarka
Nazino
Karaganda
Salekhard
Magnitogorsk
Vorkuta
Soloivetsky
Dmitlag
Butyrka
Majdanek
Sobibor
Belzec
Treblinka
Chelmno
Transnistria
Auschwitz
Theresienstadt
Jasenovac
Lampedusa
Ravensbrück
Sachsenhausen
Belsen
Moringen
Mittelbau-Dora
Buchenwald
Vel D'Hiv
Drancy
Gurs
Dachau
Mauthausen
Rab
Ferramonti
Nora
Danane

© 2023, Mappa Mundi Cartography

5 | *Konzentrationslager*: Conquest and Genocide in the Nazi Empire

In February 1940, the German Communist Margarete Buber-Neumann crossed a bridge in Brest-Litovsk, a frontier town between the USSR and Nazi-occupied Poland, as part of a prisoner exchange between Hitler and Stalin. Any hopes for release, however, evaporated when Buber-Neumann, after two years in the Soviet Gulag, now became an inmate at Ravensbrück concentration camp, administered by the Nazi SS (*Schutzstaffel*). In doing so, she traded the sprawling, often disorganized Karaganda complex for a much smaller, more tightly disciplined institution. Like the Gulag, Nazi camps were sites of political terror that detained suspected "enemies of the regime" as an extrajudicial measure. When Buber-Neumann first arrived, however, political prisoners were the minority at a compound populated by prostitutes and common criminals. In the next five years, she would witness dramatic changes as Nazi camps expanded, radicalized, and increasingly concentrated Slavs, Jews, and other racial enemies. For these latter victims, camps transformed into venues of mass annihilation unprecedented in the wider history of mass confinement.

Ravensbrück was only one outpost in a larger universe of Nazi camps, which included SS *Konzentrationslager*, POW camps, civilian labor barracks, and an infamous, administratively distinct network of extermination camps. Above all, the ominous complex at Auschwitz-Birkenau, with its relentless hunger and toil, its mechanical and methodical extermination, and its gas chambers and crematoria, has framed dominant perceptions of Nazi *Konzentrationslager* and of concentration camps more generally. And the testimonies of Holocaust survivors like Primo Levi (1919–87) and Elie Wiesel (1928–2016) have understandably dominated collective memory. As an SS supervisor at Ravensbrück told Buber-Neumann, "Auschwitz is the most horrible place the mind of man could conceive."[1] Yet the Auschwitz of 1944 represented a horrific and genocidal extreme within a diverse and dynamic Nazi camp system – one that changed dramatically over time, responded to events, and incarcerated a wide variety of "problem populations" according to competing, chaotic, and often contradictory agendas. This chapter considers the development of Nazi camps and the degree to which they both emerged and diverged from larger global histories. It also considers continuities with colonial camps, while identifying the ways in which Nazi *Konzentrationslager* departed radically from previous experiences. Hitler declared that concentration camps were foreign inventions, which "we merely read up on ... in the encyclopedia and then later copied."[2] To what extent was this true?

Early Camps

Just as the hardships of World War I triggered political revolution in the Soviet Union, the indignity of defeat, along with humiliating peace terms – foreign occupation and the loss of overseas colonies like South-West Africa – fueled a politics of grievance and revenge in Germany. As diplomats signed the Versailles Treaty (1919), thousands of German civilians and POWs languished in Allied internment camps. Four years of war had militarized society and traumatized its soldiers. For some, the violence of the trenches generated a pacifist politics that disavowed war and embraced the Weimar Republic's (1918–33) cosmopolitan, social-democratic vision. Yet war had also brutalized an entire generation, inuring it to anonymous, dehumanized violence. There was "something Treblinka-like" about the battle of the Somme (1916), the historian John Keegan remarks in reference to the infamous death camp, the "long docile lines of young men, shoddily uniformed, heavily burdened ... plodding forward ... to their own extermination inside the barbed wire."[3] For alienated and disillusioned figures like Adolf Hitler (1889–1945), a directionless, unemployed vagrant who lived in homeless shelters prior to World War I, the discipline of army life was formative – and the violence redemptive. Some veterans never truly demobilized but embraced military might, masculine vigor, and the stark divisions of "us and them" that characterized the racist and far-right politics of fascism and ultranationalism. In the process, they vowed to avenge Germany's losses, while organizing politics and society like a giant army camp.

As early as 1920, Hitler embraced the idea of detaining "security risks" and "useless eaters" in mass numbers, and he justified such actions with reference to global precedents: "in South Africa," he proclaimed, "the British deported 76,000 women and children [it was actually over 200,000] to concentration camps."[4] But the camp's allure extended beyond aspiring tyrants: the Great War had normalized the concentration of social and political suspects as a central practice of modern government. Even Germany's moderate, postwar democratic president, Friedrich Ebert (successor to August Bebel, who had criticized Germany's treatment of the Nama and Herero in South-West Africa), invoked emergency powers from 1920 to 1923 to detain political suspects. With Russia's Civil War threatening to spread, suspected Communists, along with "undesired foreigners," mostly Eastern European Jews, were detained in what critics labeled "concentration camps." With wide public support, the city council of Frankfurt likewise concentrated "gypsies" and vagabonds in 1926, while the Weimar Republic, facing an economic crisis and mass unemployment, established paramilitary work camps in 1931 to deter work-shy men from abusing welfare payments and to reform them through physical labor.[5]

Elaborating upon longstanding traditions of mass detention, the Nazis immediately erected camps when they seized power in 1933. Fascist dictatorship, with its paramilitary Brownshirts (who wore khaki uniforms inherited from colonial *Schutztruppe*), injected military frameworks into a society it considered weak and effeminate. From the French Revolution to the Bolsheviks, mass detention without trial was a hallmark of political revolution, and the Nazis were no different. Following the Reichstag fire in 1933, an emergency decree endowed Hitler with temporary powers, similar to martial law, to place over 100,000 political suspects, mostly Communists, into "protective custody" – as in Weimar, the Bolshevik specter offered a major motivation for early camps, and for Western powers to tolerate them. The logic resembled the preemptive detention of suspected spies and saboteurs during World War I, though in Nazi Germany the suspension of rights lasted for the duration of the regime and was justified by war against domestic enemies rather than foreign powers.

Strict punishments and forced labor intimidated opponents into silence and submission. But in 1934 the future of Nazi camps remained uncertain. Within months, most prisoners were released, and while the paramilitary SS leader Heinrich Himmler's (1900–45) *Inspektion der Konzentrationslager (IKL)* department provided permanent bureaucratic structure, camps dwindled in size and number. By 1936 all that remained were 4,000 prisoners in four official camps. Inmate populations would not surpass those of concentration camps in the South African War until 1942, or those of regular German prisons until 1943. And when the Nazis achieved a sense of permanence and normalization by the mid-1930s, some senior officials argued the remaining *Konzentrationslager* should be dissolved.

Yet as technologies of discipline and indoctrination, camps retained widespread appeal. With an emphasis on communal membership, military barracks, industrial factories, and Hitler Youth camps helped forge and fortify a communal *Volk* (a people or nation). Indeed, camps were the basic disciplinary apparatus of the Nazi regime. Likewise, "the healing effects of productive work and tight discipline" at *Konzentrationslager* would educate inmates "to become useful members of the National Socialist state," the *Munich Illustrated News* maintained in 1933. Following a period of convalescence, however, the Nazi regime radicalized in the run-up to World War II. "Action Workshy Reich" in 1938 once again swelled camp numbers by detaining 10,000 vagrants, beggars, and prostitutes. Though the Nazis' contempt for social and sexual deviance was extreme, it emerged from more general patterns of modern governance that generated workhouses and prisons. The appropriation of the Moringen workhouse near Hannover as a concentration camp made the connection explicit. So did Berlin's Rummelsburg workhouse, which was repurposed to detain "asocials" in 1933. The slogan *Arbeit Macht Frei* ("Work Makes You Free") installed at Dachau, Nazi Germany's first purpose-built concentration camp, likewise traced its origins to nineteenth-century campaigns against unemployment and asocial behavior (chap. 1), while a sign in large white lettering proclaimed the Victorian virtues of self-help: "There is only one path to freedom: Obedience, Diligence, Honesty, Orderliness, Cleanliness, Sobriety, Truthfulness, Self-Sacrifice, and Love of the Fatherland."[6] Such, at least, was the public, acceptable face of the camps. The "death's head" insignia (itself a traditional Prussian military symbol) on the uniforms of SS guards belied more sinister dimensions.

Race Laws

In Nazi Germany, as elsewhere, membership in a national community not only depended on assimilating and transforming deviance, but on excluding and segregating racial and ethnic difference. Internal "others" would thus be treated like enemy aliens, much as they had in World War I internment camps. Hitler viewed Roma and Sinti ("gypsies"), Black Africans (particularly the "Rhineland bastards" descended from interracial unions between German women and French-African soldiers during World War I), and

Eastern European Slavs as backward and inferior. These were common sentiments with deep roots in western European and imperial history; indeed, the English word "slave" derives from "Slav." Antisemitic hatred was also widespread. Tropes of the calculating, greedy, deceitful Jew have inflected world literature from Shakespeare to Kipling. Medieval cities like Venice and Frankfurt had concentrated Jews in walled ghettos and identified them with yellow badges (chap. 1) – a practice that was abandoned during the Enlightenment but revived by the Nazis in 1939 – while Spain forcibly expelled Jews in the same year Columbus arrived in America.

Ancient hatreds, however, were superseded by modern "race science." Transatlantic eugenics increasingly represented Jewishness as a race rather than religion, with innate biological traits. Like Hitler, the American industrialist Henry Ford (1863–1947) depicted Jews as a "vicious, antisocial, and destructive" force whose defective moral and mental traits were a genetic rather than cultural or religious disability.[7] In the specific context of interwar Germany, moreover, Jews were malleable scapegoats. As bankers and merchants, they symbolized the greed and empty materialism of bourgeois capitalism. Yet Jews were also consummate communists, the Nazis maintained, responsible for the Bolshevik revolution and the elevation of the Soviet Union (an existential geopolitical threat) to superpower status. As rootless, transnational cosmopolitans, moreover, Jews were particularly offensive to ethnic-nationalist mindsets that sought to draw clear boundaries between us and them. Though logically incoherent, such visions were central components of the Nazis' ultimately contradictory and self-destructive ideology.

Apart from a brief period following *Kristallnacht* in 1938 (see "Transatlantic Pogroms" below), Jews did not dominate *Konzentrationslager* populations until 1942. But the Nuremberg Race Laws (1935) inaugurated an exclusionary logic that would ultimately transform Nazi camps into instruments of racial extermination. At the center of Nazi ideology was a pitiless social Darwinism that divided humanity into superior and "inferior" races – Africans, Asians, Slavs, and Jews. The latter, ultimately destined for extinction, should be segregated from racially pure Aryans, Hitler maintained, or else miscegenation would degenerate the Reich's racial stock. Such ideas had colonial origins. In particular, Hitler had read the German eugenicist Eugen Fischer (1874–1967), whose fieldwork inspecting corpses from Nama and Herero concentration camps led him to conclude (incorrectly) that African skulls bore features of intellectual deficiency. One of Fischer's students, the infamous Auschwitz medical officer Joseph

Mengele (1911–79), believed the same applied to Jews. Jim Crow laws in the American South also offered a "blueprint" and "classic model," the historian James Whiteman argues, for a segregated society that prohibited interracial marriage and defined Jews with biological criteria.[8] Similar to the "one drop rule" in America, anyone with three Jewish grandparents was racially Jewish. *Mischling*, with one or two grandparents, were similarly tainted and ultimately detained behind wire.

America's designation of Native Americans, Filipinos, and other groups as non-citizens, despite their residence in American territories, also inspired provisions of the Nuremberg Laws that stripped Jews of their German citizenship. Yet Nazi antisemitism differed from colonial racism in key respects. Long confined to reservations and plantations, Native Americans and enslaved Africans were powerless and impoverished – destined by Providence to perish. Hitler, however, regarded Jews as powerful aggressors and perpetrators of a global conspiracy. Depicted, at times, as primitive indigenes, wandering and unsettled, they were also a foreign occupying force, Hitler believed, who dominated German politics and business, and who pulled the strings of both global capitalism and communism. War against international Jewry would thus be a dubious act of "colonial liberation," as well as a defensive act, preserving Western civilization from an "Asiatic" onslaught. Hitler first conjured such delusions while confined in a prison cell for high treason following the Beer Hall Putsch of 1923. He would seek redemption, as a proclaimed ultranationalist, by imprisoning his enemies in concentration camps.

TRANSATLANTIC POGROMS

Mob violence against racial minorities has a long global history. Pogroms against Jews in Russia's pale of settlement (1881–2, 1903–6) prompted mass migrations, while the Hamidian Massacres (1894–6) foreshadowed the Armenian genocide. And in the United States, paramilitary groups like the Ku Klux Klan ("the fascists of America") targeted Jews, immigrants, and Indigenous peoples, though their main victims were African Americans. America's worst race massacre occurred in Tulsa, Oklahoma, on May 31, 1921. Fears of declining social status and economic resentment intersected with racial hatred as white mobs attacked the country's wealthiest African American community, Greenwood or "Black Wall Street." Some 300 people were killed and property damage amounted to $33 million (modern figures), for which victims were never compensated. Siding with the looters, the National Guard interned approximately 6,000 Black men in makeshift camps under martial law. Detainees were only released if vouched for by a white resident, and they had to carry green identity cards in public. Such violence ultimately intimidated 1.5 million southern Blacks to migrate north between 1910 and 1940.

Nazi Germany followed a similar script on November 9, 1938, with *Kristallnacht*, "the Night of the Broken Glass." In Tulsa, familiar fears of miscegenation motivated the massacre – a Black teenager was falsely accused of assaulting a white girl – while in Germany, antisemitic violence followed the assassination of a Nazi diplomat. With implicit government encouragement, rioters, along with Hitler Youth and paramilitary stormtroopers, smashed the windows of 7,500 Jewish businesses, along with countless synagogues and homes. Ninety-one Jews were killed and 30,000 were temporarily detained in concentration camps, marking the first time Jews outnumbered "asocials" and political prisoners in Dachau and other camps. Property damage was economically devastating, and the Nazi state seized all insurance claims. German Jews were also fined $5.5 billion for the assassination. As in Tulsa, the abiding goal was to vent racial and economic grievances while intimidating Jews to emigrate.

Tulsa has been described as "America's own Kristallnacht." Is this a legitimate comparison? What are the similarities and important differences between these two pogroms? If Tulsa represented something of a climax to racial violence in the United States, *Kristallnacht* was only a beginning. Why?

A Colonial War?

In contrast to camps in colonial Africa, Nazi *Konzentrationslager* emerged in a peacetime (albeit tumultuous and revolutionary) context. But it was World War II that transformed them into the deadly mass phenomenon we remember. From 22,000 prisoners on the eve of the conflict, camps counted more than 700,000 inmates by 1945 – not including the many millions concentrated in 1,143 fenced ghettos across occupied eastern Europe. Though Himmler's Inspectorate of Concentration Camps entered the war as a permanent bureaucratic institution, camps improvised and radicalized according to wartime contingencies. Life and death inside them, and the labor and violence inmates endured, did not result from rigid, preordained blueprints, but from the vagaries of military victory, occupation, and defeat.

World War II combined the total-war dynamics of 1914 with the indiscriminate violence of colonial conflict. As war militarized society, governments across Europe arrested enemy aliens as a security measure, reviving internment policies from World War I. Britain detained Axis civilians, America and Canada interned ethnic Japanese (chap. 7), and Germany arrested Polish intellectuals and political prisoners, expanding concentration camps in the process. Particularly on the Eastern Front, however, Hitler's ambitions violated military norms that had previously governed conflict between European powers. Here, he unleashed the barbarism of colonial conquest. Hitler's war, the historian Mark Mazower comments, reflected a "desire to explore, expand, identify, and control territory and peoples that had taken [Europeans] to Africa, the Americas, and the remotest islands of the Pacific."[9] A strident nationalist, Hitler was also an empire builder. *General Plan Ost*, drafted during Operation Barbarossa (the 1941 invasion of the Soviet Union), envisioned a vast German empire stretching from central Europe to the Ural Mountains, which would form an "eastern wall" against "Asian barbarians." In sum, the historian Jürgen Zimmerer contends, Germany's invasion of Poland, Russia, and Ukraine constituted "the largest colonial war … in history."[10]

The loss of Namibia and other African colonies at the end of World War I remained a principal grievance at the Treaty of Versailles (Britain drafted a report in 1918 condemning abuses at Nama and Herero concentration camps to justify its annexation of German colonies). Hoping to transcend the failed imperialism of Germany under Kaiser Wilhelm (who abdicated in 1918), however, Hitler marginalized "Africanists" lobbying to reconquer South-West Africa. And in contrast to other fascist leaders like Mussolini, who deployed fighter planes and mustard gas to conquer Ethiopia, Africa's last independent nation, Hitler pursued colonial ambitions in Europe itself. An extensive continental land empire, he believed, would ensure Germany the great power status necessary to compete with the Soviet Union and United States. To that end, Nazi insiders employed the language of imperial racism. Erich Koch (1896–1986), *Reichkommissar* for occupied Ukraine, described Slavic people as "white niggers" and "natural slaves." The Nazi governor of occupied Poland, Hans Frank (1900–46), proclaimed eastern Europe would "be treated like a colony," while Hitler himself referred to Poles and Russians as "a mass of born slaves, who feel the need for a master."[11]

An admirer of the British Empire, the Führer further insisted that Germany should "learn from the English, who, with two hundred and fifty thousand men ... govern four hundred million Indians."[12] Eastern Europe, accordingly, would become Germany's India, and "Slavs would provide the German equivalent of the conquered native populations of India and Africa."[13] Concentration camps would transform occupied Poland and Ukraine into twentieth-century slave states, in which natives would have "but one justification for existence – to be used by us economically."[14] Germany thus revived the paradigm of the plantation. But in contrast to British imperialism, the Nazis dismissed talk of "civilizing missions" and "white men's burdens" as outdated liberal sentimentalism. "Anyone who talks about cherishing the local inhabitant and civilizing him" would themselves go "straight off into a concentration camp!" Hitler warned.[15]

The Nazis' abiding goal, however, was not simply to exploit labor and resources but to open "living room" for German settlers – to pursue *Lebensraum*, as first proposed by the nineteenth-century colonial geographer Friedrich Ratzel (chap. 3). In this context, senior Nazi members like Hermann Göring (1893–1946), son of South-West Africa's first colonial governor, and Franz Ritter von Epp (1868–1947), a *Schutztruppe* commander during the Nama-Herero genocide, transmitted the logic of German settler colonialism to Hitler's inner circle. The American West also provided inspiration. As in North America, Germany's "Wild East" – envisioned as analogous to the Great Plains of Canada and the United States – would generate a new race of virile Aryans who would stamp German *Kultur* on an untamed Slavic landscape. With echoes of American "manifest destiny," Nazi observers claimed the Slavs (like Native Americans) had failed to settle the wilderness or implant their own culture into eastern soil (as wandering cosmopolitans or itinerant travelers, Jews and "gypsies" also lacked roots in the soil). German periodicals, meanwhile, recounted life among German setters on the American frontier, and they carried stories about "the extermination [*Ausrottung*] of the redskins," which settlers pursued "in a completely systematic and business-like manner."[16] Yet while frontier fantasies animated Nazi mythology, the coordination of SS units by a centralized bureaucratic state and coercive settlement schemes that compelled ethnic Germans, sometimes against their will, to settle in newly conquered lands suggested an authoritarian variant of settler colonialism that clashed with the American historian Frederick Jackson Turner's celebration of the frontier as a space of individualistic freedom.[17] In this context, the planned industrial slaughter of total war on the Eastern Front far exceeded the violence committed by scattered, nineteenth-century settler militias.

Hitler believed his slave states in the east would require 10–15 million workers maximum. The remaining 40–50 million superfluous Slavs and 11 million Jews were destined for extinction: settler expansion depended, once again, on the elimination of the native. Conquest in the east, Hitler proclaimed, would resemble "the war waged on the Indians in North America." The "natives will have to be shot," he added: "our sole duty is to Germanize the country by the immigration of Germans, [while] regarding the natives as Redskins." In this way, the burning of Polish villages and the murderous rampage of mobile SS squadrons "extended to 'civilized' European peoples methods hitherto reserved for … 'savages,'" the Marxist dissident Karl Korsch observed.[18] Yet while British settlers had fantasized about North America as a *tabula rasa*, an empty land ready for peaceful occupation, Hitler had no such illusions: in place of a multigenerational process of settler incursion, the Nazis would truncate time (a revolutionary goal shared by Stalin's Five-Year Plans) to conquer the East in one violent paroxysm of murder and forced relocation.

Having denigrated Slavs as uncivilized, Nazi troops committed war crimes against the "Asiatic soldiers of the Red Army," while targeting civilian populations with scorched-earth warfare and ethnic cleansing. In the summer of 1941, German Panzer divisions made devastating advances into the Soviet Union. *Einsatzgruppen* shock troops murdered civilians on the spot and burned their villages, while nearly 3 million Soviet soldiers perished in brutal POW camps; 27,000 survivors were eventually transferred to new *Konzentrationslager* at Majdanek and Birkenau. Yet as imperial armies had discovered previously, the sustained occupation of hostile territories and populations was a challenging proposition. In the historian Dirk Moses's judgment, the "vicious partisan warfare" that accompanied invasion "stood in the continuity of colonial wars."[19] In Poland and Belarus, partisan fighters hiding among the civilian population launched guerrilla strikes against occupying forces, while the French Resistance achieved the same in western Europe. Elsewhere, Jewish guerrillas, like Primo Levi in Italy (before his capture and deportation to Auschwitz), actively resisted Nazi occupation. In response, Hitler called for the "complete elimination of all active and passive resistance," including ruthless and vigorous measures against "Bolshevik inciters, guerrillas, saboteurs, [and] Jews."[20]

The 1941 "Night and Fog" decree and concomitant Commissar Order on the Eastern Front mandated the execution or imprisonment of political leaders and suspected resistance fighters, though "pacification" measures applied more broadly as collective punishment – including farm burnings, mass shootings, and concentration camps – terrorized eastern Europe's civilian population. Once again, confinement and concentration emerged as tactics of military occupation. The SS detained Jewish populations in urban ghettos before their removal to camps, and in order to separate partisans from civilians, the Wehrmacht established "dead zones" from which all persons, food reserves, and livestock – "anything that moved," to echo Herbert Kitchener from the Anglo-Boer War – were removed. In Ukraine, Himmler replicated Lothar von Trotha's "extermination order" in South-West Africa when he ordered "all the Jewish men … shot [and] all the Jewish women driven into the marshes,"[21] while in the "bandit-infested" zones of Belarus, Nazi troops deported civilians, including women and children, to labor camps. Potentially loyal subjects, meanwhile, were concentrated in fortified villages or *Wehrdöfer*, where they could be monitored and indoctrinated.[22] In this way, at least, "there was a functional parallel to colonial practice," the historian Jonas Kreienbaum comments, "the concentration of population groups as a counter-guerrilla measure."[23]

The similarities should not be overstated, however. In many cases, "anti-partisan" action was nothing but cynical cover for mass murder according to racial and political rather than military or counterinsurgency agendas. And the "Jewish problem," in Nazi minds, was never simply a military matter. Germans themselves, rather than Slavs or Jews, were Indigenous victims facing a foreign oppressor, Nazis believed. As "parasites" and "bacteria" that infected the body politic and controlled global media and elite financial networks – or who orchestrated the Soviet menace from the east – Jewish invaders lurked, according to Nazi delusions, in hidden underworlds, conspiring to destroy the German *Volk*. In contrast to Slavs, a "backward" but potentially useful population of colonized slaves, Jews were the enemies of German civilization, the Nazis maintained. In a rhetorical reversal, they were colonizers who had occupied and dominated Germany. Their elimination, then, was not an instrumental matter of military conquest but part of an existential struggle to redeem the German race. Instead of temporary internment, Nazi ideologues demanded a permanent ethnic cleansing. Antisemitic hatred was thus more virulent than prejudice against "uncivilized Slavs" or against Australian and American Aboriginals who were simply "in the way."

The destruction of European Jews thus departed from previous practices of colonial conquest. But the "final solution" and the ultimate transformation of camps into instruments of mass murder developed in stages, and relied, at first, on traditional tactics. Following the invasion of Poland in 1939, Reinhard Heydrich (1904–42) proposed a *Judenreservat* or "Jewish reservation" that would concentrate some 300,000 members of the "Jewish tribe" under SS supervision near Lublin, Poland. Adolf Eichmann (1906–62), meanwhile, revived an old imperial idea, floated by antisemites as early as the 1870s and considered by Herbert Kitchener during the South African War (chap. 3): mass deportation to the island colony of Madagascar. As Nazi forces made deep incursions into Russia, Siberia presented another arena, as it had for Stalin, to exile undesirable groups. In each case, however, practical considerations intervened. British naval power closed shipping lanes to Madagascar, while Soviet victories on the Eastern Front in late 1942 forestalled the *General Plan Ost*'s vision to colonize European Russia and push undesirables east of the Urals. With alternatives foreclosed, and with wartime violence presenting new and radical possibilities, Nazi officials started transporting mass numbers of Jews, Russians, and Poles to concentration camps. And as inmate populations burgeoned, from 53,000 in 1940 to 224,000 following defeats at Moscow (1941–2) and Stalingrad (1942–3), camps transformed from cells isolating political prisoners and asocials into venues for racial repression, brutal forced labor, and mass extermination.

WHO REMEMBERS THE ARMENIANS?

Adolf Hitler wagered the world would either ignore or forget about Nazi atrocities. Such, at least, was the lesson of North American history. "When we eat wheat from Canada," he observed, "we don't think about the despoiled Indians."[24] Such was also the lesson of more recent genocides. In August 1939, a week before the invasion of Poland, Hitler allegedly ordered his troops "to send to death mercilessly and without compassion, men, women, and children of Polish derivation and language. Only thus shall we gain the living room we need." Pondering these impending war crimes, he purportedly added: "Who, after all, speaks today of the annihilation of the Armenians?"[25]

One person who did remember the Armenians was the Polish-Jewish jurist Raphael Lemkin, who coined the word "genocide" in 1944 with specific reference to the plight of Armenians, Jews, and Native Americans. Another was Jewish-Austrian writer Franz Werfel, whose novel *The Forty Days of Musa Dagh* (1933) recounted the heroic armed resistance of a small community of Armenians living near Aleppo amid the deportations, massacres, and concentration camps of the Armenian genocide (chap. 3). The book would gain immense popularity among Jews imprisoned in Nazi ghettos and concentration camps, who passed copies hand to hand as a symbol of hope and a model of partisan resistance. When planning an armed revolt against impending deportations, for example, the Jewish council at Białystok recorded: "We are ... left with only one possibility: organizing collective resistance ... at any price; to view the ghetto as our 'Musa Dagh,' and to add a chapter of honor to the history of ... our movement."[26] The Armenians of Musa Dagh were rescued by French naval ships. But Europe's Jews had no savior.

What if the world had remembered the Armenians? Can history provide lessons and prevent us from repeating past mistakes? Or is the public powerless against powerful dictators who manipulate history to suit their own ends?

Life Behind the Wire

Fantasies of imperial domination abounded in the pronouncements of *Ostland* officials. But the loss of Germany's African empire in 1919 meant that colonial tropes about "subhuman" racial populations were rarely matched by actual expertise. Though the Kaiserreich's colonial *Konzentrationslager* were well known, few Nazi officials had concrete, practical experience with their construction or internal management. At a granular level, then, local experience at prisons, workhouses, and army camps inspired the geometric barracks, electrified barbed wire, and quadrilateral watchtowers of Buchenwald and Dachau – much as local models like native "pontok" huts had inspired the sack-and-stick "wigwams" of Windhoek (figure 5.1).

Discipline, roll calls, and military drills were clear army imports, while corporal punishment, including the infamous *Anbinden* (chap. 3), derived from pre-1918 penitentiary regulations in Prussia, Heinrich Himmler claimed. Similarly, Prussian workhouses inspired punishments like solitary confinement and regimes of silence at feeding times,[27] while an apparent

FIGURE 5.1 Windhoek concentration camp in South-West Africa, 1904 (*left*); the SS concentration camp at Dachau in Germany (*right*) also reflected local architecture. (Source: National Archives of Namibia; US Holocaust Museum.)

emphasis on the "healing effects of productive work and tight discipline" rehearsed agendas at modern prisons. As Jewish prisoners swelled camp populations after *Kristallnacht*, and particularly after Operation Barbarossa, meanwhile, officials deployed familiar medical tropes as they "isolate[d] incurable political, social, and racial 'parasites' from the rest of society."[28]

In the early phases of World War II, an emphasis on cleanliness and spartan efficiency governed camp life. Confined at the Ravensbrück women's camp, where segregation by sex reflected fears about the reproduction of undesirables, Buber-Neumann encountered a "realm of orderliness" run on "strictly military lines." Following encounters with apparent dirt and disorder in the colonial world, European culture came to prize cleanliness and sanitation as markers of civilization. But the Nazis took such proclivities to manic extremes. For them, social, political, and especially racial outcasts infected the German social body and needed to be cleansed. The result, Buber-Neumann described, was a "pedantic nightmare" of sanitary rigor, at least until wartime chaos transformed camps into disease-ridden slums. "Dust was removed everywhere, even from the beams across the hut" – SS overseers "went round with white gloves" to check. Meanwhile, "pettifogging rules" mandated that "feet must not be put round the legs of stools for fear of marks." At times, such "Prussian chicanery" made Buber-Neumann nostalgic for the "lousy mud huts" and comparative dirt and disorder of the Soviet Gulag. Yet hygienic discipline, at least in the early phase of Nazi *Konzentrationslager*, prevented epidemic disease, and Nazi camps provided "luxuries" like showers and sausage breakfasts unheard of in the Gulag.[29]

If Nazi apologists portrayed camps as benign rehabilitation centers, however, they were deceiving themselves. The camp SS – a cadre of privileged functionaries, whose zeal distinguished them from apathetic Gulag guards assigned to the archipelago as punishment – institutionalized violence and brutality from early on. In Buber-Neumann's account, corporal punishment on a "special whipping block," and eventually firing squads and even gas chambers, awaited inmates who violated camp rules – a contrast, she felt, to the less violent penalties of the Gulag.[30] Like their Soviet counterparts, however, the SS mobilized the tactics of "divide and rule" by turning the *Konzentrationslager*'s wide diversity of inmates against each other. In order to make inmates "legible," authorities classified and identified them with an intricate system of colored badges: green for "criminal," black for "asocial," red for "political prisoner," blue for foreign "forced laborer," yellow for "Jew," brown for "Roma/Sinti," and pink for "homosexuals," whose persecution represented a temporal and symbolic break from the tolerant sexual climate of Weimar Germany.

Camp survivors habitually reserved their greatest resentment for prisoner functionaries, known as *Kapos*, who exchanged rewards (better rations and accommodation, and even trips to the SS brothel) for maintaining discipline, often outdoing the SS's brutality in the process. At Auschwitz, Primo Levi described the "pure bestiality" of a *Kapo* named Alex, "a violent and unreliable rogue" interned for criminal rather than political or racial offenses who "never let slip an opportunity of proclaiming his pride in his pure blood." Invariably, the SS displayed their "satanic knowledge of human beings" by choosing only the most brutal inmates for positions of authority within their system of "prisoner self-administration." For the political theorist Hannah Arendt, the *Kapos* represented the camp's gravest offense, for they blurred moral distinctions between victim and perpetrator. Levi's own will to survive was driven, in part, by the need to bear witness – and to pass moral judgment. "The poor brute Alex ... would be amazed," Levi wrote, "that on the basis of his actions, I judge him and ... innumerable others like him, big and small, in Auschwitz and everywhere."[31] The *Kapos*, though, were by no means exceptional: they reminded Buber-Neumann of the barrack brigadiers, often criminals, in the Gulag.

As the war progressed, logistical breakdown replaced tight discipline, particularly as absolute destruction on the Eastern Front flooded camps with hundreds of thousands of inmates – Polish partisans, Russian POWs, and above all, Eastern European Jews. Starting in 1942, camps proliferated in size and number, but terrible overcrowding resulted in extreme hunger, dirt, disorder, and outbreaks of disease. Gone was the regime of cleanliness described at Ravensbrück. "Prisoners [now] died like flies of typhoid, tuberculosis, dysentery, pneumonia, and other causes," Buber-Neumann observed.[32] Increasingly, Nazi camps resembled the chaotic and improvised installations of colonial war. In such situations, inmates engaged in a desperate struggle. Concentration camps, Levi commented, constituted a "gigantic biological and social experiment," inspired by colonial eugenics and racial "science," in which only the fittest and most productive would survive. Extreme shortages generated an intricate barter economy in which everything could be traded – or stolen – in an effort to avoid beatings from *Kapos* or lethal work brigades. For Levi, "death beg[an] with the shoes." When conducting heavy labor, ill-fitting footwear led to ugly sores and ulcers, which might culminate in gangrene and death.[33] Such circumstances, though unsettling, were not unprecedented: *valenki* boots were vital to survival in the Soviet arctic, while on tropical slave plantations, barefooted laborers got "ulcers on their feet," which "if neglected ... to a dangerous degree ... disable[d] them from walking."[34]

One common tie that unites Nazi *Konzentrationslager* with other episodes of mass confinement was the exploitation of labor. At first, work was "part and parcel of the 'process of reeducation,'" Buber-Neumann observed, "and labor productivity had nothing whatever to do with it." Indeed, "if there was nothing else to do, piles of sand would be carted from one place to another and back again."[35] Amid pervasive wartime labor shortages, however, economic motives transformed *Konzentrationslager* into mass factories. As increasingly vital components of the war economy, more so even than their Gulag counterparts, camps detained a broadening array of "enemies of the state," real and very often imagined, to work at mines and munitions factories. At Mauthausen inmates worked in stone quarries; at Dora-Mittelberg they produced V-2 rockets in an enormous underground bunker; and subcamps of Auschwitz enslaved inmates for agricultural work on SS farms. In his book comparing American plantations with Nazi concentration camps, the historian Stanley Elkins concludes the latter were "a special and highly perverted instance of human slavery."[36] Inmates agreed. "We are slaves," Primo Levi wrote, "deprived of every right, exposed to every insult."[37]

As in South-West Africa, where camps supplied private conglomerates (chap. 3), Nazi camps rented out slave labor in public-private partnerships to corporations like Siemens and Bayer, which erected their own satellite camps close to workplaces. The Monowitz compound at Auschwitz was essentially a synthetic rubber factory run by IG Farben, extracting forced labor with the same brutality and lethality (albeit different technology) as Congolese rubber plantations. In contrast to premodern slave systems, however, Nazi *Konzentrationslager* combined unfree labor with the tactics of industrial production. Women working 11-hour shifts at the "SS slave shop" in Ravensbrück, where they sewed military uniforms, encountered the same techniques as Victorian factories or today's Third World sweatshops: mechanized assembly lines, division of labor, preset quotas.[38] Working in the relative comfort of heated workshops, however, such inmates avoided the hardships of outdoor labor. Before securing a position as a chemical specialist in a Monowitz laboratory, an opportunity that no doubt saved his life, Primo Levi hauled timber and steel at a construction site in subzero temperatures. If the camps had lasted any longer, he wrote, "a harsh language would have been born … [to] express what it means to toil the whole day in the wind."[39]

But the war, and thus the camps, ended before new vocabularies emerged. Camp labor could not prevail against the mobilized economies of the democratic West – just as plantation slavery was, arguably, never as productive as free wage labor. Ultimately, then, *Konzentrationslager* were much better at killing than producing. In total, at least 1.7 million SS concentration camp inmates perished in a destructive and unsustainable system that instrumentalized human life (many more would die, the following pages note, in a distinct network of extermination centers). Approaching inmates not as human beings but as disposable units of labor, camps sent the sick and weak to gas chambers when they were no longer able to work. At the worst camps, the life expectancy was approximately three months; system-wide, the annual death rate exceeded 60 percent.[40] Like at German POW camps in World War I, and Shark Island in South-West Africa, which achieved a preliminary, pre-industrial version of the Nazis' more systematic "annihilation through labor" policy, an enduring proclivity for immoderate violence proved counterproductive to the Nazi war effort. Dead bodies could not work. Yet the paradox is only apparent, for Nazi war aims were not limited to battlefield victory, but to the destruction of "subhumanity." To this end, the history of concentration camps intersects (though does not entirely overlap) with that of the Holocaust.

THE CAMP AND THE PLANTATION

Concentration camps and slave plantations emerged under different circumstances, but they retain structural similarities. Psychologists have compared the trauma chattel slaves and *Konzentrationslager* inmates endured upon entering new lives of captivity and toil. With no fixed term of imprisonment, both groups faced uncertain futures that led to depression and despair. After arduous journeys in sealed cattle cars (an experience not dissimilar to the "Middle Passage"), prisoners entering Nazi camps encountered a difficult period of adjustment that resembled the dangerous "seasoning period" on the plantation. "If you survive the first three months you will survive the next three years," inmates maintained. Dehumanizing rituals, like medical exams and the tattooing (or branding in the case of plantation slaves) of identification numbers, initiated inmates while stripping them of dignity and rights. Like slaves, camp prisoners were not valued as human beings but as instruments of production. Meanwhile, SS guards (like plantation overseers) demanded absolute obedience and enacted powers of life or death. In a system of "perverted patriarchy," as the historian of American slavery Stanley Elkins calls it, inmates (like enslaved people) even came to internalize their own racial subjection, recognizing *Kapos* and SS guards as all-powerful father figures, akin to a master.[41]

Yet important differences remain. Nazi camps were much larger than even the most substantial Caribbean plantations. And while camps and plantations both enforced unfree labor, Nazi racism, and the desperate wartime context in which it operated, demanded both the exploitation of labor *and* the extermination of subhuman laborers in the process. Camps had gas chambers; plantations did not.

A Double Extermination

The Madagascar Plan and Jewish "nature reserves" were important psychological precursors to the Nazi "final solution," for they envisioned a Europe free of Jews. The long global history of concentration camps also offered apparent justification to Nazi spokesmen, who made regular reference to the concentration camps of other empires. In 1941, propaganda minister Joseph Goebbels set *Ohm Krüger*, one of the era's most popular films, at a concentration camp in Boer War-era South Africa. As blatant anti-English propaganda amid the ongoing "Battle for Britain," the film simultaneously projected Nazi practices – brutal colonial conquest, indiscriminate violence against civilians, and the use of concentration camps – onto Britain in an effort to distract from and exonerate the still greater crimes the Nazis were then committing. Filmed only a few miles from the notorious Sachsenhausen concentration camp outside Berlin, the film helped normalize camps to the German public at the very moment Nazi *Konzentrationslager* were developing in ominous new directions. As recounted in this book's introduction, Hermann Göring, the son of German South-West Africa's first colonial governor, pioneered such dissimulation in his heated exchange with the British ambassador to Germany. Violent practices thus became justifiable if Germany's enemies had done the same.

Yet while the global history of camps provided convenient comparative fodder, the Nazi Empire's pursuit of industrialized genocide has no moral or historical equivalent. Hannah Arendt distinguished the "purgatory" of prewar Nazi camps (and those of other regimes like colonial Britain and the Soviet Union), designed to isolate undesirable elements, from the "hell" of Nazi Germany's most brutal *Konzentrationslager*, which systematically destroyed bodies and souls.[42] Comparisons between Nazi camps and colonial or Soviet precedents – not to mention the German historian Ernst Nolte's controversial suggestion that Hitler's camps were merely "mirror images" of the Gulag – must carefully balance broad similarities with the distinct singularity of Nazi crimes. In his moving memoir, originally titled *If This Is a Man*, Primo Levi testifies to the erasure of humanity at Auschwitz, the largest and most infamous Nazi camp. Forced to survive through theft and betrayal and detained within an "eternal present" of unending hunger and insults, inmates lost all sense of time or space. Auschwitz, Levi continued, turned men into "sordid puppets" who moved like "automatons"; walking cadavers stripped of dignity and individuality, they lacked the will to resist or even consent to the regime. Jewish inmates referred to the walking dead as *Musselman*, whose bent form resembled Muslims in prayer; physically and psychologically broken, they were soon liquidated in the gas chambers. For Levi, the "resolution to annihilate us first as men in order to kill us more slowly afterwards" spoke to the "double sense of the term 'extermination camp.'"[43]

Camps also annihilated women. At Ravensbrück, a women's-only camp administered by male SS officers but overseen by 150 female guards, 50,000 inmates, some accompanied by their children, perished from overwork, starvation, and disease – a situation that challenged gender norms

FIGURE 5.2 Though camps like Auschwitz liquidated the majority of women and children in gas chambers, a minority survived in labor battalions. (Source: Yad Vashem.)

envisioning women as unsuited to either enforcing or enduring physical punishment. Other camps concentrated men and women together. Here, shaven heads and shapeless uniforms erased gender identity (figure 5.2), as did the hunger and overwork that disrupted women's menstrual cycles. Some feared their ordeal would leave them permanently infertile, causing them to lose their "womanhood," though others faced a daily struggle to find sanitary pads: "You took the undergarment slip they gave you, ripped it and made little rags, and guarded those little rags like they were gold," one inmate recounted.[44] Nazi camps even deadened parental instincts. In extreme cases, survivors recall mothers, faced with impossible choices and unimaginable duress, committing infanticide in order to liberate their children from the living hell surrounding them.[45] Conversely, Elie Wiesel, in his memoir *Night*, speaks of the relief he felt when his father died; for this once devout student of the Talmud, God also perished in that moment.

However horrific, the testimonies of survivors like Levi, Buber-Neumann, and Wiesel are atypical – because they survived. At the Wansee Conference (January 20, 1942), Hitler's inner circle devised the "Final Solution to the Jewish Problem," transforming Nazi genocide into something more systematic and premeditated than the decentralized killings of colonial conquest. The six resulting extermination camps, administratively and phenomenologically distinct from SS *Konzentrationslager*, were unprecedented technologies of industrial murder. To Arendt's typology, the historians Joël Kotek and Pierre Rigoulot add another term, *Gehenna*, a specifically Judaic vision of hell in which souls are immediately destroyed, to describe the final phases of the Jewish (and Roma/Sinti) Holocaust.[46] Auschwitz and Majdanek combined the functions of concentration and extermination camps, systematically working prisoners to death while liquidating those unable to work. In a moment of outsized significance, medical personnel, endowed with exceptional, extrajudicial powers, classified incoming prisoners. Those "judged capable … of working usefully for the Reich"[47] were assigned barracks; the sick and elderly, as well as the vast majority of children and women, whose youth and reproductive capacity threatened the genocidal aspirations of Nazi biopolitics, were summarily liquidated. Age and gender, then, became matters of life and death.

In a refinement of genocide, meanwhile, the extermination factories at Chełmno, Belzec, Sobibor, and, most infamously, Treblinka, existed solely for the purposes of mass murder. New arrivals, mostly from Polish ghettos and SS camps, were forced indiscriminately into gas chambers, regardless of physical profile. Some 2.7 million of the Holocaust's nearly 6 million victims were killed in this manner, their bodies incinerated in onsite ovens. At least a million more perished from hunger, work, or disease while concentrated in ghettos or camps, while mobile SS death squads in the forests of Poland and Ukraine killed the remaining 2 million in a murderous rampage that took a mental toll on even the most fanatical antisemites.[48] In this context, gas chambers and extermination centers achieved a quick, sanitized, serialized death that reduced the act of murder to a technocratic operation – and thereby shielded German soldiers from the psychological burden of killing.

Lacking barracks or worksites, extermination facilities like Treblinka were less "camps" than processing centers for the disposal of human bodies. And in contrast to concentration camps, which have provided historians with rich inmate testimonies, Treblinka had practically no survivors. It therefore exists uneasily within the global history of mass confinement, on the extreme outer edge of a diverse but brutal spectrum of Nazi camps. Yet such facilities were unique not in their elements but in their genocidal application. Like an industrial assembly line, the division of labor among *Kapos* and SS guards achieved maximum efficiency in the production of corpses. Bureaucratic planning, train transports, and Zyklon B gas, a pesticide used in the 1920s to fumigate the clothing of migrants at the US-Mexico border, and which the Nazis adapted to "euthanize" sick concentration camp inmates, materialized the horrific potential of racial hatred, ethnic nationalism, and the elimination of "unwanted" populations. Treblinka was an extreme and murderous conclusion to a spiraling dynamic of ethnic cleansing only imperfectly realized in the atrocities of the colonial world.

Global Fascism

In the decades immediately following World War II, fascism was largely discredited. Yet in the 1930s, the militarized politics of autocratic leadership, national rebirth, and ethnic purity represented a dynamic and appealing force that confined suspected "enemies" across Europe and as far afield as East Asia and Latin America (chaps. 6 and 7). In Spain, the military dictator Francisco Franco (1892–1975) concentrated republican partisans, communists, and other dissidents in camps stretching from the French border to North African *presidios*. Inmates suffered from starvation and arbitrary violence while toiling in labor battalions under the caustic slogan "Punishment Redemption through Work." Franco's *Inspección de Campos de Concentración* visited Sachsenhausen in Berlin while Himmler inspected Spanish camps in 1940, contributing to a transnational playbook of fascist internment.

In Italy, Hitler's closest collaborator, Benito Mussolini (1883–1945), like Franco, confined political dissidents and other "dangerous" populations in repurposed island colonies like Lampedusa and agricultural penal camps first established in the nineteenth century. Italy's occupation of Libya (1911–43) likewise depended on the concentration of rebellious populations (figure 5.3), including almost the entire nomadic population of the Jebel Akhdar uplands, in camps and behind a 300-mile "frontier wire" – a common tactic of colonial counterinsurgency. And when Mussolini's forces invaded Ethiopia in 1936, they concentrated suspected resistance fighters and their families in order to pacify the country. Transported to Danane in occupied Somalia, thousands of men, women, and children perished from epidemic disease, while inmates at Nora labored in open quarries and died of sunstroke in 50°C heat.[49] Camp authorities "gave [us] nothing, no cloth, blanket, or carpet to sleep on," the prisoner Michael Tessema testified.

FIGURE 5.3 Al-Coefia concentration camp in occupied Libya (1932). Mussolini's empire in North Africa suggests a "missing link" between colonial and fascist violence. (Source: Archivio Storico Diplomatico Ministero degli Affari Esteri.)

Rations consisted of "four hard biscuits (*galeta*) in a day," and contaminated water killed 3,175 out of 6,500 inmates. More troubling still, women in the camp "were absolutely naked. There was not even a piece of cloth to hide their delicate organs," and in one case, a guard whipped the mother of a dead infant, forcing her to dig her child's grave.[50]

Brutality in Africa soon migrated to Europe, particularly after Mussolini's official turn to antisemitism in 1938. By Nazi standards, camps like Ferramonti, which concentrated Italian Jews, were relatively benign. Inmates lived behind barbed wire but frequented a camp library, school, theater, and synagogue; the vast majority survived, though several thousand, once "liberated" by the United States Army, were reinterned as enemy aliens at Oswego, New York. Italian concentration camps in occupied Slovenia and Croatia, however, were more menacing. Here, settler colonial dynamics prevailed as Italian forces ethnically cleansed native Slavs in order to make room for Italian settlers. Mussolini's forces burned down villages, executed insurgents, and concentrated suspected guerrillas and civilian hostages. At Rab, inmates died from cold, hunger, and disease in leaky tents – a pattern repeated by the murderous pro-Nazi regimes of Croatia, Slovakia, and Romania, where the killing fields of Transnistria approached the horror but lacked the systematic rigor of Nazi death camps. Under President Jozef Tiso (1887–1947), an antisemitic Catholic priest, militias rounded up 89,000 Slovakian Jews, detaining them in transit camps before deporting them to Auschwitz. The Ustaše, Croatia's ultranationalist government, also liquidated Jews and Romani. Mortality rates at the infamous Jasenovac concentration camp were eclipsed only by Nazi extermination factories. Croatian guards, however, murdered inmates individually, with knives and axes – a contrast to the institutionalized slaughter of Birkenau or Treblinka. The Balkans, then, earned a reputation for violence that would be reprised in future generations, as Bosnian Serbs, motivated by the ultranationalist politics of Slobodan Milošević (1941–2006), went on to massacre 8,000 Muslim Bosniaks at Srebrenica in 1995, while detaining thousands more at camps like Omarska, where suspected partisans and their families faced torture, rape, and extrajudicial killings.

France's history of wartime camps is especially vexed. As an Allied power, France interned Axis enemy aliens, including Jewish refugees from the Third Reich, along with left-wing pacifists. Following military defeat in 1940, however, France's collaborationist Vichy regime adopted fascist iconography, established a uniformed paramilitary force, the *Milice*, and replaced the Third Republic's secular egalitarianism with an authoritarian ethnic and antisemitic nationalism that emulated Nazi Germany. Camps like Gurs, first built to accommodate refugees from the Spanish Civil War (1936–9), soon detained Jews and illegal immigrants in dehumanizing conditions. Like Italy, Vichy France also turned North Africa into a space of confinement for racial and political enemies, including Jews, communists, and Arab dissidents. And while France did not operate death camps, violent nighttime raids captured foreign and French Jews, stripping them of civil rights and detaining them, under appalling conditions, in stadiums like the Vél d'Hiv or in the modernist apartment blocks of Drancy. From here, authorities shipped some 76,000 Jewish inmates to concentration and extermination camps in Germany and Nazi-occupied Poland. Presented with the option of saving Jewish children by keeping them in France, the antisemitic Vichy minister Pierre Laval chose, instead, to deport them to Nazi Germany on the premise that families should not be separated. Thus did Vichy camps acquire their moniker "the antechamber of Auschwitz."

Conclusion

As Germany faced a two-front assault in the dying days of World War II, the Nazi regime and its Italian and Vichy collaborators disintegrated. In the final phase of their existence, life in crowded and now chaotic

Konzentrationslager oscillated between hope and despair. Evacuation marches into "darkest Germany" killed thousands of prisoners as Soviet and Allied troops advanced. Others, hastily relocated to decommissioned prison ships like the *SS Cap Arcona* – an expedient revival of nineteenth-century carceral measures – sadly perished from errant Allied bombings in the Bay of Lübeck. By 1945, many inmates were too sick or emaciated to survive, while others would suffer years of psychological readjustment to life on the outside. Nonetheless, for Primo Levi, the liberation of Auschwitz by Soviet forces was a moment of euphoria, in which he felt himself become a man again. Margarete Buber-Neumann likewise relished the "gift of liberty," though as a former Gulag inmate, her fate under Soviet occupation remained tenuous. Indeed, the Soviet Union, fortified by victory, repurposed Sachsenhausen and other former *Konzentrationslager* east of the "iron curtain" as outposts of the Gulag archipelago.

As symbols of unfreedom and inhumanity, Nazi camps loomed large in postwar politics: they featured prominently at the Nuremberg trials (1945–46), which convicted the Nazi leadership of war crimes. Yet if the horrors of *Konzentrationslager* discredited the Nazi regime, it did not put an end to camps. In the words of Herbert Blank, an anti-Nazi imprisoned during World War II, "one should not be put off by the fact that during the Hitler years the term 'camp' was corrupted." That "says everything against Hitler but nothing against camps," which remained valid tools, he maintained, for converting "the morally ailing … back into productive and healthy members of society."[51] Showcasing the degree to which camps had become essential tools to modern statecraft across the moral and ideological spectrum, West German authorities, amid postwar dislocation, billeted displaced persons in former Nazi camps (chap. 8), while Dachau became a work camp for the education of "wayward women and lazy men" – a fulfillment, perhaps, of the Nazis' early depiction of camps as disciplinary and educational institutions, twentieth-century versions of the industrial workhouse.[52]

Notes

1 Margarete Buber-Neumann, *Under Two Dictators: Prisoner of Stalin and Hitler*, trans. Edward Fitzgerald (London: Pimlico, 2009), 230.

2 Paul Moore, "'And What Concentration Camps Those Were!': Foreign Concentration Camps in Nazi Propaganda, 1933–9," *Journal of Contemporary History* 45, no. 3 (2010): 672.

3 John Keegan, *The Face of Battle: A Study of Agincourt, Waterloo, and the Somme* (London: Pimlico, 2004), 255–6.

4 Harold Marcuse, *Legacies of Dachau: The Uses and Abuses of a Concentration Camp, 1933–2001* (Cambridge: Cambridge University Press, 2001), 20.

5 Christian Goeschel and Nikolaus Wachsmann, "Before Auschwitz: The Formation of the Nazi Concentration Camps, 1933–9," *Journal of Contemporary History* 42, no. 3 (2010): 529–30.

6 Marcuse, *Legacies of Dachau*, 28, 29.

7 Enzo Traverso, *The Origins of Nazi Violence*, trans. Janet Lloyd (New York: New Press, 2003), 135.

8 James Q. Whiteman, *Hitler's American Model: The United States and the Making of Nazi Race Law* (Princeton: Princeton University Press, 2017).

9 Mark Mazower, *Hitler's Empire: How the Nazis Ruled Europe* (New York: Penguin, 2009), xxxix.

10 Jürgen Zimmerer, "Colonialism and the Holocaust: Towards an Archaeology of Genocide," in *Genocide and Settler Society: Frontier Violence and Stolen Indigenous Children in Australian History*, ed. A. Dirk Moses (New York: Berghahn, 2004), 49.

11 Benjamin Madley, "From Africa to Auschwitz: How German South-West Africa Incubated Ideas and Methods Adopted and Developed by the Nazis in Eastern Europe," *European History Quarterly* 35, no. 3 (2005): 438.

12 Hugh Trevor-Roper, ed., *Hitler's Table Talk, 1941–44* (New York: Enigma Books, 2000), 15. Owing to transcription and translation errors, historians debate the exact wording of Hitler's private dinnertime statements.

13 Ian Kershaw, *Hitler, 1936–45: Nemesis* (New York: W.W. Norton, 2001), 405.

14 Hitler cited in David Olusoga and Casper W. Erichsen, *The Kaiser's Holocaust: Germany's Forgotten Genocide and the Colonial Roots of Nazism* (London: Faber and Faber, 2010), 339.

15 Trevor-Roper, *Hitler's Table Talk*, 466.

16 H. Glenn Penny, *Kindred by Choice: Germans and American Indians since 1800* (Chapel Hill: University of North Carolina Press, 2013), 233.

17 Elizabeth Harvey, "Management and Manipulation: Nazi Settlement Planners and Ethnic German Settlers in Occupied Poland," *Settler Colonialism in the Twentieth Century: Projects, Practices, Legacies*, ed. Caroline Elkins and Susan Pedersen (New York: Routledge, 2006), 95–112. For Turner's famous "frontier thesis," see Frederick Jackson Turner, *The Frontier in American History* (New York: Henry Holt and Company, 1920).

18 Traverso, *Origins of Nazi Violence*, 71, 50.

19 A. Dirk Moses, "Empire, Colony, Genocide: Keywords and the Philosophy of History," in A. Dirk Moses, ed., *Empire, Colony, Genocide: Conquest, Occupation and Subaltern Resistance in World History* (New York: Berghahn, 2008), 37.

20 Mazower, *Hitler's Empire*, 170.

21 Zimmerer, "Colonialism and the Holocaust," 67.

22 Christian Gerlach, *Extremely Violent Societies: Mass Violence in the Twentieth-Century World* (Cambridge: Cambridge University Press, 2010), 190; Peter Lieb, "Few Carrots and a Lot of Sticks: German Anti-Partisan Warfare in World War Two," in *Counterinsurgency in Modern Warfare*, ed. Daniel Marston and Carter Malkasian (Oxford: Osprey, 2008), 74–83.

23 Jonas Kreienbaum, *A Sad Fiasco: Colonial Concentration Camps in Southern Africa, 1900–1908*, trans. Elizabeth Janik (New York: Berghahn, 2019), 231.

24 Trevor-Roper, *Hitler's Table Talk*, 69.

25 Stefan Ihrig, *Justifying Genocide: Germany and the Armenians from Bismarck to Hitler* (Cambridge: Harvard University Press, 2016), 347–8. Historians debate the exact wording of Hitler's August 22, 1939 Obersalzberg Speech.

26 Ihrig, *Justifying Genocide*, 367.

27 Goeschel and Wachsmann, "Before Auschwitz," 529–32.

28 Marcuse, *Legacies of Dachau*, 28.

29 Buber-Neumann, *Two Dictators*, 192–3, 178.

30 Buber-Neumann, *Two Dictators*, 179.

31 Primo Levi, *Survival in Auschwitz*, trans. Stuart Woolf (New York: Touchstone, 1996), 67, 90–1, 110.

32 Buber-Neumann, *Two Dictators*, 246.

33 Levi, *Survival in Auschwitz*, 87, 34.

34 Dr. Collins, *Practical Rules for the Management and Medical Treatment of Negro Slaves in the Sugar Colonies* (London: J. Barfield, 1803), 69.

35 Buber-Neumann, *Two Dictators*, 175.

36 Stanley Elkins, *Slavery: A Problem in American Institutional and Intellectual Life* (Chicago: University of Chicago Press, 1959), 104.

37 Levi, *Survival in Auschwitz*, 41.

38 Buber-Neumann, *Two Dictators*, 225.

39 Levi, *Survival in Auschwitz*, 123.

40 Mortality rates varied greatly across time and space. For statistics, see Nikolaus Wachsmann, *KL: A History of the Nazi Concentration Camps* (New York: Farrar, Straus, and Giroux, 2015), 627–8; and Karin Orth, "The Genesis and Structure of the National Socialist Concentration Camps" in *Encyclopedia of Camps and Ghettos, 1933–45: Volume I*, ed. Geoffrey P. Megargee (Bloomington: Indiana University Press, 2009), 194. The figures here do not include the 2 million Jewish inmates killed in the administratively distinct extermination camps of Treblinka, Sobibor, Belzec, and Chełmno.

41 Elkins, *Slavery*, 110, 104. See also Marc Buggeln, "Were Concentration Camp Prisoners Slaves?: The Possibilities and Limits of Comparative History and Global Historical Perspectives," *International Review of Social History* 53, no. 1 (2008): 101–29; and Kitty Millet, *The Victims of Slavery, Colonization and the Holocaust: A Comparative History of Persecution* (London: Bloomsbury, 2017).

42 Hannah Arendt, *The Origins of Totalitarianism* (New York: Harcourt, 1968), 45.

43 Levi, *Survival in Auschwitz*, 27.

44 Jo-Ann Owusu, "Menstruation and the Holocaust," *History Today* 69, no. 5 (2019), https://www.historytoday.com/archive/feature/menstruation-and-holocaust.

45 Esther Hertzog, "Subjugated Motherhood and the Holocaust," *Dapim: Studies on the Holocaust* 30, no. 1 (2006): 27.

46 For an English-language discussion of Kotek and Rigoulot's distinction, see Robert Jan Van Pelt, "Paradise/Hades, Purgatory, Hell/Gehenna: A Political Typology of the Camps," in *The Routledge History of the Holocaust*, ed. Jonathan C. Friedman (New York: Routledge, 2011), 197.

47 Levi, *Survival in Auschwitz*, 20.

48 For statistics, see "How Many People Did the Nazis Murder?," *United States Holocaust Museum*, accessed September 26, 2023, https://encyclopedia.ushmm.org/content/en/article/documenting-numbers-of-victims-of-the-holocaust-and-nazi-persecution.

49 James Walston, "History and Memory of the Italian Concentration Camps," *Historical Journal* 40, no. 1 (1997): 174.

50 "Testimony of Michael Tessema," accessed October 1, 2023, https://campifascisti.it/file/media/Testemony%20of%20Michael%20Tessema.pdf.

51 Herbert Blank cited in Marcuse, *Legacies of Dachau*, 159.

52 Marcuse, *Legacies of Dachau*, 166.

6 | Asian Archipelagos: War, Empire, and Revolution in the East

In 1960, Hongda ("Harry") Wu rode in the back of an army jeep destined for the Beiyuan Detention Centre in Beijing's northern suburbs. Arrested as a "counterrevolutionary rightist," he shared his ride with a "dirty and disheveled" vagrant, likely caught stealing food during China's Great Famine (1958–62) or rounded up in an urban sweep in preparation for May Day celebrations. Over the preceding decades, the extremism of the 1930s and the upheavals of World War II had played out on a global stage. Authoritarian polities like imperial Japan conducted brutal displays of military violence against POWs and forced laborers in the 1930s and 1940s, while the right-wing government of nationalist China detained political opponents during the Chinese Civil War (1927–49). But for Harry Wu (1937–2016), the outspoken son of a wealthy banker, the Communist system rose in front of him like "a great wall."[1] While the Soviet Empire extended into eastern Europe following its victory in World War II, the world's largest network of Communist concentration camps developed in East Asia. Founded in 1949, Mao Zedong's People's Republic of China (PRC) confined Wu and millions of others in a vast system of "reform through forced labor" camps, while North Korea, Cambodia, and other countries emulated Sino or Soviet models when constructing their own sprawling camp networks.

The global dissemination of mass confinement highlights the degree to which ruling elites across the world appropriated camps as potent tools of governance and repression. Asia's carceral archipelagos stemmed from political connections between East and West and the global circulation of ideas and expertise. German, Soviet, and American advisors consulted with their counterparts in modernizing client states. Far from passive recipients, however, non-Western societies actively modified and sometimes

149

radicalized the camp to suit their own ends. This chapter examines the global proliferation of camps from imperial Japan and nationalist China in the 1930s to post-World War II gulags established by Mao and other Asian dictatorships. In doing so, it traces transnational connections while considering the ways in which non-Western cultures assimilated and transformed approaches to mass encampment.

Japanese Empire

Ultranationalism and aggressive military expansion were by no means limited to Nazi Europe. As participants of the "global '30s," Japan was a key partner in Germany's fascist world alliance. Following the Meiji restoration (1867), Japan, a self-conscious Western protégé, imported European and American advisors, many with experience managing Native Americans, to help colonize "uncivilized" populations. Internalizing Western colonial concepts of race and civilization, authorities in nineteenth-century Hokkaido forced the Indigenous Ainu into monitored settlements that removed them from their traditional culture and communities. Japan likewise bisected Taiwan's eastern highlands with electrified fencing, dividing "raw barbarians [seiban]," including insurgent Indigenous people, from "cooked barbarians [jukuban]," which it subjected to Japanization programs in "protected villages" that provided military and social security to concentrated residents. The project recalled longstanding Chinese policing on either side of the Great Wall, though the opening of "savage children's educational institutes" reflected Western influence.[2]

As Japan extended its imperial ambitions into mainland Asia, it approached Korea and Manchukuo, its client state in northern China, as vast settler colonies. In this context, the Chinese Communist leader Mao Zedong (1893–76) condemned the Japanese for "recall[ing] a past ... that witnessed the extension of the British Empire to North America" and "that saw the [Spanish] overrun Central and South America."[3] For Mao, guerrilla strikes were potent tactics in the struggle against Japanese imperialism. Harried by Chinese insurgents – or "bandits," the "vermin of the community," as Japanese generals called them[4] – occupation forces razed villages and turned to violent search-and-capture raids to clear rebellious zones and relocate 5.5 million Koreans, Chinese, and Manchus to more than 10,000 "protected villages." Such tactics resembled Cuba's reconcentrados and British concentration camps in South Africa. But Japan also innovated: the provision of security, healthcare, food, and pro-Japanese propaganda marked a developing counterinsurgency tactic, *minshin hāku* (seizing the people's heart) that Western powers would later replicate in Malaya and Vietnam (chap. 7). Japan, however, failed to win the hearts and minds of a population it deemed racially unfit. Echoing Nazi perceptions of East European Slavs, Uno Shintaro, a Japanese officer, confided: "[W]e never really considered the Chinese humans ... we concluded that the Yamato [Japanese] race was superior."[5] By the 1930s, then, Japan increasingly assimilated the military ambitions and racial worldview of its partners in Nazi Germany.

World War II in Asia was more protracted than in Europe, lasting from Japan's invasion of Manchuria (1931) to its final nuclear showdown with the United States (1945). It also portended an ominous new chapter of Asian camps. In an effort to showcase its modernity and civilization, Japan introduced military internment to East Asia in World War I with relatively salubrious facilities, recreational activities, wholesome food, and modern medical treatment for German and Austrian aliens. In contrast, Japanese camps in World War II are best remembered by 132,000 Allied POWs, transported on abysmal "hell ships" from Malaya, the Philippines, and the Dutch Indies to worksites in Japan and occupied Burma, and, less prominently, by 125,000 civilian internees, whose testimony at the Tokyo War Crimes tribunal (1946–8) revealed torture, forced labor, and wretched living conditions. Neglect and abuse stemmed from familiar logistical challenges inherent to an overstretched empire, which struggled to supply captives with resources or control the violent impulses of colonial "men on the spot." But vengeance also motivated violence. Japan's ambiguous identity as both a "civilized" and an industrial nation equal to Europe *and* as a colonized Asian country allowed it to take the posture, when convenient, of colonial liberator. As it extended its own empire across Southeast Asia, Japan turned the imperial tables, imprisoning European colonists in former garrisons that once held Asian convicts and political prisoners. At Changi prison in Singapore, Sikh soldiers, turned by Japan, guarded British POWs – a form of conscious racial humiliation that subjected white Europeans to treatment previously reserved for dark-skinned colonials.

Yet Japanese forces committed still greater atrocities against Chinese, Korean, and Southeast Asian populations. Fueled by jingoistic war fever and fantasies of Japan's special racial fitness, "the conflict [in East Asia] was essentially a colonial war," the historian Steven Lee remarks, "with Japanese troops fighting guerrilla and warlord armies."[6] Faced with partisan attacks against railways and supply lines, Japan regarded armed resistance in China as a colonial rebellion rather than an official war, thereby denying

Chinese captives the status of POWs under international law. In order to "pacify" the countryside, the Taiyuan concentration camp detained nearly 100,000 war captives. Described as "Japan's Auschwitz" by the prisoner Liu Qinxiao, a member of Mao Zedong's Eighth Army, the camp subjected inmates to forced labor, illness, and starvation.[7] Many more were shot on the spot, as massacres at Hebei, Changjiao, and most famously, Nanking, attest. Survivors flocked to refugee camps, 175 in Shanghai alone, run by the Chinese national government and monitored by the Red Cross.

Japan's "kill all, burn all, loot all" policies killed 4 million civilians and enslaved many more. As total war demanded the ruthless exploitation of human and natural resources, public-private ventures conscripted more than 6 million Koreans and Chinese in Japan and Manchuria. The Chadian detention center, near Beijing, interned Korean workers to produce rice, though forced laborers also worked in mines and factories. Corporations like Mitsubishi and Nippon Steel benefited in the same way Bayer and Siemens profited from Nazi *Konzentrationslager*. Further afield, forced labor along the Siam-Burma railway, dramatized by the 1957 film *The Bridge on the River Kwai*, was especially deadly. Crowded thatched-roof barracks recalled conditions endured by captive or conscript laborers who lived and died in work camps along European railway projects stretching from Congo to Indonesia.

Yet while Western POWs faced infamous hardships – like the Bataan Death March in the Philippines – they were treated "with comparative consideration," one survivor concedes. By contrast, "coolie camps" housing conscripted Asian laborers, an abused but silent majority, resembled "charnel houses." One witness detailed "corpses rotting unburied in the jungle, [an] almost complete lack of sanitation ... frightful stench, overcrowding, and swarms of flies."[8] Though brutalized as an inferior race, such workers were targeted less for their ethnic or political affiliation than their instrumental utility – for their value as unpaid laborers. Along with war captives, financial incentives (that never materialized) and outright coercion co-opted thousands. In Malaya, Japanese authorities even screened free films at local cinemas; soldiers then locked the doors and forcibly deported those entrapped to Burmese work camps. In other cases, vagrants (often displaced by war) were detained and deported to distant worksites. Such practices extended earlier colonial policies in Hokkaido and Korea, where the *kangoku beya* (jail house system) threatened or even kidnapped local populations, forcing them into confined and segregated living quarters, where they worked as "semi-slaves" in mines and on railways.

SEX SLAVES AND GUINEA PIGS

Forced laborers in Japanese camps were predominately male. But Japan's notorious "comfort stations" detained Korean and Chinese women as sex slaves, forcing them to service Japanese soldiers in guarded brothels. Japan's most gruesome war crimes, however, occurred at a secretive facility, Unit 731, at Pingfang on the outskirts of Harbin in occupied Manchuria. Here, barbed-wire cells detained Chinese political dissidents, Communist sympathizers, ordinary criminals, vagrants, the mentally disabled, and Allied POWs. Disguised as a lumber mill, the sprawling complex was run by the "Epidemic Prevention and Water Purification Department" under the auspices of the military police (here as elsewhere, medical terminology offered a euphemism for atrocity). Instead of extracting labor, the camp conducted biological experiments on live human subjects. Inmates received injections of infectious diseases disguised as vaccinations; others underwent experimental surgeries that removed organs or amputated limbs. Researchers even removed prisoners' stomachs, stitching their esophaguses to their intestines. Japanese doctors published their results in academic journals, writing that their studies had been conducted on "Manchurian monkeys." The unit also unleashed biological weapons, including anthrax, on the surrounding population, killing up to 400,000. One such weapon, carrying bubonic plague-infected fleas, was apparently scheduled to be dropped on San Diego, California, in September 1945, just weeks after American nuclear bombs brought World War II to an end.

Research at Unit 731, like the sadistic experiments of Dr. Mengele at Auschwitz, had little scientific merit. Yet the Pingfang camp did produce militarily useful knowledge. After the war, the United States government gave immunity to Unit 731 officials in return for data they gathered about biological weapons, while dismissing rumors about atrocities as Communist propaganda.[9] Undoubtedly the victim of such violence, Communist China would likewise conduct medical experiments during the Mao era, "vaccinating" healthy prisoners with diseases as if they were "human guinea pigs."[10] So would Cambodia, where the Khmer Rouge, having liquidated all Western-trained doctors, performed gruesome procedures – extracting intestines, slitting throats – at the menacing Security Prison 21.

Camps, according to Giorgio Agamben, reduce inmates to "bare life," to agentless human animals whose biological existence depends entirely on camp authorities.[11] In a vacuum of civil rights and legal oversight, are such atrocities inevitable?

Confucian Concentration Camps

As it pursued an imperial blitzkrieg across East Asia, Japan was both a menace and a model. Following a "century of humiliation" at the hands of Western powers, Chinese Nationalists, known as the Guomindang (GMD), endeavored to modernize and militarize along Japanese lines. Inspired by pan-Asian nationalism, Sun Yat Sen (1866–1925), the founding father of modern China, encouraged Japanese forces to liberate Filipino insurgents detained in American "reconcentration camps" (1899–1901, chap. 3). Meanwhile, Sun's successor, Chiang Kai-shek (1887–1975), openly admired Japan's discipline and power when he moved to Tokyo to enlist in the Imperial Japanese Army Academy in 1906. After serving two years, he returned to China to depose the decaying Manchu dynasty in the Xinhai Revolution (1911). Chiang also looked to Europe for inspiration. Though he rejected Communism, Chiang traveled to Moscow in 1923 to study Soviet politics and military doctrine, and as leader of a unified nationalist China from 1928, he invited German military advisors like General Alexander von Falkenhausen to Beijing. Soon, he styled himself "Generalissimo" in emulation of the ruthless military strongmen of Europe's far right. The appeal of military strength and fascist vitality were clear: Chiang's paramilitary "Blue Shirts" were Chinese analogs of Mussolini's Blackshirts and Hitler's SA.

As Chiang's forces unified China into a modern republic, they met resistance not only from local warlords and Japanese invaders, but from a rival claimant to a liberated China: Mao Zedong's Communist Party. As an uneasy Communist-Nationalist alliance against imperial Japan gave way to intermittent civil war (1927–49), Communist guerrillas launched strikes against Chiang's forces. In the 1930s, GMD jurists looked to Nazi *Konzentrationslager* – as they existed before their transformation into tools of racial genocide and slave labor in World War II – as "efficient means ... to quell communist opposition and pacify society." Following von Faulkenhausen's advice to liquidate Communist guerrillas and intern their civilian supporters, Chiang detained Maoist war captives, as well as liberal intellectuals and suspected Japanese spies, in what foreign observers described as "fascist concentration camps." As Dai Li, director of GMD Intelligence, noted, "[yes] we had concentration camps (*jizhongying*)," though "in times of war every state has organized similar institutions, detaining political prisoners ... as well as enemies and spies who do harm to national security."[12]

Opened in 1938, camps like Xifeng and Shangrao provided models for larger networks of secretive GMD detention sites that existed beyond the reach of Chinese law (figure 6.1). Living conditions varied over time: rations and sanitation were generally poor, though one American observer applauded the "extraordinarily comfortable" barracks he inspected. The abiding emphasis, however, was on creating loyal citizens rather than destroying human life – to "correct" inmates' thinking and return them to a role in society that did not entail opposition to the GMD. Though Chiang Kai-shek employed convict laborers, sentenced by regular judicial processes, to work at munitions factories and on public works – an "agricultural colony" at Pingwu reclaimed "wasteland," while convicts billeted in "peasant sheds" at Guizhou built coffins[13] – political prisoners, like the future Vietnamese Communist Ho Chi Minh, described relatively light labor routines at these facilities. Work, then, was less a tool of corporal punishment and economic production than of moral transformation and political instruction. Regular "study meetings" and anti-communist indoctrination patterned camp life. To this end, officials coined new terminology: the camp became a *daxue*, or "university"; cells were "study rooms"; and inmates were "people in self-cultivation" or, to employ a medical metaphor, "convalescents." Those who transformed their values and beliefs were rewarded with higher wages and greater freedoms.[14] Yet camps exhibited a darker side. In the 1930s, GMD authorities regularly used the "cat-o'-nine tails," a weapon imported from the British enclave at Hong Kong and often used at American slave plantations.[15]

Chiang's camps highlighted the transnational synthesis of foreign and local traditions. While Nazi Germany provided inspiration for detaining communists, Soviet models of collective living also informed arrangements. Noting that Soviet camps resembled factories and farming villages, GMD criminologists embraced communal barracks rather than individual cells. Britain and America also influenced Chinese developments. Chinese modernizers had long turned to Western blueprints, sometimes via the conduit of Japanese models. Built in 1907, the Beijing No. 1 Prison, based on London's Pentonville Reformatory, introduced a Western focus on inmate rehabilitation (chap. 1), while penal colonies like Green Island, which operated until 1987 off the coast of Taiwan, appropriated longstanding practices of carceral exile. Throughout the twentieth century, then, "thought reform" and "education through labor" found an especially receptive cultural environment in China, where the ancient teachings of Confucius and Mencius emphasized self-cultivation and the essential malleability

急烽集中营示意图

FIGURE 6.1 Xifeng, the "Confucian concentration camp," highlights the transnational circulation and adaptation of internment practices. Rooting the GMD's authoritarian rule in Chinese traditions, barracks at Xifeng soon bore Confucian names like Loyalty (*zhong*) and Filial Piety (*xiao*). (Source: World History Connected.)

of humankind. But security concerns also dominated. In 1942, the Sino-American Cooperation Organization imported American specialists to train Chinese secret service agents. Its main prison, a "special detention center" at an abandoned Chongqing coal mine, confined Communist suspects behind electrified barbed wire and subjected them to torture and interrogation, performing similar functions to future camps like Guantanamo Bay (chap. 7). Popularly known as the "White House," the camp became an enduring symbol of repression in the People's Republic of China (PRC) – a regime that established its own expansive camp system.[16]

The Chinese Gulag

With victory over imperial Japan in World War II and with the retreat of Chiang Kai-shek to Taiwan in the subsequent Civil War (1946–9), the Chinese Communist Party (CCP) under Mao Zedong announced a radical break from the imperial and republican past. Yet the promise of reeducation through labor endured through a vast new system of Communist forced-labor camps. As a revolutionary polity, militarized and brutalized by decades of civil war and foreign occupation, Communist China, like the Soviet Union, pursued an ambitious modernization campaign while rooting out "class enemies" and suspected "counterrevolutionaries" (including fellow Communists who did not ascribe to Mao's belief that peasants rather than industrial workers were the revolutionary vanguard). The Jiangxi "Soviet," an organization of Maoist guerrillas supported by Moscow, first imprisoned GMD officials and POWs in the 1930s. As the CCP cemented power, it extended detention to a widening array of political suspects along with vagrants, prostitutes, and gang members who were "mopped up" amid postwar civil unrest. Across the ideological divide, then, Chinese camps existed as flexible institutions of social control and political reeducation. Yet in contrast to nationalist China, Communist camps expanded exponentially in the years after the Civil War. Inmates under Chiang numbered in the thousands. Mao imprisoned millions.

The CCP inherited an existing network of poorhouses, homeless shelters (*shourong suo*), GMD camps, and imperial-era institutions like Shanghai's Tilanqiao prison, designed by British engineers, along with the Chadian detention center, built by Japan and refurbished by Chiang. Yet the CCP's carceral demands far outstripped existing capacity. Prison shortages soon forced detainees to inhabit leaky tents, makeshift huts, or, in remote frontiers, improvised yurts, while they constructed more permanent barracks at a growing continental system of "reeducation through labor" camps (*laodong jiaoyang*), a form of administrative detention, and the much larger "reform through labor" camps (*laodong gaizao*) for inmates convicted, under the criminal code, of more serious offenses. Known generically as *laogai*, this archipelago of camps was larger than the Soviet Gulag in absolute though not per capita numbers, imprisoning up to 40 million inmates. And despite moderations in the Deng Xiaoping era (1978–89), and administrative renaming and reform in 1994 and 2007, labor camps lasted into the twenty-first century as institutions of criminal punishment and – following pro-democracy protests in Tiananmen Square (1989) and Hong Kong (2020) – of periodic political repression.

Like Soviet camps, laogai served the dual purposes of political terror and criminal justice, mixing dissidents and intellectuals with vagrants, thieves, and murderers. Like Chiang Kai-shek, Chairman Mao looked for foreign support and inspiration. Following the Civil War, a coterie of political and military advisors traveled from Moscow to Beijing, revitalizing longstanding cooperation between two countries that shared a significant land border. Much as they did for East European satellite states – Poland, Romania, and East Germany – Soviet bureaucrats circulated blueprints for penal reform and criminal punishment. An expression of filial piety, "learn from Soviet big brother" became a rallying cry, as Soviet experts helped PRC authorities draft new legal codes. Particularly after the Sino-Soviet split (1956–66) and during the popular radicalism of the Cultural Revolution (1966–76), however, criminal punishment in China could be even more violent, arbitrary, and politicized than in the Soviet Union, prioritizing class struggle and social transformation above all else.

As Chinese Communists transitioned from guerrilla insurgents to agents of a one-party state, a paranoid siege mentality targeted suspected counterrevolutionaries and foreign agents. In the 1950s, an ideology of struggle, inherited from years of civil war and from Marxist-Leninist philosophy, fueled numerous campaigns to contain and "fence off" undesirables. To purify society, "all erroneous thoughts, all poisonous weeds" needed to be contained, Mao ordained, before they "spread unchecked."[17] Following in Soviet footsteps, the Campaign to Suppress Counterrevolutionaries (1950) and the "Three and Five Antis" campaigns (1951–2), ostensibly designed to combat bribery and tax evasion, violated democratic precepts by purging political dissidents and intellectuals who criticized party orthodoxy. Meanwhile, the Anti-Rightist Campaign (1957–8) initiated a violent class struggle. Like "the designation of witches in Europe during the Middle Ages," the prisoner Liu Zongren recounts, thousands were imprisoned without trial or due process.[18] Such was the fate of Harry Wu, whose prosperous background and Western missionary education made him doubly suspect. Like the Soviet Union, China also suspected its own POWs and targeted ethnic minorities, including Mongols and Uyghurs (see chap. 7). In 1959, the prisoner Han Wei-tien observed "thousands of captured nomadic people," including guerrilla separatists from Tibet, flowing into his camp at Telingha.[19] In its early years, then, the "people's democratic dictatorship" detained more than half a million political prisoners in what the historian Jean-Luc Domenach calls the PRC's "founding terror."[20]

As in the Soviet Gulag, however, "ordinary criminals" often outnumbered "politicals," growing from 35 percent to 60 percent of inmates during the 1960s, and constituting 90 percent of the camp population by the end of the twentieth century.[21] With Mao's contempt for the rule of law, which he considered a tool of bourgeois oppression – were property laws not forms of institutionalized theft from the working class? – the CCP often conflated criminal and political offenses. And as emergency wartime powers lingered into peacetime, party leaders exercised immense discretionary powers. Anything constituting a threat to party rule, from "loafing" to "sabotage," could be construed as a crime, and in order to justify their detention, political suspects were often pressured to confess to fabricated criminal charges. Yet given the upheavals of war, revolution, unemployment, and growing poverty, criminal offenses like robbery, assault, drug abuse, and illegal migration to urban centers abounded. The forced collectivization of Mao's "Great Leap Forward" (1959–62) was as economically disastrous as Stalin's Five-Year Plan, while frenzied quests to destroy class enemies deprived the country of capital and expertise. Meanwhile, the "Four Pests Campaign" (1958) presaged an ecological tragicomedy – one that compounded hardships generated by state procurement and unsound farming methods – when it all but eradicated the Eurasian sparrow, resulting in an explosion of crop-eating insects. Famine soon followed, flooding the camps with penal convicts. "Most of the new arrivals," Wu observed in 1961, "were not political prisoners like me but villagers picked up for theft or vagrancy, like so much human trash."[22] Liu Zongren also witnessed "hordes of gangsters, street thugs, opium addicts, and prostitutes," as well as "juvenile delinquents" and other "social scum" rounded up by police and detained at Chadian.[23] As in the Soviet Union, then, camps appropriated and superseded prisons as sites of criminal punishment.

Work and Punishment

The laogai's internal organization demonstrates clear Soviet connections. Indeed, Luo Ruiqing, the founding Minister of China's Public Security Bureau, even hung a portrait of Felix Dzerzhinsky, head of the Soviet Secret Police, in his office.[24] Apart from a revolutionary focus on political struggle and control, China's geography of detention resembled the expansive archipelago described by Solzhenitsyn. On the border with Siberia, the fearsome Xingkaihu complex, a Chinese Kolyma, terrorized prisoners. Like Stalin's Gulag, distance, cold, and harrowing boxcar journeys – "the train was like a big coffin for us," the writer and prisoner Pu Ning writes – were inherent aspects of punishment, as camps spread into distant frontier provinces like Qinghai and Xinjiang. Forced laborers like Han Wei-Tien, a GMD "counterrevolutionary," constructed the Qinghai-Tibet highway, a strategic military artery, desecrating the graves and destroying the grassland livelihoods of Tibetan and Mongolian nomads in the process. Though prisoners felt solidarity with the tribesmen they displaced – they were "fellow travel-lers," as Han put it – authorities regarded them as "pioneers" who would "construct a new Shanghai in the Gobi Desert."[25] In this way, laogai camps fulfilled a recurring colonial dream while extending state power across a vast continental empire, building railways and canals, reclaiming waste-lands, and settling distant regions with ethnic Han Chinese. Like the Soviet Union, internal exile (the *qiang-zhi-jiu-ye* job placement system) required released prisoners to live in proximity to camp.

Camp infrastructure also built on Soviet precedents. Many laogai camps were established as turnkey operations, based on Russian blueprints, though they were less centralized and standardized. Like their Soviet counterparts, Chinese camps were located around worksites, often at great distances from population centers, and they presented comparable penal architectures. Watchtowers and electrified barbed wire encircled some camps, but walls and fences often proved unnecessary in remote regions like the Xinjiang Uyghur Autonomous area, where the desert imposed its own barrier. Sublime mountains and scenic forests also trapped inmates in unwalled prisons. And as Communist China transformed into a Stalinist police state, tight surveillance networks monitored the general population, making escape futile – anyone without papers soon attracted attention from the Public Security Bureau.

Local conditions also inflected arrangements. Thanks to decades of war and centuries of Western imperial domination, China was even more impoverished than the Soviet Union, leaving Mao with few resources to devote to prisoner comfort. Camps, accordingly, repurposed existing build-ings or consisted of filthy huts made of mud clods. For Bao Ruo-Wang, an accused counterrevolutionary, the camp at Chadian farm resembled "a nineteenth-century factory or mill," while the prominent writer and "rightist intellectual" Zhang Xianliang likened his compound in the remote Ningxia autonomous region to "an old mule shed."[26] As with the GMD's "Confucian concentration camps," Chinese traditions also prevailed. Like tsarist Russia, the Manchu Empire (1636–1911) had transported convicts to distant worksites and agricultural labor colonies under sentences of penal exile. Then, as now, the barren Xinjiang and Qinghai provinces symbolized the dangers that awaited criminal or political prisoners. Even the Great Wall – both a symbol of Chinese civilization and a technology of confinement – was built by convict labor. Soviet systems of penal servitude thus found fertile ground in China, where law was conceptualized more as a tool of the state than a means of protecting individual rights, and where political culture had traditionally placed few limits on the power of state officials to mobilize forced labor. As such, the historians Yenna Wu and Philip Williams attest, "the modern day use of forced labor and prison camps has an ancient pedigree in China, which cannot be accurately portrayed as merely a Soviet grafting onto a Chinese rootstock."[27] Though an admiring disciple of Stalin, then, Mao might also be considered a latter-day Chinese emperor; his lieutenants, Liu Zongren added, were "just another batch of court officials ... building personal privileges and accumulating wealth."[28]

Whatever its inspiration, labor dominated laogai life. Over 19 years, Harry Wu, a self-styled "Chinese Solzhenitsyn," worked at an agricultural colony, a coal mine, a steel factory, and even in a chemical laboratory – a privileged position that afforded him better rations, a heated workplace, and a reprieve from destructive physical labor, much as it did for Primo Levi at Auschwitz (chap. 5). In scenes reminiscent of Solzhenitsyn's *One Day in the Life of Ivan Denisovich*, Wu described early morning roll calls, which organized workers into ranks and squadrons, who then marched under armed escort to worksites, where "four red warning flags mark off the territory in which the prisoners are to work." "Anyone wandering outside of this restricted area [was] immediately shot," he added. Rations, meanwhile, were calibrated to ambitious daily labor quotas enforced by squad leaders and public security cadres. And like the Gulag's collective living and working conditions, military-style battalions organized workers, who lived and slept together in communal barracks. "One of the [laogai's] most distinctive characteristics," Wu notes, is "organization along military lines."[29] In place of bunkbeds, however, Chinese prisoners slept on traditional earthen *kangs*, which are heated from below, an innovation Siberian Gulag inmates might have appreciated.

MODERN SLAVERY

China's laogai arguably constituted the twentieth century's largest system of slavery. Just as Solzhenitsyn compared Gulag guards to slave drivers and inmates to serfs, laogai prisoners were essentially "state slaves," Harry Wu maintained, "whose labor force [could] be exploited" and whose "health, safety, and work environment [were] completely ignored."[30] "When inspecting new arrivals," Wu continues, guards "walked around us, patting our chests, feeling our shoulders, neglecting only to open our mouths and examine our teeth."[31] Another inmate, Zhang Xianliang, was similarly reminded "of how a breeder would ... inspect the inside of a horse's mouth before purchasing it."[32] Though labor dominated camp life, historians of the laogai, like those of Stalin's Gulag, debate its economic efficacy. Chinese authorities lauded the "many benefits," economic and political, of "a workforce numbering ... as much as the whole workforce of Bulgaria" that "does not need insurance or wages" and can "build great things."[33] Yet historians estimate laogai production (in 1988) amounted to only 0.2 percent of China's total GDP.[34] Nonetheless, laogai detachments proved important to national reconstruction following the Civil War. And even today, Chinese prisoners manufacture a wide variety of products, from cotton and steel to textiles and automotive parts, which are sold to global markets. A 1997 study suggested up to one third of Chinese tea was grown by laogai labor, which was then blended with the regular supply before export.[35] In 1782, abolitionists in Britain organized a highly effective sugar boycott to protest slavery at Caribbean plantations. Might consumers see similar results by forsaking Chinese tea?

Hungry Bodies

Conditions within the laogai, as in the Soviet Gulag, mirrored those in the outside world. During the collectivization and forced industrialization of the "Great Leap Forward," labor quotas intensified on both sides of the wire, while countrywide famines (1958–62) augured the worst period inside the camps. Just as memoirs from Auschwitz and Kolyma highlight the intricate politics of soup – inmates like Levi and Solzhenitsyn jockeyed in line hoping for thicker helpings from the bottom of the pot – Chinese prisoners obsessed over the steamed *wotou* bun: its size, ingredients, and texture. Transferred to a new camp at Qinghe farm, Wu's heart sank when he saw the *wotou* served – "an ivory color, almost white, and too flaccid to hold its shape" consisting of "twenty percent corn flour, eighty percent ground, fermented corncob." As it turned out, however, the "double steaming method" at Qinghe had unintended benefits. Not only did it "increase the volume of food, allowing empty stomachs to [feel] full," but it had "an extreme laxative effect." Whereas previously, inmates had endured an "unsufferable constipation" in which "many ... had helped dig the lumps of feces from each other's anuses," the bowels now flowed freely.[36]

Yet relief was short-lived. As hunger persisted, inmates faced a pitiless struggle to survive. At the height of famine, authorities lowered work
quotas, enabling inmates to scavenge for food, eating insects and frogs,
or searching for grain stored underground by mice and rats. Recalling
scenes from the Andover Workhouse scandal (chap. 1), inmates even ate
human bone marrow. Having encountered a tangle of hibernating snakes,
meanwhile, Wu huddled "like an animal" over his prey; he then "tore off
their skins with [his] teeth and ripped out their insides."[37] If Maoist zealots
described counterrevolutionaries as "packs of wild animals,"[38] dehumanizing camp conditions turned rhetoric into reality. "Since you found yourself
living in a cage," Pu Ning observed, "it behooved you to act as a caged
animal. Without some beastliness, some wildness, you couldn't survive."[39]
Just as the Gulag reminded Evgenia Ginzburg of "a gigantic poultry farm"
that kept prisoners "cooped up in open cages," laogai inmates compared
conditions to pig pens and industrial chicken farms.[40] Much like the leg-
endary bedbugs of Kolyma, moreover, laogai fleas were "so numerous as
to leave red bumps all over a prisoner's body." Though authorities shaved
prisoners' heads to prevent lice – a Soviet innovation rarely practiced in premodern China – showers and baths were nonexistent. As Zhang Xianliang
recounted, "hungry inmates [would] pick off lice and munch them down."[41]
Such was a fitting environment for so-called "capitalist parasites."

Conditions were not always so bad. Rations improved in the late 1960s,
Liu Zongren remembers, and impoverished villagers even asked to "live
inside the Big Compound," which offered "a secure, almost luxurious life"
in comparison.[42] At the height of the 1961–2 famine, however, prisoners
resembled living corpses, inhabiting a liminal state between life and death.
One inmate at Qinghe Farm, Chen Ming, was apparently carted away as a
corpse, only to escape the grasp of death and wake up in the morgue.[43] In
scenes that could equally apply to the final days of Dachau or Buchenwald,
Wu described prisoners whose "mouths hung slightly open below hollowed
cheeks. Their gaunt necks seemed unnaturally long. Their blank faces
gave no sign they had noticed our arrival." And with a start, Wu wondered
whether [he] looked the same, recoiling "from the thought that these rav-
aged people were my mirror."[44] At Auschwitz, Primo Levi had a similar
revelation: though "there [was] nowhere to look in a mirror … our appearance stands in front of us, reflected in a hundred livid faces, in a hundred
miserable and sordid puppets."[45] Yet while Mao's camps were brutal tools
of repression, they did not commit the genocidal crimes of Nazi Germany.
"Because we didn't kill them," Mao's heir apparent Liu Shaoqi maintained,

"we can let them work, and possibly they will at some time in the future turn into good people."[46] Death, then, was an outcome of hunger and disease rather than willful extermination.

As he reached the advanced stages of starvation, Wu was selected for Qinghe farm's subcamp 585, the "Prison Patient Recovery Center." While medical euphemisms have often disguised twentieth-century atrocities, the compound, in this case, released prisoners from forced labor and fed them with a special bean gruel designed to build their strength. The "People's government and the Communist party don't want you to die," a guard informed Wu, "but to be reformed into new socialist people." This act of "revolutionary humanitarianism," however, was double-edged. Though food could be given, it could also be taken away. Not only were rations calibrated to inmates' political attitudes and labor potential, they were strategically withheld to compel compliance. Party cadres informed Wu, following a period of forced starvation in a cell too small to stand in, that he would be saved from death, but only if he transformed into "a new socialist person." The first step was to confess his "crimes": "leniency to those who confess, severity to those who resist" became the laogai's most repeated slogan.[47]

Reformed Minds

An abiding emphasis on "thought reform" distinguished laogai camps. Though historians like Steven Barnes have placed reform and rehabilitation at the center of the Soviet Gulag, particularly in the often-forgotten labor colonies and special settlements (chap. 4), the laogai's emphasis on indoctrination differed sharply from the cynical environment Gulag prisoners like Solzhenitsyn encountered, where fulfilling work quotas and obeying rules was all that practically mattered. Indeed, while Solzhenitsyn dismissed the Gulag's Cultural and Educational Department as a farce, laogai authorities approached Mao's moralizing mandate to create "new socialist citizens" with genuine enthusiasm. In this way, they blended traditional Chinese concepts – to "renovate the people" (*xin min*) and "civilize the masses through education" (*jiaohua*), also exhibited at GMD camps – with an emphasis, shared by Western criminology, on work as a civilizing and rehabilitating force.[48] The focus on thought reform was thus compatible with a deeply entrenched Chinese disposition to bring the wayward self into line with the communal order. Labor and collective life would help socialize "parasites, consumers, and criminals" who had lived selfishly off other people's work. Yet as Yenna Wu points out, the Chinese term *gaizao*, from which *laogai* derives, traditionally applied to inanimate objects rather than human beings. As such, it connoted a blunt instrumentality that envisioned inmates less as autonomous individuals than as "pliant tools of the party," subject to coercive reprogramming.[49]

Just as premodern China practiced footbinding, the laogai enforced "headbinding," Harry Wu remarked.[50] Apart from socializing labor, with its romanticized proletarian overtones, the laogai enforced an intensive regimen of political indoctrination. For Mao, an original and independent theorist within the Marxist oeuvre, socialism not only entailed the redistribution of property or the transformation of material conditions, but the internalization of an ethos. Like Benthamite prisons, laogai camps did more than punish the body – they aimed to transform the soul. Similar to GMD concentration camps a generation previous, regular political study meetings, often lasting two to three hours per day, embraced the slogan "Reform first, production second." Upon entry, prisoners wrote critical reflections, in which they confessed their crimes through a detailed autobiography. Inmates then read and discussed political texts collectively, including articles from the official organ of the CCP, *The People's Daily*, as well as speeches and writings by Mao, Marx, Lenin, and Stalin. Weekly "struggle meetings," often dedicated to a weekly theme, also monitored inmates' progress. "In each small group on Sunday evening," Zhang Xianliang recounts, "convicts would sit cross-legged on their bunks, and, like true believers, confess their sins."[51] For an atheist regime, Communist China's emphasis on penance resembled the Christian confessional – much as statements by its high priest, Mao, codified in the *Little Red Book*, carried the weight of the Bible.

Group therapy offers another analog. Led by party cadres to ensure doctrinal compliance, prisoners were encouraged, collaboratively, to uncover and assess deviant attitudes and behaviors. Yet violence was inherent to the process. Those who resisted faced solitary confinement and traditional torture methods. Stress positions like the "tiger bench" and "hanging a chicken by its feet" were "so excruciating that the prisoner often screams just before losing consciousness."[52] During the Cultural Revolution, meanwhile, Red Guard paramilitaries revived traditions of popular violence by invading the camps and assaulting inmates. Though camps mobilized peer pressure to enforce compliance – a natural tactic in a society that valued group conformity over individual expression – laogai authorities were, at times, adept at dividing prisoners against each other: "Never call one another brothers. Do not attempt to build up affection," a camp placard read.[53] Criminal felons exploited political prisoners much like the *Kapos* of Nazi *Konʒentrationslager*. And at periodic "struggle sessions," inmates were encouraged to publicly denounce and humiliate each other, a process that often culminated in the violent beating of an "exposed" counterrevolutionary. In a dedicated struggle session, Harry Wu suffered a compound fracture to his arm when he was bludgeoned with a shovel.

Did thought reform work? The question is debatable. For Wu, Mao's injunction to "learn from the peasants" resulted in little more than learning to cheat and steal. Liu Zongren concurred: camps allowed criminals to "swap their methods for breaking the law," turning "pickpockets into burglars" and "street brawlers into killers."[54] Struggle meetings, meanwhile, often vented personal animosities rather than reforming deviant thoughts. The constantly shifting orthodoxies of the Cultural Revolution, in which sacred party officials were suddenly purged, also compromised efforts to instill a clear and consistent political message. Far from a moral transformation, then, Wu witnessed an erosion of the ethical principles that once guided his life. By forcing inmates into a Darwinian struggle to survive, camps fostered an individual selfishness at odds with Communism's socializing impetus. And while Wu gained a genuine appreciation for the suffering of China's peasantry, his camp experience only fortified his resistance to the regime. For some, however, the strategic combination of "severity to those who resist and leniency to those who confess" engendered a Pavlovian compliance. The prisoner Bao Ruo-Wang confessed to feeling "an admiration that bordered on love" for his camp commandant, who had expressed genuine concern for his political rehabilitation: "I am here to help you undergo reform," he announced. "If you ever have problems – ideological, political, or whatever – come and see me and we'll talk them over. My door's open twenty-four hours a day." "Call it what you like," Bao concluded: "if that was brainwashing, I am for it."[55]

CAMP SOCIETIES

"The French Emperor Napoleon said the soldier that does not want to become a general is not a good soldier." Thus began an address delivered to uniformed primary school students, saluting the Chinese flag and singing the national anthem at the Institute for Professional Sport. Dedicated to forging the next generation of Olympic medalists, the Shanghai sports

camp subjects five-year-olds, selected nationwide according to strict physiological criteria, to four hours per day of intensive exercise and psychological conditioning. Though the camp produces elite athletes, its physical
and emotional toll has shocked Western observers.[56]

The political scientist Gregory Kasza has classified the PRC, along with
North Korea, imperial Japan, the Soviet Union, and Nazi Germany, as "conscription societies," which organize civilian populations as if they were mass
armies.[57] In China, laogai camps developed into organizational motifs for
society more generally. For Harry Wu, labor camps were simply augmented
versions of the "larger bird cage" that constituted Communist China. State
farms and factories, like Soviet *kolkhozes*, were essentially open prisons in
which labor brigades and production squads faced constant supervision
and control. Like camp inmates, citizens and workers, whether in the office or factory, were subject to similar processes of self-confession, group
study, and collective struggle. Today, the laogai's influence is evident everywhere, from schools and workplaces to a hierarchical pipeline of "Olympic factories." Chinese citizens have internalized camp discipline. China, by
some accounts, is a giant camp.

Yet while camps are emblematic of authoritarian regimes, fitness "boot
camps" in the United States enact military-style discipline, and summer
youth camps offer communal living and transformative education. Why
are these latter "camps" so widely accepted in the democratic West? How
do they differ from their Chinese counterparts?

Laogai's Offspring

Communism, like fascism, facilitated the transnational circulation of coercive practices. Though Mao condemned Western imperialism, Communist
China was (and emphatically is) an empire in its own right, displacing and
exploiting minorities and extending its influence to satellite states abroad. In
Vietnam, Ho Chi Minh (1890–1969), himself a Communist insurgent under
Mao and a former prisoner of Chiang, followed China's example by establishing his own (more temporary and less brutal) system of labor reform
and political prisoner camps. In Cambodia, meanwhile, the Khmer Rouge's
quest to create an agrarian utopia in the 1970s departed from the Soviet
focus on industrialization but drew inspiration from Mao, who romanticized

the peasantry as the proletarian class of underdeveloped Asian societies. Yet while Chinese and Vietnamese officials cast their camps as "humanitarian" reeducation centers, the Cambodian leader Pol Pot (1925–98) killed nearly 25 percent of the country's population, some 1.5–2 million people. In an instance of what Harry Wu terms "classicide,"[58] Khmer forces evacuated towns and cities, deporting business people and intellectuals (including anyone wearing eyeglasses, a marker of wealth and learning) to facilities like Security Prison 21 and to bloody killing fields, where suspects were murdered with scythes and axes. In an effort to "purify" the country of corrupting foreign influences, the Khmer Rouge also liquidated ethnic Vietnamese, Thai, Chinese, and other minorities, along with Buddhists and Muslims. Combining Soviet class struggle with far-right xenophobia, the historian Ben Kiernan observes, Pol Pot cleansed Cambodia's imagined heartland to make room for an idolized ethnic-Cambodian peasantry, much like Hitler's quest for *lebensraum*.[59] Yet while Cambodia transformed into a giant forced-labor camp – peasants worked 12 hours a day to fulfill wildly impractical quotas – its killing fields had no pretense to labor or reform. Like the murderous plains of Transnistria, like Polish forests overrun by Nazi death squads, or like Treblinka, though without industrial technology, the sole purpose was genocide.

If Cambodia's killing spree was fleeting and unsustainable, the totalitarian dictatorship of North Korea has institutionalized political repression with a permanent system of labor and reeducation camps. Soviet and Chinese blueprints provided direct inspiration – the country's founder, Kim Il-Sung (1912–94), appointed as his security chief Pang Hak-Se, a man born and raised in the USSR, while the "Great Leader" himself had trained with Maoist guerrillas. Like Chinese laogai, however, Korean camps also reflect the peculiar cultural and geopolitical circumstances of the regime. Though the deaths of Mao and Stalin initiated a period of moderation within the Chinese and Soviet gulags, Korean camps, still in existence today, only expanded and radicalized as the Kim dynasty tightened its grip on power.

Like its predecessors, the North Korean gulag (*kwan-li-so*) was an offspring of military conflict and Communist revolution. Early efforts to detain political opponents within the Korean Workers' Party expanded dramatically during the Korean Civil War (1950–53), which partitioned the 38th parallel with an East Asian iron (or "bamboo") curtain. Despite a ceasefire, however, emergency measures extended indefinitely as security forces concentrated anyone deemed "noxious" to the state: landlords, capitalists, criminals, and suspected foreign agents. Deploying familiar botanical metaphors, propagandists vowed to "desiccate the seedlings of counterrevolution, pull them out by their roots, exterminate every last one of them."[60] In practice, though, crimes as trivial as listening to South Korean radio have landed ten-year sentences.

Korean prisoners endure heavy labor, frigid temperatures, and perpetual starvation that rival conditions within the worst camp systems in human history. Like Harry Wu, the North Korean defector Kang Chol-Hwan scavenged for amphibians at Yodok concentration camp – "the way to eat a salamander is to grab it by the tail and swallow it in one quick gulp," he discovered – and he even bred rodents as a food source. Treated like vermin himself, Kang came to appreciate rats, which he once considered "scary and disgusting," as "touchingly kind animals." Like Primo Levi, luck and ingenuity helped Kang survive (working at a chemistry lab once again helped avoid the worst of a frigid winter), but as his confinement continued, he struggled to retain his humanity: "ceding to hunger, acting like an animal, these are things anyone is capable of." A "person dying of hunger," he continued, "will grab a rat and eat it without hesitation. Yet as soon as he begins to regain his strength, his dignity returns, and he thinks to himself, I'm a human being, how could I have descended so low?"[61] The prisoner Shin In Guen was likewise so hungry he regurgitated his food in order to eat it again; following his 2005 escape from Kaechon (Camp 14)'s "total control zone," he has had to "slowly learn how to be a human being."[62]

Like Mao's laogai, though perhaps less convincingly, North Korean camps preach rehabilitation. Weekly self-criticism sessions force prisoners to denounce each other. Yet inmates "understood that it was just a routine," and guards really cared only about production quotas. "Instead of turning us into stalwart admirers of [the] Great Leader," Kang concluded, the camp "taught us how to rebel, jeer, and mock anything vaguely whiffing of authority." At times, pervasive surveillance and the rote memorization of Kim Il-Sung's speeches triggered performances of ritualized veneration: "Why did you leave this world, which had become so happy under the wise governance of our Great Leader?" one inmate, mourning a relative's death, instinctively cried upon seeing a nearby snitch. Yet according to dissidents (admittedly a problematic source), the camps created even fewer converts than their Chinese counterparts. The propaganda was so crude inmates were bound to reject it, Kang writes. Cruelty was also counterproductive. Much like the performative violence of early modern Europe (chap. 1), public displays of humiliation (being forced to walk like a dog or smell human excrement over a cesspit) only alienated inmates. So did gruesome

FIGURE 6.2 Inmates at camps across Communist Asia endured horrific starvation, as depicted by the North Korean artist Kwon Hyo Jin, whose images were submitted to a United Nations Commission of Inquiry. (Source: United Nations.)

public executions. Forced, in a bestial display, to participate in a public stoning, inmates regarded the victims as heroes. Even committed Communists, like Kang's grandmother, came to realize "the regime was closer to Hitler's world than anything Marx or Lenin had envisioned."[63]

Promises of reform rang especially hollow at camps for "incurable enemies" sentenced to life imprisonment for "contaminating" society. For irredeemables like Shin In Guen, "traitorous blood" could never be "washed away."[64] Meanwhile, North Korea's emphasis on race and heredity marked an ominous development in the Communist tradition, one that indeed placed its camps closer to Hitler's than Stalin's. Simply put, Kang writes, "North Korea believes in eugenics, that people of undesirable origins should disappear or at least be prevented from reproducing."[65] More than a social construct, then, class identity and political allegiance became genetic traits. Just as Cambodia murdered the infant children of counterrevolutionaries – "to dig up grass, one must also dig up the roots,"[66] the Khmer Rouge declared – Korean guards eradicate family lineages by kidnapping the babies of inmates. Meanwhile, female prisoners caught having sexual relations endure savage punishments: their breasts are ripped off, or they are raped with the end of a shovel. Pregnancies caused by ubiquitous sexual assaults by guards, who routinely address female inmates as "bitch," often result in the execution of both mother and unborn child. Yet unlike the Khmer Rouge, which considered the nuclear family a bourgeois construct to be obliterated, the family unit remains intact within the North Korean gulag. Sentenced together, families eat together, work together, and inhabit their own huts rather than communal barracks. Faced with horrendous starvation, however, natural bonds between parents and children sometimes break down: Shin In Guen betrayed his own mother for a handful of rice. He felt no remorse as he watched her execution.[67]

The Korean focus on the family produces other peculiarities. The practice of imposing punishment across three generations suggests a cultural syncretism between Western institutions (concentration camps) and Korean culture.[68] Punished for the sins of his paternal grandfather, Kang suggested the camp's policy of maintaining the cohesion of the family unit reflected the resilience of Confucian traditions. Though Harry Wu's family in China was never detained, they publicly disavowed him in order to save face. In Korea, a more extreme case, only Kang's mother, unrelated by blood to the family's counterrevolutionary patriarch, was absolved. Moreover, the emphasis on generational crimes mirrors – and serves, perversely, to justify – the enduring tyranny of the Kim family. Considering their rulers divine, North Koreans venerate a trinity: the grandfather (Il-Sung), the father (Jong-Il), and now the son (Jong Un).

Conclusion

In the 1930s and 1940s, camps became truly global phenomena. The xenophobia and militarism of the European far right, with its aura of vitality and strength, also flourished in Asia. But the Communist bloc, extending across the Eurasian continent, generated the largest and most enduring systems of encampment. Amid war and revolution, centralized planning, and hubristic schemes to radically transform human and material relations (to uproot and replant the human garden), camps provided potent tools to reform and reforge Asian societies. Rejecting individual rights, freedom of expression, and the rule of law as bourgeois constructs, Communist camps were menacing tools of repression, as inmates detained today in North Korea and China attest. History repeated itself, as both tragedy and farce, as dictatorial rulers, bolstered by increasingly outlandish cults of personality, extended wartime states of exception to detain political opponents together with criminal convicts. Yet as they followed Western templates of discipline and punishment, Confucian communal and family values reoriented the purpose and governance of camps, just as Mao and Kim repurposed Marxist ideology to reflect local realities.

Communism's worldwide spread cannot be explained by violence and repression alone, however. In the waning era of Western imperialism and the global inequality it fostered, the spectres of Marx and Mao were, to many, a force for liberation. As Communist and anticolonial freedom fighters across Asia and Africa demanded independence, liberal and imperial powers, led by America, Britain, and France, used their own camps, the next chapter suggests, to quash resistance and maintain domination. And even after decolonization and Communism's global demise, geopolitical struggles like the "war against terror" have provided impetus for new camps, whether for Islamic terror suspects at Guantanamo Bay or Uyghur Muslims in western China.

Notes

1 Hongda Harry Wu and Carolyn Wakeman, *Bitter Winds: A Memoir of My Years in China's Gulag* (New York: Wiley, 1994), 47, 37.

2 Vivian Blaxell, "Seized Hearts: 'Soft' Japanese Counterinsurgency Before 1945 and Its Persistent Legacies in Postwar Malaya, South Vietnam and Beyond," *Asia-Pacific Journal* 18, no. 6 (2020): 1–19.

3 Mao Zedong, *On Guerrilla Warfare*, trans. Samuel B. Griffith (New York: Praeger, 1961), 95.

4 Noboru Yamaguchi, "An Unexpected Encounter with Hybrid Warfare: The Japanese Experience in North China, 1937–1945," in *Hybrid Warfare: Fighting Complex Opponents from the Ancient World to the Present*, ed. Williamson Murray and Peter Mansoor (Cambridge: Cambridge University Press, 2012), 252.

5 Haruko Taya Cook and Theodore F. Cook, *Japan at War: An Oral History* (New York: New Press, 1993), 153.

6 Steven Lee, "The Japanese Empire at War, 1931–1945," in *The Oxford Illustrated History of World War II*, ed. Richard Overy (Oxford: Oxford University Press, 2015), 40.

7 Tom Phillips, "China Rebuilds Its Forgotten 'Auschwitz' to Remember Japan's Brutality," *The Guardian*, September 1, 2015, https://www.theguardian.com/world/2015/sep/01/china-rebuilds-its-forgotten-auschwitz-to-remember-japans-brutality.

8 Robert Hardie, *The Burma-Siam Railway: The Secret Diary of Dr. Robert Hardie, 1942–1945* (Cirencester: Quadrant Books, 1983), 109, 106.

9 Sheldon Harris, *Factories of Death: Japanese Biological Warfare, 1932–1945, and the American Coverup* (New York: Routledge, 2002).

10 Klaus Mühlhahn, *Criminal Justice in China: A History* (Cambridge: Harvard University Press, 2009), 244.

11 Giorgio Agamben, *Homo Sacer: Sovereign Power and Bare Life*, trans. Daniel Heller-Roazen (Stanford: Stanford University Press, 1998).

12 Klaus Mühlhahn, "The Dark Side of Globalization: The Concentration Camps in Republican China in Global Perspective," *World History Connected* 6, no. 1 (2009), https://worldhistoryconnected.press.uillinois.edu/6.1/muhlhahn.html.

13 Frank Dikötter, *Crime, Punishment and the Prison in Modern China* (New York: Columbia University Press, 2002), 349–52.

14 Mühlhahn, "Dark Side of Globalization."

15 Frank Dikötter, "The Promise of Repentance: The Prison in Modern China," in Frank Dikötter and Ian Brown, eds., *Cultures of Confinement: A History of the Prison in Africa, Asia, and Latin America* (Ithaca: Cornell University Press, 2007), 293.

16 Dikötter, "Promise of Repentance," 295.

17 Mao Zedong, *Quotations from Chairman Mao* (Beijing: Peking Foreign Languages Press, 1966), chap. 2.

18 Liu Zongren, *Hard Time: 30 Months in a Chinese Labor Camp*, ed. Erik Noyes and James J. Wang (San Francisco: China Books, 1995), 161.

19 Pu Ning, *Red in Tooth and Claw: Twenty-Six Years in Communist Chinese Prisons* (New York: Grove Press, 1994), 162–3.

20 Jean-Luc Domenach, *China: L'Archipel Oublie* (Paris: Fayard, 1992).

21 Mühlhahn, *Criminal Justice*, 258.

22 Wu, *Bitter Winds*, 53.

23 Liu, *Hard Time*, 67–8.

24 Philip Williams and Yenna Wu, *The Great Wall of Confinement: The Chinese Prison Camp through Contemporary Fiction and Reportage* (Berkeley: University of California Press, 2004), 49.

25 Han Wei-Tien, as recounted by Pu Ning, *Red in Tooth*, 57, 114, 171, 64.

26 Bao Ruo-Wang and Rudolph Chelminski, *Prisoner of Mao* (New York: Coward, McCann & Geoghegan, 1973), 176; Zhang Xianliang, *Grass Soup*, trans. Martha Avery (Boston: David R. Godine, 1995), 190.

27 Williams and Wu, *Great Wall*, 28.

28 Liu, *Hard Time*, 161.

29 Hongda Harry Wu, *Laogai: The Chinese Gulag* (New York: Routledge, 2018), 67, 64.

30 *Laogai Prisoners, the Slaves of the Communist Regime: Testimony at Congressional-Executive Commission on China* 109 Cong. (2015) (Testimony of Harry Wu, Executive Director of Laogai Research Foundation), https://www.cecc.gov/sites/chinacommission.house.gov/files/documents/hearings/2012/CECC%20Hearing%20Testimony%20-%20Harry%20Wu%20-%207.31.12.pdf.

31 Wu, *Bitter Winds*, 69.

32 Williams and Wu, *Great Wall*, 107.

33 Mühlhahn, *Criminal Justice*, 223–4.

34 James D. Seymour and Michael R. Anderson, *New Ghosts, Old Ghosts: Prisons and Labor Reform in China* (Armonk, NY: M.E. Sharpe, 1998), 209.

35 Michael Chapman, "Chinese Slaves Make Goods for American Malls," *Human Events* 53, no. 25 (1997); see also Wu, *Laogai: The Chinese Gulag*, 36–49.

36 Harry Wu, "Laogai: Inside China's Forgotten Labor Camps," in *Enslaved: True Stories of Modern-Day Slavery*, ed. Jesse Sage and Liora Kasten (New York: Palgrave, 2006), 120–21.

37 Wu, *Bitter Winds*, 105, 134.

38 Mühlhahn, *Criminal Justice*, 182.

39 Pu Ning quoted in Mühlhahn, *Criminal Justice*, 260.

40 Ginzburg quoted in Robert Conquest, *Kolyma: The Arctic Death Camps* (London: Macmillan, 1978), 28; Pu Ning, *Red in Tooth*, 36.

41 Zhang quoted in Wu and Williams, *Great Wall*, 85, 95.

42 Liu, *Hard Time*, 95, 216.
43 Harry Wu, "Extract from *Thunderstorm in the Night*," trans. Bernard Cleary, in *Writers Under Siege: Voices of Freedom from Around the World*, ed. Lucy Popescu and Carole Seymour Jones (New York: NYU Press, 2007), 163.
44 Wu, *Bitter Winds*, 114–5.
45 Primo Levi, *Survival in Auschwitz*, trans. Stuart Woolf (New York: Touchstone, 1996), 27.
46 Mühlhahn, *Criminal Justice*, 224.
47 Wu, *Bitter Winds*, 131, 184.
48 Mühlhahn, "Dark Side of Globalization."
49 Williams and Wu, *Great Wall*, 8–9.
50 Wu, *Bitter Winds*, 87.
51 Zhang, *Grass Soup*, 210.
52 Wu and Williams, *Great Wall*, 131.
53 Liu, *Hard Time*, 37–8.
54 Liu, *Hard Time*, 194.
55 Bao and Chelminski, *Prisoner of Mao*, 138.
56 Eric Lehnisch, dir., *Chinese Gymnast: A Champion's School* (Boulogne-Billancourt: Tony Comiti Productions, 2006).
57 Gregory Kasza, *Conscription Societies: Administered Mass Organizations* (New Haven: Yale University Press, 1995).
58 Harry Wu, "Classicide in Communist China," *Comparative Civilizations Review* 67, no. 11 (2012).
59 Ben Kiernan, "Twentieth-Century Genocides: Underlying Ideological Themes from Armenia to East Timor," in *The Specter of Genocide: Mass Murder in Historical Perspective*, ed. Robert Gellately and Ben Kiernan (Cambridge: Cambridge University Press, 2003), 29.
60 Kang Chol-Hwan and Pierre Rigoulot, *The Aquariums of Pyongyang: Ten Years in the North Korean Gulag*, trans. Yair Reiner (New York: Basic Books, 2001), 79.
61 Kang, *Aquariums of Pyongyang*, 104, 116, 142
62 Blaine Harden, *Escape from Camp 14: One Man's Remarkable Odyssey from North Korea to Freedom in the West* (New York: Penguin, 2012), foreword.
63 Kang, *Aquariums of Pyongyang*, 127, 135, 103, 141, 101.
64 Harden, *Camp 14*, 25.
65 Kang, *Aquariums of Pyongyang*, 146.
66 Philip Spencer, *Genocide since 1945* (London: Routledge, 2012), 70.
67 Harden, *Camp 14*, 26, 45, 107–8.
68 Sungmin Cho, "The Origins and Evolution of the North Korean Prison Camps: A Comparison with the Soviet Gulag," in *The Soviet Gulag: Evidence, Interpretation and Comparison*, ed. Michael David-Fox (Pittsburgh: University of Pittsburgh Press, 2016), 282.

7 | (Post)colonial Concentration: Liberal Camps from World War II to the War on Terror

In April 1945, a Nazi soldier blindfolded the 16-year-old Janina Cywinska, a Polish inmate at Dachau concentration camp, before preparing to execute her. After waiting, she does not remember how long, for a bullet that never came, another soldier removed her blindfold. When she looked at him, she saw a Japanese man. "Oh no," she responded, "you guys won and now you are going to shoot us." But these were not the forces of Axis Japan. Instead, the soldier, a member of the decorated 522nd Field Artillery Battalion, consisting of second-generation Japanese Americans, many of them enlisted directly from US internment camps, replied, "We are liberators. We are American soldiers."[1]

The ironies of encampment abound. As Allied forces revealed the grim horrors of Auschwitz and Dachau, the British prime minister Sir Winston Churchill (1874–1965) appointed a parliamentary committee to document Nazi atrocities. Yet just a decade later, Churchill's government in colonial Kenya concentrated a million ethnic Kikuyu in a "pipeline" of camps and "protected villages." And while France celebrated its partisan resistance against Nazi occupation, the government of French president Charles de Gaulle (1890–1970), a celebrated French Resistance leader, presided over a network of "*regroupement* camps" that confined 2.3 million Algerians in the 1960s. And apart from interning Japanese Americans, the United States now operates a network of black sites and interrogation cells, with Guantanamo Bay at its center.

This chapter examines camps erected by liberal, colonial, and postcolonial regimes during World War II (1939–45), the Cold War (1945–91), and the more recent "war on terror." As iron curtains divided the world into Soviet and American spheres of influence, Africans and Asians demanded the rights and freedoms they had been promised but never granted. Yet as

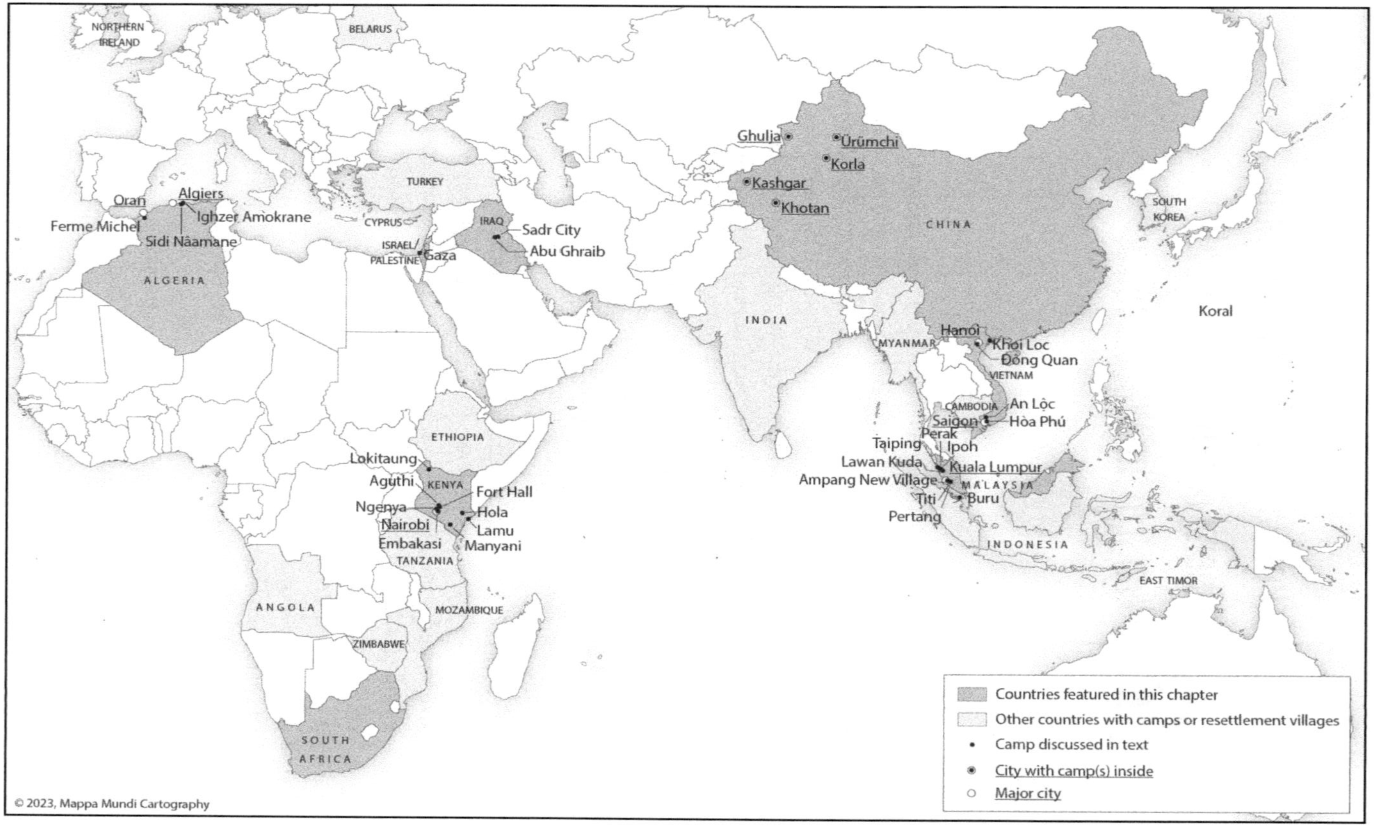

MAP 7.1 Counterinsurgency camps in the post–World War II period.

Countries featured in this chapter

Other countries with camps or resettlement villages

• Camp discussed in text

◉ City with camp(s) inside

○ Major city

© 2023, Mappa Mundi Cartography

colonized subjects rose up – in the rubber plantations of British Malaya, the Casbah of Algiers, the "white highlands" of Kenya, and Israel's Gaza Strip – imperial powers, including those that identified as liberal democracies, revived and refashioned nineteenth-century tactics of counterinsurgency to erect a global matrix of barbed wire. Conceived as military expedients, camps confined "terrorists" and guerrillas while sorting and surveilling civilians. But deeper dynamics of race and space, of labor demand and humanitarian reform also framed operations. Why did the liberators of Dachau and critics of Stalin and Mao concentrate so many behind barbed wire? How did doctrines of racism, development, and democracy frame the continued proliferation of camps? How did enclosures established by liberal democracies compare to the camps of authoritarian regimes like Nazi Germany and the Soviet Union? And how have rising global and imperial powers in the twenty-first century – China in particular – adopted camps in their efforts to settle and control colonial peripheries?

Wartime Internment

History does not necessarily repeat, but it often rhymes. "Small wars" in the nineteenth century first generated "concentration camps" as recognized instruments of colonial war (chap. 3). In the twentieth century, Britain and France developed democracies at home – a contrast to continental land empires like Nazi Germany, the Soviet Union, and China – but enforced emergency powers and dictatorial rule overseas. Camps flourished in these spaces. In Egypt, Alfred Milner, previously the British high commissioner of South Africa during the Anglo-Boer War (1899–1902), transported 3,000 suspects to camps in the Seychelles amid colonial unrest in 1919, while in Ireland, Britain's oldest colony, General John Maxwell, formerly the military governor of Pretoria, detained suspected terrorists in the Easter Rebellion (1916). During colonial Palestine's Arab Revolt (1936–9), likewise, a British "Black and Tan" paramilitary, trained in Ireland, erected the infamous Tegert Wall, a replication of Boer War blockhouses, to cordon the countryside, while barbed wire, imported from Mussolini's Italy, turned Arab villages into holding cells where suspected insurgents and their supporters could be monitored and classified. "Good" and "bad" cages at villages like Halhul divided the population: the former provided shelter and education, while the latter deprived suspects of food and water – many had to drink their own urine. As Zionist militias demanded an independent Israel during World War II, meanwhile, Britain applied similar tactics to Palestine's Jewish population. "We may yet teach Hitler something new about ... concentration camps," a colonial agent commented.[2] Yet the detention of Jews in Palestine emerged less from antisemitic impulses (though those were not entirely absent) than from longstanding traditions of colonial counterinsurgency aimed at unlawful or "uncivilized" combatants who threatened colonial rule and were thus denied the rights of POWs under international law.

Such practices continued during World War II, as Allied forces mobilized colonial manpower and resources while repressing native dissent. Police in colonial Nigeria detained 30,000 political suspects, including women and children, while Kenya imprisoned a larger proportion of its population, including activists for labor and land reforms, than any other colony in British Africa. Meanwhile, British India's Andaman penal colony (chap. 1) burgeoned, with more than 100,000 suspects, held without trial or charge for the duration of World War II. And as refugees fled the Japanese occupation of Burma in 1942, with its ubiquitous forced-labor camps, Britain imposed a peculiarly colonial system of classification: "blacks" deemed dangerous and disloyal were imprisoned; "whites" deemed safe were released; while "greys," depicted as "patients" "infected" with treasonous ideas, were sent to "rest camps" (as Raj agents euphemistically called them) for "rehabilitation."[3] Even as Britain combatted fascism, then, racial hierarchies and emergency powers denied basic rights to colonial subjects. For them, distinctions between imperialism and fascism were not always clear: Fanon noted "the totalitarian character of colonial exploitation" in French Algeria, while the West African journalist Isaac Wallace-Johnson lamented that Britain had turned Africa "into one large concentration camp."[4]

Throughout World War II, military detention extended to Europeans, who themselves were "treated like the natives of Bengal," as one critic put it. Reviving the internment camps of World War I, national security concerns, both real and imagined, facilitated the mass confinement of enemy aliens, though countries like Britain established internment tribunals in an effort to distinguish between friendly and dangerous foreigners. Detaining the latter on domestic soil, "Camp 020" and the "London Cage," a military intelligence facility near Hyde Park, were the most notorious outposts within a covert network of interrogation cells and British transit camps that tortured suspected Nazis and their sympathizers using techniques honed in the empire.[5] Overseas colonies also offered convenient holding zones. Detention camps in the Himalayan foothills detained Axis POWs, while Canada, Australia (long a site of penal exile), and the Isle of Man (an offshore

Crown Dependency), confined captured combatants and civilian internees, ranging from Nazi sympathizers to German-Jewish refugees, 805 of whom tragically perished when a German U-boat sunk the Newfoundland-bound prisoner transport *SS Arandora Star.*

As conflict spread globally, wartime emergency powers, coupled with racial animus, also generated camps on American soil. Starting in February 1942, President Roosevelt's Executive Order 9066 empowered federal troops to sweep cities and farms on the west coast of the United States, rounding up civilians of Japanese ancestry, detaining them in "assembly centers" located on racetracks and livestock pavilions, and then "evacuating" them to "relocation camps" surrounded by barbed wire. In this way, 120,000 ethnic Japanese, over two-thirds of whom were American citizens, were "wiped off the map," as John DeWitt, general of the Western Defense Command and architect of the internment, described it. In Canada, likewise, the War Measures Act facilitated the removal of 22,000 "persons of Japanese racial origins," including citizens and World War I veterans, to camps in the interior, where inmates labored on sugar beet farms in Taber, Alberta, or on orchards in the Okanagan Valley. The presence of libraries and recreational facilities indicate Japanese internment camps were very different from Auschwitz or Buchenwald – more residents were born than died – yet inmates were nonetheless held against their will, on the basis of race, not for anything they had done but for who they were. And "interior housing projects" as officials called them, were often little more than tents and shacks: "with language like that," the Canadian novelist and internee Joy Kogawa noted, "you can disguise any crime."[6]

Canadian and American "concentration camps," as President Roosevelt and chief justice Robert Owens called them (in an era before the term had become indelibly associated with Nazi atrocities[7]) were products of a long history of white supremacy and Western colonial settlement. Since the nineteenth century, Asian migrants had been demonized as carriers of disease – a "yellow peril" that "bred like rats" and took jobs from white Americans. Wartime internment would thus place Japanese farmers in racial quarantine, "herding" them off to the badlands, far removed from white settler society, as one newspaper advocated.[8] Japanese Americans posed virtually no threat to national security, classified War Department memos concluded. Yet in contrast to German and Italian nationals, who were never interned *en masse*, populist fears of a Japanese Fifth Column, an "enemy within," coupled with the racial humiliation of rapid Allied defeats to imperial Japan in the Pacific, amplified anxieties. Eugenic discourses likewise cast ethnic Japanese as "an enemy race." Despite citizenship and acculturation, DeWitt maintained, "racial strains [were] undiluted." "If they have one drop of Japanese blood," US Colonel Bendetsen concurred, "they must go to camp."[9]

Racism also intersected with economic resentments as labor-intensive, high-yield fruit farming brought Japanese Americans financial success, despite laws restricting Asian land ownership. In this context, white farmers like Austin Anson, head of the Salinas Vegetable Grower-Shipper Association, advocated purging western farms along ethnic lines: "If all the Japs were removed tomorrow ... the white farmers can take over and produce everything the Jap grows. And we do not want them back when the war ends, either."[10] "Catching every Japanese in America ... and putting them in concentration camps," Congressman John Rankin added, would "let[us] get rid of them now."[11] Given three days' notice and instructed to bring with them only what they could carry, Japanese Americans were forced to sell homes and businesses at a fraction of their cost, permitting a major transfer of wealth and land to white farmers. In journeys that reminded the internee Miné Okubo (1912–2001) "of some of the stories told on shipboard by European refugees bound for America," trains transported evacuees to camps in the remote interior (figure 7.1). "It was a desolate scene," Okubo wrote: "Hundreds of low black barracks covered with tarred paper were lined up row after row."[12]

Efforts to evacuate the west coast "exclusion zone" resembled, in broad strokes, colonial counterinsurgency efforts to clear demarcated areas of supposedly disloyal civilians. As such, Japanese internment suggested a contorted reenactment of the "concentration zones" of the Philippine-American War (1899–1902), where General DeWitt received his first commission. Yet since Japanese Americans posed no military threat – "the very fact no sabotage has taken place to date is a disturbing and confirming indication that such action will be taken," DeWitt claimed[13] – the operation became a farce. Similarly absurd efforts by the War Relocation Authority (WRA) to reform inmates with "Americanization classes" existed in tension with the racial essentialism and constitutional violations that facilitated encampment. Justifying forced relocation to the mid-and-montane west with the "language of America's Frontier Myth," government agents nonetheless cast camps as "colonies" and "pioneer communities," instructing internees to bring "work clothes suited to pioneer life."[14]

Encoded within longer histories of Western conquest and development, the "lofty American landscape" and "splendour of nature" would, WRA

FIGURE 7.1 Miné Okubo's camp was a non-place: "All residential blocks looked alike" and "people were lost all the time," she wrote. Dehumanizing conditions – inmates slept in livestock pens – and faceless bureaucracy completed her dehumanization: "my family name was reduced to No. 13660."[15] (Source: Miné Okubo Charitable Trust.)

observers claimed, have a "positive spiritual influence" on internees, who cultivated desolate deserts and unproductive marshes while earning one-tenth the market rate for their labor.[16] In reality, however, mass confinement proved damaging and counterproductive, splitting up families and turning loyal citizens against the American government. Okubo did, at times, feel like a "prospector lost in the middle of the desert," but only because she couldn't find potable water.[17] Watchtowers and barbed-wire fences, meanwhile, demarcated a prison atmosphere at odds with frontier freedom. "Like the reservations created for Native Americans," inmates quickly realized, "the camps were places for those that had lived and worked in America but were emphatically considered not American." The location of many camps on Native reservations like Fort Sill, Oklahoma, underlined solidarities with broader histories of racial exclusion and colonial confinement, as did expressions of solidarity from Jewish and African American communities.[18]

Cold War Counterinsurgency: Southeast Asia

Imprisoned as racial others and potential saboteurs, 33,000 Japanese Americans, many of them internees, eventually joined segregated US Army units to fight against the Nazi-Japanese Axis. Meanwhile, the wartime ambitions of imperial Japan faltered against motivated local populations. Just as Polish and Soviet partisans evaded camps and fortified villages (Belorussian *Wehrdöfer*, chap. 5) to disrupt Nazi forces, guerrillas from British Malaya – many trained by colonial commandos according to lessons learned fighting Boer and Arab insurgents – conducted raiding campaigns against Japanese occupying forces. But as World War II came to a close, and as superpower rivalry armed competing communist and capitalist forces in an age of proxy conflict, the Communist Malayan Liberation Army (MLA), led by the anti-imperialist guerrilla Chin Peng (1924–2013), turned its antagonism from the Japanese Empire to the British. As India declared independence (1947), and as Southeast Asia, with its lucrative tin mines and rubber plantations, became Britain's next imperial crown jewel, Malayan guerrillas launched a new era of asymmetric warfare that ultimately liberated former colonials across Asia and Africa, from Hanoi to Algiers.

Reclaiming its imperial footing after Japanese defeat, Britain faced the "Malayan Emergency" (1948–60) with troops trained in India, Ireland, and Palestine, and with familiar concerns about race and economy. Malaya's ethnic tapestry, institutionalized by the British census, consisted of Austronesian Malays, Indigenous *Orang Asli*, and a sizeable minority of migrant Chinese workers, many of whom had settled on rubber plantations in the nineteenth century but had been displaced by Japanese raids. It was primarily, though not exclusively, these communities, inhabiting the jungle fringe beyond the reach of the colonial state, from which the MLA drew material and ideological support. Amid looming Cold War tensions, meanwhile, the association of ethnic Chinese with Maoist guerrillas aligned Chin's campaign, in Western minds, with the specter of international communism, drawing American interest and support for Britain. Malay Communists had been "infected with mysterious pathologies," officials feared, though depictions of "lawless bandits," "thugs," and "terrorists" also drew from older repertoires of colonial policing. As a "floating population," cosmopolitan but illiterate, liminal and alien, Chinese "squatters" were also "illegal immigrants," Britain maintained, even though many had lived in Malaya for generations. Britain accordingly rounded up 24,000 ethnic Chinese for deportation to China, holding them in squalid transit camps.[19] The exclusion of East Asian migrants was thus a pan-Pacific affair, reaching from Malaya to California. Yet as Mao Zedong seized power in Beijing in 1949 (chap. 6), he blocked further transfers, closing the country as an outlet for "undesirables."

With exile foreclosed, colonial authorities embraced the familiar tactics of confinement and containment. As guerrillas scattered across Malaya's jungles, and as the "illness of terrorism" spread, British generals divided the Malay Peninsula into demarcated "red" (Communist), "yellow" (safe), and "blue" (dubious) zones, placing each sector into spatial quarantine. In this context, colonial security outweighed human rights, as paramilitary forces, empowered by emergency declarations, "neutralized" red zones with sweeping arrests. While flying columns scoured the countryside, however, air power and carpet-bombing updated counterinsurgency tactics as napalm and Agent Orange flushed out suspected insurgents and destroyed the crops that fed them and the jungle that concealed them. In this way, colonial forces "weeded out" not only vegetation but peasants with it, setting a precedent for sweeping measures in Vietnam, Algeria, and beyond (see map 7.1). If the sociologist Zygmunt Bauman is right to list gardening alongside medicine as a defining allegory of modern statecraft,[20] then herbicides and chemical weapons complemented the fences and barbed wire of nineteenth-century counterinsurgencies.

For those weeded out, British bureaucracy applied familiar taxonomies: "black" (irredeemable), "grey" (slated for rehabilitation), and "white" (loyal). Converted prisons and former quarantine stations along with purpose-built enclosures like the Ipoh detention camp, with its watchtowers and three-meter barbed-wire fence, imprisoned "blacks" under emergency regulations. Detainees complained of water torture and "sharp bamboo sticks [forced] into fingertips" – revelations that prompted Malaya's criminal investigation department to adjudge conditions "worse than those experienced by internees under [the] Jap [sic] regime." Meanwhile, enclosures like "Taiping Rehabilitation Camp" claimed to reeducate greys into "good lads" who "read the gospel of the glory of British rule," as the deputy head of rehabilitation described his mission.[21] Yet such efforts largely failed: nicknamed Taiping University by Communist partisans, the camp only convinced detainees of their cause.

With yet another permutation of encampment, meanwhile, Britain forcibly resettled 763,000 rural Chinese (12 percent of Malaya's total population) into 582 "new villages," as it called them, surrounded by watchtowers, electrified fences, and 770 tonnes of barbed wire. Trusted residents could leave, but it was still "like living in a chicken cage," Li Gui Mei, a resident of Ampand New Village, recalls. Lee San Choy at Lawan Kuda noted similarly: "it was like ... living in a concentration camp! When you entered or exited the village, the security guards would do a body search on you. We were not allowed to take rice, flour, sugar, or salt out of the village in order to prevent the Malayan Communist Party from obtaining those supplies."[22]

The effort to cordon civilians from guerrillas reanimated Boer War concentration camps and Cuban *reconcentrados*, though languages of "protection" justified the measure, in official minds, as a humanitarian intervention. Local precedents also pertained. As part of their *minshin hāku* strategy (chap. 6), "the Japs [*sic*] put barbed wire around Titi and Pertang, garrisoned these towns with troops and made all Chinese of the locality live within the defended areas ... Could we not try the same?" a local district officer proposed.[23] The "new villages," then, were instruments of security and surveillance. Yet the provision of shelter, healthcare, and, above all, political education aimed to "immunize" the populace against communism while creating pliant subjects. Rewards for those who pledged loyalty to Britain, in the form of better rations, economic opportunities, and community development – the provision of roads, dams, and public hospitals – laid the basis for a new "population-centric" counterinsurgency doctrine known as "hearts and minds." In modern war, as in modern prisons, power would be exercised not only against the body, but on the soul. In the process, Malaya's new villages constituted the "most important social engineering project" in modern Southeast Asia, the author of the operation's officially commissioned history asserts.[24]

NATIVE CONCENTRATION

Chinese Communists were not the only demographic concentrated behind wire. Britain considered Malaya's tribal population, the Indigenous *Orang Asli*, who inhabited guerrilla-infested mountains and rainforests, another potentially insurgent force. Britain corralled them, accordingly, into a segregated system of new villages. The goal was to "protect" the *Orang Asli* from Communist influence, though Britain also severed them from their traditional cultures and ancestral lands. Living conditions were egregious: while Britain spent $180 per capita on Chinese new villages, it spent only $16 for Indigenous people in Malaya, leading to a death rate of 16 percent.[25]

Following Malaysian independence in 1957, the *Orang Asli* remained a marginalized group. When the Malayan Communist Party launched new uprisings in the 1970s, the postcolonial state revived British tactics by "regrouping" Indigenous communities into "resettlement villages" managed by the Department of Aborigines, a holdover from colonial times. Set out in a basic grid pattern, with numbered lots and identity passes to monitor egress and ingress, villages isolated *Orang Asli* from the conditions of their indigeneity. The goal was to transform them, with hygiene, housing, and Islamic education, into submissive subjects, if not modern citizens. Like *Orang Asli*, Bedouin nomads in Algeria (see below) faced similar *regroupement* camps and sedentarization campaigns, dramatically upending their Indigenous way of life. And such schemes continued, after independence, as "socialist villages" under the mantra of agrarian reform. In this way, Aboriginal policy and modern development schemes are rooted in the tactics of military occupation. Might the same be said for Native reserves and reservations in Canada and the United States?

A Generalizable Model

Whether or not Malaya's new villages created "modern men and women," they offered pools of casual labor that served the capitalist interests of tin and rubber companies. The new villages' success in disrupting guerrilla supply lines, meanwhile, prompted officials to declare Malaya a generalizable model. Camps and concentrated villages soon spread – to other colonies (Kenya, Rhodesia, Cyprus), to other empires (French Algeria, Portuguese Angola and Mozambique), and to postcolonial states like Indonesia (in Kalimantan and East Timor), India (in Assam), and Turkey (in Kurdish Anatolia). (See map 7.1.) With active American support, "Operation Rat Killer" (1951–2) in South Korea interned suspected Communists rounded up from city streets,[26] while Indonesia's authoritarian, anti-Communist regime corralled left-wing partisans into camps like Buru (1969–79) – an island outpost of "Suharto's gulag."[27] As an instance of transnational learning, however, Indochina was emblematic. As Communist and anticolonial insurgencies spread across Southeast Asia, British experts like General Gerald Templer (1898–1979), a leading ideologue of anti-guerrilla detention, advised American officials in Vietnam, while the US State Department commissioned a six-volume report outlining the lessons of Malaya.

The Vietnam War (1955–75) combined the dynamics of decolonization and Cold War rivalry. Starting in 1952, French colonial authorities in
northern Vietnam fortified loyal villages, called *agrovilles*, under the banner
"pacification through prosperity." At Khoi Loc and Đông Quan, the war
correspondent Bernard Fall observed, France followed "British [Malayan]
prototypes line for line."[28] Meanwhile, Ngô Đình Diệm's (1902–63) newly
independent government in South Vietnam (1955) accepted American
intervention when facing Ho Chi Minh's Communist Vietcong forces in
the North. The result, by 1962, was an ambitious scheme, based on Malayan
precedents, to resettle 12 million rural Vietnamese, deemed susceptible
to Communist influence, into 12,000 "strategic hamlets" that purported
to protect residents from military recruitment while disseminating pro-
Western political indoctrination.

As in Malaya, strategic hamlets entailed a mass reconfiguration of society:
motivated by the American economist Walt Rostow's book *Stages of
Economic Growth: A Non-Communist Manifesto* (1960), which identified
urbanization and commercial farming as precursors to capitalist "take off,"
Vietnamese concentrations put "traditional" farmers into contact with the
modern world.[29] In this, they shared a common agenda with modernizing
regimes, both communist and capitalist, across the twentieth century, which
physically reorganized rural populations into planned, self-sufficient communities amenable to social and political control. In postcolonial states like
Ethiopia, which pursued a Soviet-style collectivization of its population
in the 1970s, or Tanzania, where the "Ujamaa" project resettled 7 million
peasants, fortified gridiron "villages" emerged as globally circulating technologies of agrarian reform and economic development. The coercion they
entailed, however, suggests a shared genealogy with colonial policing and
military counterinsurgency.

In Vietnam, however, minimal investment (less than $5 per capita) hardly
dissuaded concentrated populations from Communism's allure. Similarly,
watchtowers and triple rows of sharpened bamboo stakes (figure 7.2) –
erected both to protect inmates from Communist forces and to curtail the
movement of inmates – failed to broadcast the benefits of freedom. If "strategic hamlets" and "new villages" were euphemisms for concentration camps,
America's "hearts and minds" campaign rested on a foundation of violence.
Though George Orwell's concept of "Newspeak," elaborated in his novel
1984, condemned the lies of Stalinist Russia, the concept also applied to liberal empire: "defenseless villages are bombarded from the air," he wrote,
"the inhabitants driven out into the countryside, the cattle machine-gunned,

FIGURE 7.2 Malayan new villages like Perak (*left*) and Vietnamese strategic hamlets (*right*) concentrated populations in small, contained spaces that offered an antithesis to the illegibility of insurgency. (Source: Ipoworld.org; Everett Collection Historical/Alamy.)

the huts set on fire with incendiary bullets," and "this is called *pacification*."[30] Protected villages failed to provide residents with security – indeed, hamlets like An Lộc and Hòa Phú became magnets for Vietcong raids – and while American military spokesmen preached the virtues of "development," inmates, in effect, became forced laborers on public works projects. As such, the historian Michael Lantham contends, "US policies ignored the contradiction between the promotion of freedom and the construction of forced-labor camps."[31] And as Vietcong forces captured Saigon in 1975, consigning many American collaborators to Communist reeducation camps (chap. 6), the hamlets became symbols of failure. As components of Cold War and postcolonial conflict, however, mass resettlement and forced concentration remained widespread, as decolonizing Africa attests.

Settler Colonial Concentration: Kenya and Algeria

As Kikuyu men entered the giant detention camp at Manyani, Kenya, white officers shouted "*piga, piga asana*" (beat them, keep beating them). Each detainee, stripped naked, stepped through a disinfectant cattle dip before donning yellow shorts and red wristbands stamped with a number, symbols of their subjection.[32] The inmates of *regroupement* camps in French Algeria complained of similar dehumanization. "One morning," an inmate at Sidi Nâamane recounts, "soldiers with machine guns ... entered our village and expelled us without warning." Resettled from "forbidden zones" where natives could be shot on sight, "we built huts out of reeds" and "were

packed like pigs, eight to ten in a room."[33] "Like Roman colonizers ...
exulted by the passion of ordering and creating," to quote the sociologist
Pierre Bourdieu, French and British militaries imposed an alien order, at
odds with Indigenous cultures, ecologies, and agricultural rhythms.[34] In
this, they aspired – but failed – to achieve an abiding colonial fantasy: to
create a *tabula rasa*, to occupy native land, and to perpetuate, indefinitely,
the structures of colonial entitlement.

As the Mau Mau Rebellion in Kenya (1952–60) and the Algerian War of
Independence (1954–62) threatened British and French imperialism, something more primal than Cold War ideology motivated European colonists:
the control of land and the maintenance of privileged lifestyles. In contrast
to Southeast Asia, where extractive industries and fears of Communist
infiltration motivated counterinsurgency, Kenya's "White Highlands" and
Algeria's Mediterranean environs constituted prized settler colonies. Here,
entrenched European settlers developed racially segregated societies while
embracing an authoritarian politics at odds with the democratic norms of
western Europe. Though France's bloody nineteenth-century conquest
of Algeria aimed to "expel the native and if necessary, destroy him,"[35]
Indigenous Algerians did not succumb to disease like Australian or North
American natives. Instead, 1 million French settlers dominated 9 million
Arabs and Berbers, whom they corralled into cantonments and sedentary
villages, which offered pools of low-wage labor. Though Arabs paid a
higher proportion of taxes than French settlers, successive Indigenous
Acts denied them citizenship and political rights. Kenya's fertile highlands,
which sustained European agriculture above 1,500 meters, also harbored a
substantial settler population of smallholding Boers from South Africa and
a plantocracy of aristocratic British landlords who appropriated 65 percent
of arable land. Indigenous Kikuyu, Meru, and Embu, meanwhile, were concentrated on crowded reserves that operated much like Black homelands
in South Africa and native reservations in the United States (chap. 2). Yet
marginal tribal land could not sustain Kenya's growing native population:
instead, many worked as sharecroppers on white plantations or migrated
to the burgeoning slums of Nairobi, where pass laws and master-servant
legislation regulated their movement.

While camps in Kenya and Algeria emanated from developing transnational doctrines of counterinsurgency, they were also products, the final
violent convulsions, of white supremacy and settler colonial dispossession.
In Kenya, the anticolonial Mau Mau movement and its guerrilla Land and
Freedom Army (KLFA) attacked the most visible symbols of spatial and

socioeconomic dispossession: white settlers, and especially native supporters of British rule like Chief Waruhiu, whose famous assassination in October 1952 instigated an enduring state of emergency (1952–60) that facilitated mass detention and violent interrogation. Meanwhile, the sensational murder of Europeans radicalized settler racism. To white farmers, the secretive Mau Mau oath, in which KLFA fighters declared their loyalty by drinking animal blood, suggested an extreme of tribal savagery. Alternatively, Mau Mau was a disease, a mental pathology. "For many whites," the historian Caroline Elkins observes, "Mau Mau adherents did not belong to the human race; they were diseased, filthy animals who could infect the rest of the colony." They became what "the Armenians had been to the Turks, the Tutsi to the Hutu ... and the Jews to the Nazis." And "as with any incipient genocide," they "had to be eliminated" – or else isolated in camps.[36]

"Operation Jock Scott," the opening flourish of Britain's counterinsurgency campaign, arrested 180 suspected Mau Mau leaders in 1952, including the future (largely innocent) president of independent Kenya, Jomo Kenyatta (1897–1978), exiling them to remote desert prisons on the Northern Frontier. Detaining the movement's leaders, however, did not decapitate the rebellion, prompting British authorities to adopt more sweeping measures. Scorched-earth warfare and aerial bombardment cleared the countryside, while "Operation Anvil," launched in April 1954, cordoned the city of Nairobi with barbed-wire checkpoints. Driving armored vehicles and blaring orders from loudspeakers, police conducted sector-by-sector purges to "cleanse" the capital. Those detained entered one of world history's most brutal archipelagos of detention, as colonial officials, including white settlers and native informers, classified ethnic and political suspects according to familiar and peculiarly racialized categories: "whites" (cooperative); "greys" (potentially "curable"); and "blacks," a reprobate "hard core."

The former faced deportation to reserves, where they were billeted, following Boer and Malayan precedents, in guarded villages surrounded by barbed wire. Shirley Cooke, a rare European critic, feared these squalid enclosures would "get the reputation of the concentration camps after the Boer War, memories of which live even today."[37] According to officials, however, the villages existed to "protect" loyal Kikuyu from Mau Mau guerrillas. Community development officers, imagined as benign trustees, introduced training in "civilization" – handicraft workshops, agricultural reform, and history lessons emphasizing British progress – to those "craving to acquire knowledge on European lines." As components of a colonial Five-Year Plan (the Swynnerton Development Plan), "collective homesteads" and "concentrated villages" would thus be symbols of market reform and capitalist modernization – and of Britain's stamp of authority over the countryside. As in the Soviet Union, however, it proved danger-ous, observers eventually realized, to "effect in a few months a major social revolution which took 500 years or more to achieve in England."[38] And while international sympathy for Boer women and children, many of them ancestors of Kenyan settlers, pressured British authorities to improve camp conditions in South Africa (chap. 3), thousands died in Kenya from disease and malnutrition as the reserves reached their ecological capacity.

If discourses of protection and rehabilitation were distinguishing features of liberal counterinsurgency that offered a veneer of public legitimacy on the reserves, a separate system of detention camps for "blacks" and "greys" enforced brutal interrogations that approached the extremes of totalitarian concentration camps. Though Mau Mau camps were not explicitly geno-cidal, violence was routine: screening teams thrust broken bottles, gun bar-rels, knives, snakes, vermin, sticks, and hot eggs into women's vaginas and men's rectums, while "human excrement torture" added a racialized twist: detainees had to clean nightsoil buckets barehanded, a ritualistic humilia-tion that marked Mau Mau, and Black bodies more generally, as unclean. By now, the global history of camps offered a conscious framework for critique. Arrest without trial and institutionalized torture proved "distress-ingly reminiscent of conditions in Nazi Germany," Kenya's British attorney general privately confided.[39] Prisoners agreed. At Lokitaung, inmates com-pared their "brutal and inhuman treatment ... to the Nazi concentration camp," while the notorious Manyani, purpose-built following Operation Anvil, was popularly known as "Africa's Belsen."[40] The historian Marshall Clough considered other analogies: "like Soviets during the Great Purge of 1936–9," Mau Mau "were often incarcerated on the basis of the flimsi-est evidence," though in contrast to frigid Siberia, authorities disposed of bodies by feeding them to crocodiles.[41]

WOMEN OF THE CAMPS

As preemptive measures aimed at suspect collectivities rather than con-victed individuals, fortified villages and wartime internment camps concentrated large numbers of women and children, who experienced encampment in specifically gendered ways. The Japanese American Miné

Okubo complained that "women were very self-conscious and timid about using the showers" in communal barracks.[42] Conversely, the division of Algerian *regroupement* camps into individual huts privileged Western concepts of the nuclear family while compromising extended Islamic kin networks; camp education, meanwhile, aimed to convince Muslim women to remove their veils.

Authorities also detained women as political suspects. In Kenya, Britain identified 8,000 women as "hard core" Mau Mau in addition to 73,000 men. As a prominent Kikuyu feminist and one of the first women to run for elected office in independent Kenya, Wambui Otieno (1936–2011) described the unique challenges faced by women and mothers in camp: caring for her two-year-old daughter (interrogators often used the presence of children as leverage), preparing meals, finding menstrual pads, and smuggling contraband in her brassiere. At Lamu detention camp, a white officer told Otieno to "remember that [her] name was Number 59" before pushing her "to the ground … causing a scar on [her] spine that [she] carr[ies] to this day." He then raped her multiple times over the course of two days. At the end of the ordeal, the officer "told me that he had given me a baby girl. He also said that impregnating me was a decision of the British government … They hoped that [other] Mau Mau would either kill me or hate me for having a white man's child." From Kenya to Bosnia, rape has long functioned as a tool of state violence, ethnic cleansing, and political intimidation. The rapist never revealed his name, but when Otieno later gleaned it from another guard, she immediately wrote it down on a piece of paper, which she sewed into her belt. Did she feel closure, 38 years later, when she named her rapist – chief inspector Rudolf Speed – in her memoir *Mau Mau's Daughter*?[43]

Apart from punishment and torture, Mau Mau camps attempted – and often failed – to transform inmates into pliant subjects. "Moral rearmament teams" provided lectures on the virtues of British colonialism as loudspeakers blared pro-British propaganda. Echoing slogans at Victorian workhouses, Swahili signs greeted inmates: "He Who Helps Himself Will Also Be Helped" (at Aguthi), "Labor and Freedom" (at Ngenya), and "Abandon Hope All Ye Who Enter Here" (at Fort Hall).[44] Yet demands for unfree labor compromised any "therapeutic" component to work. Camps deployed

ONE SHILLING

TRUTH about KENYA
— an eye witness account by

Eileen Fletcher

FORMER REHABILITATION OFFICER KENYA GOVERNMENT

Foreword by
LESLIE HALE
Member of Parliament for Oldham West

- *Concentration Camps*
- *White Supremacy*
- *Children Starved*
- *Tortured to Death*
- *Government Statement*

"Suffer the little children . . . ."

FIGURE 7.3 Images of children behind barbed wire provided a powerful lens of humanitarian critique for British women like Eileen Fletcher, much as they did for Indigenous activists (chap. 2) and for Emily Hobhouse in South Africa (chap. 3). (Source: *Peace News*.)

inmates to quarries and colonial infrastructure projects like the Yatta canal and Embakasi (now Jomo Kenyatta International) airport, enforcing heavy labor but teaching few skills. "It was like we were in slavery," one woman, who worked at a quarry with her child tied to her back, complained. Kenya's defense minister concurred: "[W]e are *slave traders*, and the employment of our slaves are, in this instance, by the Public Works Department."[45] Even children, detained collectively with their families at camps, on reserves, and in guarded settlements (figure 7.3), were forced to work long hours, the Quaker humanitarian Eileen Fletcher charged.

Nonetheless, the emphasis on "thought reform" continued. Christian evangelism, or "brainwashing" as the internee Gakaara wa Wanjau called it, gradually "broke" some prisoners. Every night, loudspeakers announced the names of inmates scheduled for interrogation at special "screening courts," while detainees assembled, at regular intervals, for mass "ceremonies of confession," a ritual that reverberated, remarkably, with China's laogai (chap. 6).[46] The uncooperative faced routine brutality and dehumanization, but those willing to confess their crimes, renounce Mau Mau, or inform on other prisoners received better rations, shelter, and ultimately a promise to move "up" the colonial "pipeline" and return to the reserves. "If one offers a position of privilege to a few individuals in a state of slavery exacting in exchange the betrayal of a natural solidarity with their comrades," Primo Levi observed, "there will certainly be someone who will accept."[47] This sociological maxim, an extreme manifestation of the colonial mantra "divide and rule," applied, in different ways, to Kikuyu loyalists, Jewish Kapos, and Soviet prominents. The worst violence often emanated, inmates recall, from Kikuyu collaborators, themselves former detainees.

Native "Liberation"? Algerian *Regroupement*

In Algeria, colonial "civilizing missions" likewise conflicted with the security concerns and labor demands of the French colonial state. As the Algerian Liberation Army (ALN)'s guerrilla fighters drew widespread support from the Arab population, colonial authorities forced urban Muslims to wear white identifying armbands, while assembling a network of detention that rivalled Britain's "Kenyan gulag" in brutality. In a rendition of Nazi Germany's "Night and Fog" decree, France tortured ALN suspects with gang rape and electric shocks, while dumping corpses from helicopters into the Mediterranean Sea, where they vanished without a trace. "From now on," a *Le Monde* article proclaimed, Frenchmen do not "have the right to condemn ... torture by the Gestapo."[48] In the countryside, meanwhile, France, like Britain, engaged in a dramatic makeover of colonial space and society. The Morice line, a 1,160-kilometer electrified fence, prevented would-be insurgents from crossing the border from Morocco or Tunisia. Governed by uniformity and alignment – "I like the straight line," a *Sections Administratives Spécialisé* cadre declared – the quadrillage system, an age-old counterinsurgency tactic pioneered by General Kitchener in South Africa (chap. 3), then divided rural areas into grids, demarcating "forbidden zones" in which native Arabs could be shot on sight. Employing the familiar language of disease, scorched-earth warfare and napalm then sterilized "contaminated" areas: 650,000 hectares of Algerian forests were burned in this way.[49] For over 2 million displaced farmers and nomadic tribesmen, *camps de regroupement*, at first tented habitations and later barracks built according to standardized blueprints, awaited, while another million moved to *bidonville* shantytowns on the outskirts of Algiers and Oran.

Though they were assembled with martial efficiency and strategic mandates, France, like Britain, depicted *regroupement* camps as sites of civilizational uplift that would introduce "primitive" peasants to the machine-age of electricity and airplanes while protecting them from the threat of resistance. The provision of healthcare and modern education thus helped construct the camps as conduits of literacy, development, and female emancipation. Having imagined and then created a *tabula rasa* in Algeria, *regroupement* would thus inscribe the cultural markers of the conquering power while "liberating" the country from Islamic tradition. From the Scramble for Africa to America's "Operation Enduring Freedom" (2001–21) in Afghanistan, conquest and encampment in liberal empires was in this way cast as an assertion of liberty. In the event, however, the effort fell apart under the weight of its own contradictions. The ignorance, racism, and hostility of French soldiers and the larger settler community contravened humane agendas, as did the intelligence and active resistance of Algerians, who staged strikes and demonstrations in the camps, and whose dignity could not "be bought off with candy, barley, or a crocodile smile."[50]

Far from protection and empowerment, inmates remember hunger and suffering. *Regroupement* in the countryside proved as economically destructive as Soviet collectivization: between 1954 and 1960, production of cereals dropped by 78 percent; areas reserved for citrus fruits and tobacco were reduced by 69 percent, while people in the Sahara were converted to vagrancy.[51] And like residential schools in Canada (chap. 2), camps severed inmates from traditional cultures and ecologies, leading to mass pauperization and the breakdown of ancestral modes of social reproduction. Removed from their farms and economic networks, inmates found themselves in a situation of total dependence. Yet government rations, fixed at 80 kilograms of grain per year – less than Soviet civilians received during World War II – led to starvation and disease. At camps like Ferme Michel or Ighzer Amokrane, an investigative 1959 report revealed, a child died every other day from malnutrition. The testimony of Pastor Beaumont, a sympathetic missionary, described "five children who were literally dying of hunger, another whose mother told me 'he is going to die!' and whose nurse said to me, bursting into tears: 'there is nothing to be done!'"[52] At some of the worst camps, Algerian nationalists highlighted death rates that rivaled those of Nazi concentration camps.[53] Far from symbols of progress and development, then, camps in Algeria, like their counterparts elsewhere, became markers of colonial oppression as the violent destruction of native ways of life, coupled with wartime depopulation, racial segregation, and transfers of wealth and land to the settler community, consecrated the underlying structures of settler colonialism. And while camps failed to fashion loyal subjects of an *Algerie nouvelle*, the transformation of inmates (and refugees displaced to urban slums) into low-wage laborers served the French capitalist economy with an influx of docile workers. Wartime concentration, then, exposed, *in extremis*, the colonial forces latent in Algeria since the forced agglomeration of Algerians into nucleated villages in the nineteenth century.

Enclaves and Bantustans: Israel and South Africa

Like Kenya and Algeria, Israel and South Africa exemplify the forces of settler expansion and native concentration. Born in a state of war, the newly independent state of Israel (1948) revived the tactics and emergency regulations of British colonialism by transforming Palestinian villages into "closed areas" from which no Arab could leave or enter without written permission. Meanwhile, checkpoints and military sweeps over the course of seven decades placed nearly half of all Palestinian men in the Occupied Territories under administrative detention. The military general and Israeli prime minister Ariel Sharon (1928–2014) likewise built walls around Palestinian refugee camps and divided the Gaza Strip into small squares where foliage was trimmed and orchards razed, creating a panoptic *tabula rasa* that resembled Algeria. And as the exceptional measures of an enduring counterinsurgency became routine, electrified wire, concrete walls, and automated turnstiles physically separated Gaza and the West Bank. Though such barriers immobilized Palestinians *in situ* rather than deporting them to purpose-built camps, they were mechanisms of concentration, much like Malayan new villages but on an enormous scale. Established as temporary security measures, the "open air prisons" and carceral "archipelagos," as those who live in occupied Palestine call them, facilitate an enduring – and explicitly settler colonial – imperative: "more land with fewer Indigenous people on it."[54]

South Africa offers a comparable model, albeit one motivated by white supremacy more than military occupation. Though barbed-wire fences and segregated "native locations" have long partitioned South Africa's human

BANTUSTANS IN SOUTH AFRICA AND THE WEST BANK

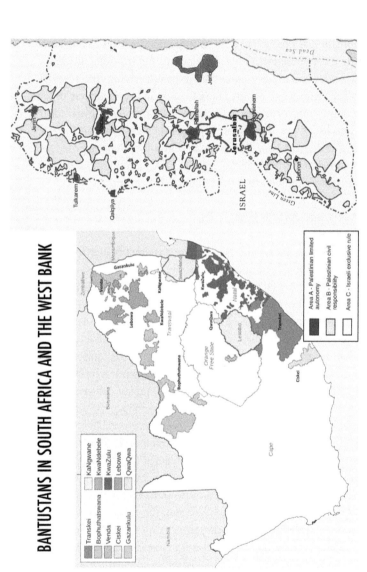

FIGURE 7.4 Faced with a hostile and sometimes antisemitic geopolitical environment, Israel today has fragmented Palestine into an "archipelago" of non-contiguous districts from which egress and ingress are forbidden or closely monitored. In an irony Ariel Sharon might not have anticipated, pro-Palestinian activists have now appropriated the language of Bantustans and apartheid to condemn the occupation. Others, like the controversial American scholar Norman Finkelstein, have described Gaza as a giant open-air "concentration camp."[55] (Source: Adapted from www.palestineportal.org. Map circa 2005.)

landscape (chap. 2), the Group Areas and Native Resettlement Acts of the 1950s, along with the Bantu Homelands Citizenship Act of 1970, inaugurated a formalized system of apartheid that concentrated designated ethnic groups in non-contiguous homelands known as "Bantustans" (figure 7.4). Like Palestinian enclaves, impoverished populations lived in squalid slums on marginal land, while derelict economies forced residents to seek employment as guest workers, monitored by intrusive pass laws and identity checks. And while notorious prisons like Robben Island interned Nelson Mandela (1918–2013) and other leaders of Black liberation, the concentration of African civilians in demarcated locations facilitated policing and surveillance. To justify the scheme, apartheid spokesmen employed "separate but equal" terminology inherited from Jim Crow America, while the limited degree of political independence granted to each territory suggested a liberal gloss of legitimacy – albeit one rejected by both Black Africans and the international community.

Others, like the white supremacist Afrikaner *Broederbond*, embraced more militant rhetoric. With traumatic memories of the South African War (1899–1902), in which British concentration camps relegated white Boers to the status of dark-skinned "savages," such forces demanded a strong authoritarian state that would guarantee white interests above equal rights and multiracial democracy. When architects of Israeli occupation like Ariel Sharon reportedly referred to South African Bantustans as explicit models for Palestine, he linked two systems of mass confinement while highlighting the historical irony uniting Boers and Jews, both as victims of concentration camps – the world's first and the world's most lethal – and as perpetrators of new carceral regimes.[56]

The War on Terror

Codified by Western militaries, new villages and mass resettlement proliferated across the decolonizing and postcolonial landscape. Facing the communist specter near American soil, the CIA-backed Guatemalan military and the United States Agency for International Development constructed "protection villages" in the 1980s to "show [peasants] who was in charge." Thus would agricultural modernization deter subversion.[57] The United States also sponsored coups d'état against left-leaning postcolonial governments in Brazil (1964), Argentina (1976), and Chile (1973), where military sweeps detained left-wing suspects in working-class neighborhoods, placing them in soccer stadiums, converted, like racetracks in Johannesburg,

Ruhleben, and Paris's Vél D'Hiv, into makeshift camps. For most, how-ever, detention was short-lived, while torture and other brutal tactics – like Algerian-inspired "death flights" dumping detainees into the ocean – were hidden from public view. And while military juntas adopted explicitly fascist iconography – the dictatorship in Argentina interrogated suspects under swastikas and photographs of Hitler[58] – the Western world quietly supported such regimes in its larger struggle against global communism. As long as it was covert, hidden from the press, and located overseas, liberal democracies tolerated mass confinement.

Yet as Cold War anxieties and postcolonial conflicts subsided – the Soviet Union dissolved in 1991, while Malaya, Vietnam, Kenya, and Algeria each won their independence – a new specter haunted Western democracies: Islamic terrorism. The discursive denigration of Algerian and Palestinian liberation fighters – previously associated with Marxism or secular nationalism – as "Islamic terrorists" foreshadowed the pivot, though America's global "war on terror," declared in the wake of September 11, 2001, signaled a new era of asymmetric conflict. Like guerrillas in the past, the enemy was amorphous: mobile and cunning (Orientalist tropes abounded), invisible yet ubiquitous, diminutive but indefinitely extended. America's invasion of Afghanistan (2002) and Iraq (2003), both suspected terrorist havens, generated familiar carceral measures: special forces encircled sites of resistance like Sadr City with checkpoints and walls to facilitate surveillance and to control and putatively protect residents from bloodshed. Effectively closed ghettos or open-air prisons, US soldiers called them "gated com-munities."[59] In general, however, American forces did not concentrate or resettle civilians *en masse*. Instead, US forces embraced the stealth and scaled-down model of covert detention, as practiced in Latin America.

Within a global network of "black sites" and clandestine interrogation centers, the chain-link cages of Guantanamo exemplify the tensions of liberal detention. Rounded up on the battlefield but denied the status of lawful combatants and the rights of POWs under the Geneva Convention, twenty-first-century terror suspects endure torture at secretive interrogation cells largely hidden from public view (though not always, as Iraq's scandal-ridden Abu Ghraib prison attests). Located in an extra-territorial enclave – a former army base in Cuba, an originary site of "reconcentration" – Guantanamo detains inmates outside the judicial oversight of the American Supreme Court. Existing in a "legal black hole," an offshore prison beyond the law, a "permanent United States penal colony floating in another world," Guantanamo has escaped the constitutional restraints of liberal democracy, which had previously challenged the existence of Japanese American internment on the mainland.[60] Like other liberal empires – Britain and France in particular – America thus exported its camps overseas to colonial peripheries that exist perpetually in what Giorgio Agamben terms a judicial "state of exception." Indeed, Guantanamo represents the concept in its classic sense.

New Empires, New Terrors

Guantanamo witnessed horrific human rights abuses: waterboarding (first pioneered in the US-Philippine War, 1899–1902), sensory deprivation, sexual humiliation, and other "enhanced interrogation" methods. As in the South African War, commentators recognized, Guantanamo showcased "a large military power using its dominance to tread a narrow line between legality and military necessity."[61] But it is not the "gulag of our time," as Amnesty International declared in 2005: the camp does not, for instance, mobilize inmate labor or detain criminal convicts, and its detainees number in the hundreds rather than millions.[62] Elsewhere, however, the global war on terror has fostered more expansive systems of mass internment. Building on the Islamophobia that proliferated globally in the wake of 9/11, Myanmar's military junta deported Muslim Rohingya to squalid ghettos and camps in 2016 as a prelude to genocide. And in 2013, following Islamist violence in Kunming, China's Xi Jinping (1953–) declared the "People's War on Terror." Vowing to eliminate the "virus" of Islam and uproot noxious "weeds" – metaphors of gardening and medicine approach the rhetorical clamor of fascist regimes[63] – Chinese security forces have concentrated 1.5 million Uyghurs, members of a predominantly Muslim, Turkic-speaking ethnic group, in the twenty-first century's largest system of concentration camps (as featured on this book's front cover). Detained collectively and preemptively at more than 380 secretive sites in suburban Ürümchi, Korla, Ghulja, Khotan, and Kashgar, and scattered across the arid steppe, Uyghur "pre-criminals" endure widespread abuse, including forced abortions and sterilizations, and torture in the "tiger chair." Meanwhile, intensive reeducation sessions – China's version of "hearts and minds" – along with "self-criticism" ceremonies reminiscent of Maoist laogai, induce inmates to learn Mandarin, sing patriotic songs, and recite Party slogans. The goal, according to Yang Tianhua, a local educational authority, is to "eradicate all malignant thought contaminated with ideological viruses from the minds of Indigenous peoples!"[64]

Discourses of terrorism have supercharged the assault on Chinese Muslims. Yet broader material and colonial processes also frame operations. Building on westward expansion under the Manchu Empire as well as Mao-era resettlement policies, ethnic Han Chinese now regard the western Xinjiang Province as an open frontier of social mobility and pioneer opportunity, an Asian analog to the American West. As settlers expropriate ancestral lands and annihilate Indigenous economies and lifestyles, which they regard as primitive and backward, Uyghur detention camps facilitate ethnic cleansing and intensive surveillance. In language familiar to any historian of the French or British empires, the Chinese state justifies mass incarceration by celebrating the "liberation" of Uyghurs from their "native way of life." Just as General Pratt, director of Pennsylvania's Carlisle Indian Industrial School, aspired in 1887 to "kill the Indian but save the man" (chap. 2), residential boarding schools in China separate families and forbid inmates from speaking their native language or practicing Islam. The goal, as in new villages and strategic hamlets, is to pacify would-be insurgents by transforming them into docile, Sinicized workers. When "Turkic farmers" arrived at state factories or cotton plantations, they "took off their grass shoes," code for primitive exoticism, "and became industrial workers," one official boasted.[65] As if to exemplify similarities with North America, the Chinese government recently, and cynically, responded to international criticism by calling for a UN investigation into Canadian residential schools – a historical rather than contemporary injustice that the Canadian government has recognized and for which it has apologized.[66] Authoritarian regimes regularly project their crimes onto their critics.

DIGITAL ENCLOSURE

While enclosure alienated eighteenth-century European peasants from their land (chap. 1), Uyghur subsistence herders are encircled by Han settlers who now constitute nearly 90 percent of Xinjiang's urban population. Twenty-first-century technology, however, has made processes of dispossession more rapid and more total, as Uyghur suspects – and Chinese civilians at large – face what the anthropologist Darren Byler terms "digital enclosure."[67] Like Xi Jinping's pandemic-era "Zero COVID" policy (2019–22) and its associated surveillance measures, Uyghur concentration camps are laboratories for more pervasive tactics of totalitarian control.

High-definition cameras, QR tracking codes, and facial recognition technology monitor movement across Muslim communities, while smartphones, geospatial apps, and artificial intelligence (AI) algorithms first developed in Silicon Valley to monitor the purchasing behavior of American consumers now scrutinize the minutia of Uyghur life. Just as Maoist apparatchiks targeted a sweeping array of "deviant" behavior, from reading foreign novels to wearing bourgeois hairstyles, China's surveillance state identifies supposed markers of Islamic extremism, like growing beards, wearing veils, or posting Quranic verses to social media, as grounds for encampment.

For Giorgio Agamben, camps embody the aspirations of state power in its purest articulation. Do Uyghur camps foreshadow, in exceptional form, a more general future in which control and surveillance, enforced by governments and corporations, and facilitated by AI, governs society as a whole?

Yet while Chinese counterterrorism and settler colonialism find parallels in the liberal West, Uyghur concentration camps should be distinguished from those erected by democratic governments. A cultural and legal emphasis on group conformity over individual rights and a near-total control of media and information have severely circumscribed free speech and public criticism, permitting Chinese officials to detain suspects more blatantly and less apologetically than their Western counterparts. Meanwhile, the centralization of power within an authoritarian regime has insulated Chinese camps from constitutional safeguards prevalent in Western democracies. Unlike Guantanamo Bay or the camps of Europe's overseas colonies, Uyghur camps operate, unproblematically, on Chinese soil, and in contrast to internment camps for Japanese Americans, which faced numerous legal challenges in the American Supreme Court, Uyghur internees have little legal or political recourse. Their internment and marginalization thus seem permanent and inexorable. Far from exceptions to the norm, Chinese camps are exemplary manifestations of a larger vision – they consecrate the totalitarian control of a one-party state. As such, their capacity for violence, particularly in the absence of legal checks and in the climate of genocidal rhetoric and intensive racial and political othering, is extreme. "What is happening in Northwest China," Darren Byler observes, "is connected to camps at the southern border of the United States" (see chap. 8) and "checkpoints in the West Bank, but its scale and cruelty takes it beyond those other sites of exceptional power over marginalized populations." As such, the camps of China's twenty-first-century empire represent a limit case of brutality and abuse.[68]

Conclusion

Even after the triumph over Hitler, European colonies were often violent places that rekindled an authoritarian will to power at odds with liberal democracy. Such were the conditions of possibility that generated camps in the first place. Yet as much as colonial administrations attempted to evade and dissimulate – the British government worked hard to prevent the Red Cross from visiting camps in Kenya and to cover up the "Hola Massacre" (1959) in which camp guards clubbed 11 Mau Mau detainees to death – public scrutiny and constitutional restraint limited the violence and duration of liberal concentration camps. Amid vigorous parliamentary debate, free speech, and a lack of censorship, critics like the Labour MP Barbara Castle in Britain responded to leaked revelations of abuse in Kenyan camps with open criticism and demands for bipartisan investigations. Despite lip service to humanitarian and reformist agendas – hallmarks of liberal confinement – revelations of murder and torture turned public opinion in Britain against the Mau Mau camps, leading to their ultimate dissolution. In France, likewise, a leaked report, published in *Le Monde* by the anticolonial critic and socialist politician Michel Rocard turned French opinion against Algerian *regroupement* camps. American imperial abuses in Vietnam likewise spawned the civil rights and antiwar movements of the 1960s. By contrast, the suppression of free speech and democratic oversight in Beijing make prospects in Xinjiang far bleaker. Should the horrors of Nazi *Konzentrationslager* or the Soviet Gulag ever return, they are more likely to do so in China or its allies – like Vladimir Putin's neo-imperialist Russia – than in the liberal West. Democracies are not immune to camps, as this chapter and the next on contemporary refugee camps make plain. Reading and writing about their crimes, without censorship or reprisal, helps ensure they won't be repeated.

Notes

1 Sonni Efron, "Japanese-American GIs Are Focus of Dachau Memories: World War II: Nisei Veterans Are Reunited with Some People They Rescued from Horror of Nazi Death Camp," *Los Angeles Times*, December 1, 1991, https://www.latimes.com/archives/la-xpm-1991-12-01-mn-872-story.html.

2 Caroline Elkins, *Legacy of Violence: A History of the British Empire* (New York: Knopf, 2022), 235.

3 Elkins, *Legacy of Violence*, 337.

4 Frantz Fanon, *Wretched of the Earth*, trans. Richard Philcox (New York: Grove Press, 1963), 41; Isaac Wallace-Johnson quoted in Leslie James, "What Lessons on Fascism Can We Learn from Africa's Colonial Past?," *Africa Is a Country*, January 24, 2017, https://africasacountry.com/2017/01/what-lessons-on-fascism-can-we-learn-from-africas-colonial-past.

5 Elkins, *Legacy of Violence*, 298–300, 267–8.

6 Joy Kogawa, *Obasan* (Toronto: Penguin, 1981), chap. 7.

7 Roger Daniels, "Words Do Matter: A Note on Inappropriate Terminology and the Incarceration of the Japanese Americans," in *Nikkei in the Pacific Northwest: Japanese Americans and Japanese Canadians in the Twentieth Century*, ed. Louis Fiset and Gail Nomura (University of Washington Press, 2005), 190–214.

8 David Neiwert, *The Eliminationists: How Hate Talk Radicalized the American Right* (New York: Routledge, 2016), 195.

9 Michi Weglyn, *Years of Infamy: The Untold Story of America's Concentration Camps* (Seattle: University of Washington Press, 1996), 77.

10 Lawrence Goldstone, *Not White Enough: The Long, Shameful Road to Japanese American Internment* (Lawrence: University of Press of Kansas, 2023), 188.

11 Weglyn, *Years of Infamy*, 54.

12 Miné Okubo, *Citizen 13660* (New York: Columbia University Press, 1946), 26, 122.

13 John DeWitt quoted in *Personal Justice Denied: Report of the Commission on Wartime Relocation and Internment of Civilians* (Seattle: University of Washington Press, 1997), 82.

14 Xiaojing Zhou, "Spatial Construction and Management of the 'Enemy Race': US Concentration Camps," in *The Camp: Narratives of Internment and Exclusion*, ed. Colman Hogan and Marta Marin Domine (Newcastle: Cambridge Scholars, 2007), 95–6.

15 Okubo, *Citizen 13660*, 136, 19.

16 Zhou, "Spatial Construction," 97.

17 Okubo, *Citizen 13660*, 142.

18 Valerie Solar, "'We Were Close to Freedom and Yet Far from It': Dislocation, Emplacement, and the Japanese American Internment," in Hogan and Domine, *The Camp*, 134.

19 Elkins, *Legacy of Violence*, 475–6.

20 Zygmunt Bauman, *Modernity and the Holocaust* (Ithaca: Cornell University Press, 1989).

21 Elkins, *Legacy of Violence*, 500–1.

22 Lai Ying-qi, "The Story of Chinese New Villages in Malaysia," *Tzu Chi Mission of Culture*, accessed November 5, 2022, http://tzuchiculture.org/rhythms-monthly-243/.

23 Elkins, *Legacy of Violence*, 504.

24 Anthony Short quoted in Christian Gerlach, *Extremely Violent Societies: Mass Violence in the Twentieth-Century World* (Cambridge: Cambridge University Press, 2010), 189.

25 Gerlach, *Extremely Violent Societies*, 215.

26 Jean-Michel Turcotte, "Civilian Internees, Common Criminals or Dangerous Communists: The International Committee of the Red Cross, the United Nations Command and Internment in South Korea, 1950–3," in *Internment Refugee Camps: Historical and Contemporary Perspectives*, ed. Gabriele Anderl, Linda Erker and Christoph Reinprecht (Bielefeld: Transcript, 2023), 133.

27 Ken M.P. Setiawan, "Arbitrary Detention in Indonesia: Buru Prison Island, 1969–1979," and Hannah Loney, "Displacement and Detention on Atauro Island During the Indonesian Occupation of East Timor," in *Detention Camps in Asia: The Conditions of Confinement in*

Modern Asian History, ed. Robert Cribb, Christina Twomey, and Sandra Wilson (Leiden: Brill, 2022), 82–99, 100–16.

28 Bernard Fall, *The Two Vietnams: A Political and Military Analysis* (New York: Praeger, 1967), 375.

29 Gerlach, *Extremely Violent Societies*, 202.

30 George Orwell, *Politics and the English Language* (London: Renard Press, 2021), 34.

31 Michael Lantham, *Modernization as Ideology: American Social Science and "Nation Building" in the Kennedy Era* (Chapel Hill: University of North Carolina Press, 2000), 187.

32 Elkins, *Legacy of Violence*, 559.

33 Michel Cornaton, *Les Camps de Regroupement de la guerre d'Algerie* (Paris: L'Harmattan, 1967), 83. (Translation mine.)

34 Pierre Bourdieu and Abdelmalek Sayad, *The Uprooting: The Crisis of Traditional Agriculture in Algeria*, ed. Paul A. Silverstein, trans. Susan Emanuel (Cambridge: Polity, 2018), 12.

35 Ben Kiernan, *Blood and Soil: A World History of Genocide and Extermination from Sparta to Darfur* (New Haven: Yale University Press, 2007), 374.

36 Caroline Elkins, *Imperial Reckoning: The Untold Story of Britain's Gulag in Kenya* (New York: Henry Holt, 2005), 49.

37 Elkins, *Imperial Reckoning*, 59.

38 Elkins, *Imperial Reckoning*, 240, 125, 263.

39 Elkins, *Legacy of Violence*, 546.

40 Elkins, *Imperial Reckoning*, 335.

41 Marshall Clough, *Mau Mau Memoirs: History, Memory, and Politics* (Boulder: Lynne Rienner, 1998), 204–5.

42 Okubo, *Citizen 13660*, 75.

43 Wambui Waiyaki Otieno, *Mau Mau's Daughter: A Life History*, ed. Cora Ann Presley (Boulder: Lynne Rienner, 1998), 82–5.

44 Elkins, *Imperial Reckoning*, 188–90.

45 Elkins, *Imperial Reckoning*, 264, 130.

46 Wanjau quoted in Clough, *Mau Mau Memoirs*, 197.

47 Primo Levi, *Survival in Auschwitz*, trans. Stuart Woolf (New York: Touchstone, 1996), 91.

48 *Le Monde* quoted in William Cohen, "The Algerian War, the French State and Official Memory," *Réflexions Historiques* 28, no. 2 (2002): 222.

49 Fabian Sacriste, "Aurès, Algeria: Regroupement Camps during the Algerian War for Independence," *Architecture & Colonialism* 10 (2017), https://thefunambulist.net/magazine/10-architecture-colonialism/aures-algeria-regroupement-camps-algerian-war-independence-fabien-sacriste.

50 Benjamin Claude Brower, "Regroupement Camps and Shantytowns in Late-Colonial Algeria," *L'Année du Maghreb* 20 (2019), https://journals.openedition.org/anneemaghreb/4616.

51 Abderrahman Beggar, "The *Camps de regroupement* During the War of Algeria," in Colman and Domine, *The Camp*, 161.

52 Cornaton, *Camps de Regroupement*, 96–7. (Translation mine.)

53 A.A. Heggoy, *Insurgency and Counterinsurgency in Algeria* (Bloomington: Indiana University Press, 1972), 223.

54 Laleh Khalili, *Time in the Shadows: Confinement in Counterinsurgencies* (Stanford: Stanford University Press, 2013), 187, 184.

55 Jeremy Scahill, "Blacklisted Academic Norman Finkelstein on Gaza, 'The World's Largest Concentration Camp,'" *The Intercept*, May 20, 2018, https://theintercept.com/2018/05/20/norman-finkelstein-gaza-iran-israel-jerusalem-embassy/.

56 Julie Peteet, "The Work of Comparison: Israel/Palestine and Apartheid," *Anthropological Quarterly* 89, no. 1 (2016): 247–81.

57 Gerlach, *Extremely Violent Societies*, 202.

58 Andrea Pitzer, *One Long Night: A Global History of Concentration Camps* (New York: Little, Brown and Company, 2017), 348.

59 Khalili, *Time in the Shadows*, 188.

60 Amy Kaplan, "Where Is Guantanamo?" *American Quarterly* 57, no. 3 (2005): 831.

61 Cahal Milmo, "Guantanamo Bay: Camp X-Ray's Origins Can be Traced Back to Boer War," *Independent*, January 18, 2002.

62 Richard Norton-Taylor, "Guantanamo Is Gulag of Our Time, Says Amnesty," *The Guardian*, May 26, 2005, https://www.theguardian.com/world/2005/may/26/usa.guantanamo.

63 Aidan Forth, "The Ominous Metaphors of Uighur Concentration Camps," *The Conversation*, January 19, 2020, https://theconversation.com/the-ominous-metaphors-of-chinas-uighur-concentration-camps-129665.

64 Sayragul Sauytbay and Alexandra Cavelius, *The Chief Witness: Escape from China's Modern-Day Concentration Camps*, trans. Caroline Waight (Pontiac: Scribe, 2021), 134.

65 Darren Byler, *Terror Capitalism: Uyghur Dispossession and Masculinity in a Chinese City* (Durham: Duke University Press, 2021).

66 Brennan MacDonald, "China Hits Back at Canada, Calls for UN Investigation into Crimes Against Indigenous People," *CBC News*, June 22, 2021, https://www.cbc.ca/news/politics/china-canada-un-calls-investigation-crimes-indigenous-uyghurs-1.6075025.

67 Darren Byler, *In the Camps: China's High-Tech Penal Colony* (New York: Columbia Global Reports, 2021), 11.

68 Byler, *In the Camps*, 27.

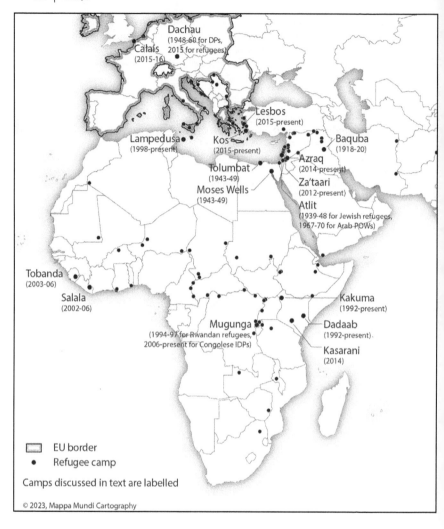

MAP 8.1 Selected refugee camps. In the twenty-first century, camps increasingly perform the function of "airlocks," hermetically sealing the developed world from African and Middle Eastern refugees.

8 | Humanitarian Containment: Refugee Camps and Migrant Detention

There are 35 million refugees in the world today. Seven million live in camps. War, natural disaster, political persecution, and economic hardship have generated a diverse network of humanitarian containment – of formal camps and self-settled shanties, of countless transit zones, island detention sites, and barren desert enclosures. Such arrangements are especially common in Africa and Asia, the former spaces of empire. Yet camps also extend across Europe's boundaries and that of its settler world. Detention facilities guard America's southern border, occupy offshore archipelagos in the Pacific, and line Europe's Mediterranean coast, marking a barrier between a prosperous North and the Global South. In the wake of the 2015 Syrian migrant crisis, German authorities even repurposed the infamous Dachau *Konzentrationslager* to billet refugees and asylum-seekers – an expedient that revived post-World War II efforts by the United Nations (UN) to provide emergency shelter at liberated Nazi camps.

The contrasts between refugee camps run by the UN and other NGOs and the brutal enclosures of Nazi Germany and the Soviet Union (or even of colonial Britain and France) are clear. To exemplify the difference, Ashkhan, an Afghan refugee at a subcamp of Dachau, the "Herb Garden," voiced his gratitude for having a roof over his head, while Dachau's mayor, a Social Democrat, believed the former Nazi camp, with its "historical burden," could perform "a socially meaningful purpose."[1] Yet refugee camps, like concentration camps, internment camps, POW camps, and other forms of mass confinement, exist to concentrate, classify, and contain unwanted categories of humanity.[2] In a world where nation states have emerged as the prime guarantors of human rights, stateless populations are doubly vulnerable. Devoid of rights, and existing in a state of "bare life," they are persecuted in the countries they flee, yet spurned by those who receive them. Such a world has produced "a new kind of human being," Hannah Arendt observed: the "kind that are put in concentration camps by their foes and in internment camps by their friends."[3] Humanitarian sympathy governs at-risk populations, yet forced migrants and other border crossers often suggest "a risk" to host societies. Confounding cause for effect, squalid camps turn refugees into the dehumanized denizens they are sometimes imagined to be. And by means of a racist conjuring trick, many refugees become, in public imaginations, the militants and terrorists they are actually trying to flee. Security, then, complements sympathy as the presiding logic of humanitarian containment: barbed wire protects refugees from violence, but it also protects host countries from refugees.

The genealogy of mass confinement underlines this ontological entanglement. Nineteenth-century workhouses and prisons (chap. 1) reflected a humane agenda of reform and rehabilitation while intensifying regimes of discipline and punishment. And as chap. 3 indicated, the terms "concentration camp" and "refugee camp" remained interchangeable until after World War II – a linguistic ambiguity that recognized the considerable coercion of concentrating vulnerable groups. The gloss of humanitarian uplift and social development likewise coexisted with racial hierarchies and violent displacements in the decolonizing world (chap. 7). By examining how the management of refugees and migrants has transformed into a "custodial regime for innocent people,"[4] this chapter places the refugee camps and asylum detention centers of the modern world within larger histories of mass confinement.

Nineteenth-Century Inheritance

Popular representations of the refugee have undergone profound historical change. Early refugees, like French Huguenots fleeing religious persecution in 1685, were readily assimilated into Protestant communities in Britain and Holland. Meanwhile, Muslim Tartars ethnically cleansed from Crimea and Algerians displaced by France's colonial invasion of 1830 found ready refuge among co-religionists in the Ottoman Empire and Morocco. Royalists and émigrés escaping revolutionary France, along with populations displaced by Polish independence, the American and Italian Revolutions, or Ottoman and Russian oppression, generated a powerful "narrative genre," the historian Caroline Shaw contends, that cast refugees as sympathetic and deserving figures.[5] Typical refugees, usually represented as men, existed in the public imagination as heroic freedom fighters. And far from economic burdens – the huddled, destitute masses that dominate perceptions today – they were often wealthy and highly "civilized." For such groups, camps never materialized, much as European countries have largely welcomed and assimilated (rather than excluded and encamped) Ukrainian refugees in the wake of Russia's 2022 invasion.

By the end of the nineteenth century, however, more negative associations emerged. In particular, Russian pogroms (1881–2, 1903–6) displaced over a million Jews, who became the quintessential refugees of the day. Antisemitic tropes characterized Yiddish-speaking "hordes," more alien and less assimilated than their western counterparts, as superfluous nomads, rootless wanderers, and social pariahs. Anxiety about "pauper and diseased alien immigrants" framed efforts in Britain, like the 1905 Aliens Exclusion Bill, to enforce border restrictions, while German and American legislation in the 1890s targeted Polish and Chinese migrants.[6] Encounters in the colonial world presented equally degraded specters. Though fugitive slaves were sympathetic figures, racist proclivities removed them to segregated contraband camps during the American Civil War (chap. 3). Devastating famines (1876–8, 1896–1902, 1932, 1943) in Asia and Latin America also displaced millions. As drought-stricken peasants sought sanctuary in wealthy towns, white colonists voiced dismay about the "gaunt refugees" who "fill our streets, wandering about … by day, and camping out on open spaces."[7] Such sights sparked compassion. But as alien apparitions, exotic and racialized, they were also specters of disease and social unrest, much like their Jewish counterparts. In this context, camps offered convenient tools to relieve the hungry while segregating and controlling them.

In Brazil, anxieties about "invasions" of backland peasants generated diminutive *palhocas* (stick shacks) in 1877 and more organized *campos de concentração* in the early twentieth century. Arranged in uniform streets and monitored by armed guards, these sites distributed aid while forestalling rebellion. And with the end of slavery in 1888, they provided captive labor for nearby public works.[8] The nineteenth century's largest system of relief camps, however, developed in colonial India. In a South Asian derivative of the "workhouse test" (chap. 1), authorities corralled nearly 10 million "famine wanderers" into camps in 1876–7 and again from 1897 to 1903 as a condition of humanitarian assistance. And while inmates sometimes ran up "whatever wigwams they pleased,"[9] the colonial government, particularly its military, sanitary, and public works departments, accepted responsibility for accommodation and discipline, thereby disseminating the camp – including templates for huts and tents, official diets, work regimens, and sanitary inspections – across emergent networks of

FIGURE 8.1 The Dharaseo famine camp in Naldurg, India, in 1877 (*above*) prefigured tented relief camps during the Bengal famine (1943) and informed the management of camps for refugees following the partition of India and Pakistan in 1947 (*below*). (Source: Andra Pradesh State Archives; Prime Minister's Museum and Library, Delhi.)

international relief. Recognizing the British Empire as a repository of camp expertise, authorities in Austria-Hungary requested assistance from Indian famine experts in 1882 to manage congregations of impoverished Jewish refugees fleeing Russian pogroms,[10] while South Africa seconded Indian civil servants conversant with famine camps to supervise refugee or concentration camps (as they were interchangeably known) during the Anglo-Boer War (chap. 3) – a measure that showcased the colonial origins of camps as flexible instruments of both anti-guerrilla internment and humanitarian assistance. The Russian famine of 1920, caused by the Bolsheviks' scorched-earth campaign, offered an additional venue for the globalization of humanitarian encampment. Directed by the British colonial expert Benjamin Robertson, the International Russian Relief Fund supervised relief works on the Indian model,[11] bringing yet more camps to the Russian landscape.

NATURAL DISASTER

Before the UN coined the term "internally displaced person" (IDP), victims of natural disasters were known simply as refugees, regardless of whether they were displaced inside or outside their home states. Following the Great Fire of London in 1666, homeless residents camped out in wagons, tents, or on open ground. With the growing capacities of modern states, however, authorities adopted more direct roles in disaster relief. The American Civil War general Philip Sheridan patrolled the streets of Chicago under martial law after the 1871 Chicago Fire, but fugitives from the blaze were left to shelter in churches or to erect improvised structures in outlying parks. In 1906, however, military authorities distributed tents and constructed nearly 6,000 timber huts, laid out in geometric rows, to billet survivors of the San Francisco Earthquake. And authorities in Japan corralled ethnic Koreans into makeshift camps, ostensibly to protect them from Japanese mobs, following the Great Kantō Earthquake (1923). In America, a formal civilian department, the Federal Emergency Management Agency (FEMA), did not replace ad hoc military relief efforts until 1979. Its accommodation of Hurricane Katrina (2005) victims, especially the impoverished Black residents of New Orleans' Ninth Ward, in sports stadiums and prefabricated mobile homes, however, was widely criticized for its incompetence and inhumanity. Has class and racial discrimination made "internal others," displaced within their own communities, as vulnerable as stateless refugees?

Wartime Refugees

Refugee camps predated the twentieth century – a genealogy often neglected by social scientists preoccupied with contemporary refugee management. But the upheavals of World War I augured a new scale of humanitarian containment. As colonial violence came home to Europe in 1914, the deserted villages of northern France bore a close resemblance to the province of Gujarat during the 1899–1900 famine, the Bombay government official and future secretary of the League of Red Cross Societies Sir Claude Hill observed.[12] And as Germany invaded Belgium, "slow caravans of old women and children trailing along the high roads" resembled "modern Jews in search of new countries." From villains in Congo (chap. 2) to victims of German aggression, Belgian refugees, as culturally and racially familiar Europeans, met warm receptions in Britain and Holland. But class prejudice also prevailed: Britain provided wealthy families with comfortable townhomes while billeting the indigent in workhouses and temporary shelters – places to which "one does not want to take good class people," aid workers remarked. Holland likewise established camps, though in order to avoid impolitic associations with the South African War, it named them refugee "villages."[13]

Other demographics provoked sharper scrutiny. In Austria-Hungary, which exploited World War I refugees for unskilled labor, a brutal camp for displaced Jews resembled a prison. "We [we]re placed under heavy guard," an inmate complained, and "in our ears echo[ed] the insults ... [of] the local population: 'dirty, cursed Jews.'"[14] A complex humanitarian politics marked refugees as both suspect and sympathetic. Amid the Bolshevik Revolution, Poland and Lithuania established "refugee concentration camps," as they were known, to distribute food and shelter to Russian émigrés while filtering out suspected Communists and Jewish undesirables who "brought with them," one newspaper remarked, "many different dangers to the true citizens of our country." Following the post-World War I disintegration of the Ottoman Empire, meanwhile, population transfers enforced by the League of Nations corralled ethnic Greek and Turkish civilians into "homelands" they had never seen. In an ominous prologue to events in Nazi Europe, Anatolian Greeks expelled from Turkey were forced to wear yellow armbands to distinguish them from locals. Other Greek refugees faced grim conditions in shelters that reminded the American diplomat Henry Morgenthau of Bolshevik "concentration camps."[15]

As it is today, the interwar Middle East emerged as a core zone of humanitarian encampment. Just as World War I codified nineteenth-century practices in a twentieth-century context, the lands of the former

FIGURE 8.2 Baquba "refugee/concentration camp," in interwar Iraq (*above*), set a template for modern refugee camps like in Lesbos, Greece, established in 2015 (*below*). The use of army tents suggests clear military influences in terms of structure and management. (Source: UK National Archives; Nicolas Economou/ Shutterstock.)

Ottoman Empire, a pivot between east and west on the doorstep of Europe, disseminated humanitarian containment, earlier showcased in the famines of colonial India. When the Armenian genocide consigned its victims to primitive extermination camps (chap. 3), affluent refugees rented private accommodation. But camps invariably concentrated the poor. Winding alleys and ramshackle huts characterized ad hoc settlements in Aleppo and Alexandropol. But the British army, incorporating its experience from previous episodes of colonial encampment, operated more formal relief centers – or "concentration camps," as officials called them in reference to Anglo-Boer War precedents – at Port Said, Egypt, and in Mosul, Basra, and Baquba, Iraq (figure 8.2).

By establishing encampment as a condition of relief, such facilities, run on military lines, injected colonial practices into the burgeoning landscape of international humanitarianism, as represented by the International Red Cross (IRC) and NGOs like the American Near East Relief (NER). As such, they operated "at the crossroads of imperial priorities, wartime crisis, and a longer philanthropic tradition that had its roots in the Victorian period."[16] Showcasing a colonial pedigree – "sanitation amongst Orientals [is] crudely primitive," Baquba's commandant remarked – a "barbed-wire Detention Camp" confined "malefactors."[17] If such measures saved lives, they also reflected a general attitude that the discipline, discomfort, and dehumanization of camp life was appropriate for subordinate colonials inured to poverty and hardship.

INTERWAR RELIEF CAMPS

The interwar period witnessed severe economic crisis. In Weimar Germany (1918–33), work camps for the unemployed preceded more sinister camps under Adolf Hitler. The liberal West likewise suffered during the Great Depression. As American unemployment surged to 25 percent, President Roosevelt's New Deal (1933–39) employed millions of men and women in state and local jobs, at national parks, and in camps attached to public works projects. Refugees escaping Dustbowl conditions in Oklahoma and the Midwest lived alongside Mexican and Asian migrants at California relief camps, where local farmers feared they would depress wages. New Deal programs were popular. But in Canada, the coercive nature of relief camps proved more controversial. Fearful that unemployed transients would threaten public order, the Conservative government of R.B. Bennett established more than 200 camps for 170,000 men. Deprived of voting rights and paid only 10 percent of normal wages, they performed heavy labor in return for shelter and rations. Wary of communism, Major-General Andrew McNaughton felt the camps would discipline "prospective members of what Marx called the 'industrial reserve army,' the storm troopers of the revolution." In reality, however, the concentration of unemployed men in military-run camps, segregated from society in remote locations, bred deep resentment. Protesting conditions, 7,000 men walked out of camps in British Columbia; dozens were later gunned down by police on July 1, 1935.[18] How do such arrangements intersect with the larger history of humanitarian containment?

European DPs

World War II generated still larger, more global displacements. Chinese civilians fled Japan's military advance; Yugoslav, Italian, and Czechoslovak refugees found shelter in Egypt; Poles escaped to transit camps in Iran following the Nazi-Soviet invasion; and Ukrainians feared they would "be scattered in small groups around the globe."[19] The same fate awaited European Jews as they fled Hitler's *Konzentrationslager*. Yet as Nazi genocide accelerated, antisemitic travel restrictions barricaded foreign nations against a Jewish "invasion." Infamously, Canada and the United States refused entry to the refugee ship MS *St. Louis*, forcing 900 Jewish asylum-seekers back to Hitler's Germany. "Receiving states" adopted "the same language and discriminating practices as persecuting states," Hannah Arendt charged.[20] And like today, national borders, fortified with police checks and passport control, complemented barbed-wire camps to contain the flow of refugees.

At the end of World War II, Europe's 40–60 million displaced persons (DPs) dominated public attention. East Europeans, many sick and starving, resisted repatriation to the Soviet Union with its ominous Gulag, while homeless civilians, former internees, ethnic Germans expelled from their homes, and emaciated Holocaust survivors required urgent care – a situation that generated nascent organizations like the UN Relief and Rehabilitation Agency (UNRRA), founded in 1943. Yet wartime prejudices prevailed. Many considered DPs, especially Jews, Poles, Ukrainians, and other Slavs, to be criminals, subversives, and potential revolutionaries, much as Nazi propaganda had portrayed them as communists and "pests." The use of Nazi camps like Dachau, Bergen-Belsen, or Moringen to billet postwar DPs highlighted deeper continuities. It is a "bitter irony," the refugee scholar Liisa Malkki writes, "that many … concentration camps in Germany," with their disciplinary spaces "suited to the mass control of people," were "transformed into 'Assembly Centers' for refugees."[21] The American government's 1945 Harrison report put it more bluntly: "We appear to be treating the Jews as the Nazis treated them except that we do not exterminate them." Many DPs, it continued, were "living under guard behind barbed-wire fences … including [at] some of the most notorious concentration camps."[22] Languishing at a Polish DP camp, Primo Levi recognized the predicament: "What use was it to have been liberated, if we still had to spend our days in a frame of barbed wire?"[23]

Even as UNRRA camps protected Jewish DPs from hostile populations, postwar pogroms, like the vicious 1946 massacre in Kielce, Poland, induced many to seek sanctuary in colonial Palestine, where Zionist militias lobbied for an independent Jewish state. Fearing Arab unrest, however, British naval ships patrolled the eastern Mediterranean until 1947, interning Jewish "illegal immigrants" at Atlit, south of Haifa, or detaining them in Cyprus, where inmates lived in drafty Nissen huts surrounded by watchtowers. Whether in Nazi Germany or British Palestine, Jews faced encampment not for what they had done but for who they were. Nonetheless, the Jewish experience reminds us that camps, as flexible technologies of biopolitical management, could save lives as well as destroy them. In 1948, camps in Cyprus boasted the world's highest birth rate, much as Armenian settlements in Aleppo and Beirut after World War I reversed years of genocide and population decline. And while Holocaust survivors faced harsh conditions – "we can treat you like the Nazis treat you," a British colonial officer purportedly declared – internees recognized that British internment camps and Nazi *Konzentrationslager* were "as different as light and darkness."[24] Hitler envisioned a "final solution" to the "Jewish question," but the camps of Cyprus were genuinely temporary waystations that ceased operations after their inmates migrated to newly independent Israel.

In Europe, some DPs – orphans, destitute widows, and the physically or mentally infirm – lingered until 1957, transforming the final camps into long-term social welfare operations, much like their workhouse antecedents (chap. 1). But while some found comfort and security behind barbed wire, the dangers and cruelties of prolonged encampment became clear. Moved by the suffering of fellow Europeans, especially amid belated revelations of Nazi atrocities, and yet wary of indiscriminate charity, Western governments feared the "demoralizing" impact of camp life. Like the collective farm, a Soviet DP added, refugee camps had "turned us into dull and banal people."[25] Amid looming Cold War conflicts, meanwhile, Western leaders worried DP camps would become Communist recruiting centers. In this context, new agencies like the United Nations High Commissioner for Refugees (UNHCR), founded in 1950, organized the repatriation of Europe's remaining DPs, while western Europe and the United States embraced a new era of postwar migration. President Truman's Displaced Persons Act (1948), a landmark of liberal internationalism – and one that highlighted the (ultimately unfulfilled) promises of the postwar détente – facilitated the immigration of nearly half a million European DPs, while Canada, lifting previous restrictions, accepted 197,000.

Immigration, repatriation, or, in the case of Jewish DPs, the provision of statehood thus emerged as preferred and durable solutions to Europe's refugee crisis. Yet the immediate postwar period suggested a historical crossroads – one in which global leaders repudiated camps (at least for displaced Europeans) at the very moment they laid foundations for a lasting regime of humanitarian containment situated in the Third World. As civil war and economic dislocation spread across Asia and Africa, colonized and racialized populations – the "wretched of the Earth," in Frantz Fanon's words – faced a future of prolonged encampment. And as Europe closed its postwar camps, the Middle East and decolonizing Africa witnessed a new proliferation of canvas tents and wire fences.

Postcolonial Displacement

Far from settling global affairs, the upheavals of World War II heralded new dislocations. Indeed, only a Eurocentric perspective could associate the post-1945 period with peace and prosperity. As a harbinger of postcolonial conflict, the 1947 partition of India and Pakistan set the tenor for decades to come. Fearing their "conditions [would] be like Jews in the Hitlerite regime," 1.2 million Hindus and Muslims fled sectarian pogroms. Some found shelter in 160 tented refugee camps near Delhi and Calcutta (figure 8.1), but the Indian government also exiled "undesirables" to remote regions like the Andaman Islands, thereby connecting modern refugee management with the infamous political prison established under British rule (chap. 1). That same year, the partition of Israel and Palestine and the resulting Arab-Israeli war – the *Nakba*, or catastrophe, as Palestinians remember it – led to the mass exodus of a people who share an antagonistic but peculiarly analogous history with the Jews who displaced them. As Palestinians became "refugees on the borders of [their] own country to make room for other refugees,"[26] an American proposal to house them in Cyprus, at camps formerly occupied by Jewish DPs, highlighted this kinship of persecution, as did the detention of Arab fighters at Atlit in 1967. Scattered across Lebanon, Syria, and Jordan, facilities operated by the UN Relief and Works Agency in Palestine (UNRWA) offered temporary respite. Yet as *Nakba* refugees yearned for a future independent state, Israel's ongoing military occupation (1967–present, chap. 7) and the fraught politics of return – many Palestinians rejected third-country resettlement for fear of losing their claim to an independent Palestine – conspired to transform UNRWA camps into permanent features of the Arab-Israeli landscape. The exception became the norm as temporary tents gave way to concrete housing blocks in the 1960s.

However singular its politics, the Palestinian conflict presaged future global developments. Originally founded as a temporary organization for European DPs, the UNHCR expanded its scope in the 1950s to Hong Kong, where it organized relief for over a million Chinese refugees fleeing Maoist repression, while UNHCR efforts in Morocco and Tunisia during the Algerian War of Independence relied on camps as economical tools for distributing aid. (Coordinating with French military authorities, the UN's removal of refugees from sensitive border areas to prevent contact with ALN guerrillas also showcased encampment's enduring counterinsurgency function.) Above all, however, the Vietnam War (1955–75) and the numerous civil conflicts of decolonizing (1956–80) and postcolonial Africa – especially in the Horn of Africa (Sudan, Somalia, Ethiopia, Eritrea) and Great Lakes region (Congo, Rwanda, Burundi, Tanzania, Uganda) – conspired to transform refugee management from the 1960s onward into a truly global problem. And as Africa became a continent of mass displacement, the archetypal refugee transformed, in Western minds, from a persecuted European fleeing Nazi or Soviet violence to a dark-skinned colonial other, whose politics were inscrutable, whose culture was alien, but who nonetheless became the subject of technocratic knowledge and professional humanitarian intervention.

Internationalist visions of global citizenship and free movement, institutionalized by the 1951 Geneva Convention on the Status of Refugees and Article 14.1 of the UN Charter of Human Rights, established legal rights of asylum for those crossing international borders due to political and religious persecution. Yet as refugees proliferated in the Global South, governments in Europe and America proved increasingly unwilling to absorb them. Eager to prevent "unacceptable levels of mass migration," the UNHCR, in coordination with Western governments, rejected proposals in the 1960s from the Organization for African Unity to expand rights of asylum to include victims of ecological catastrophe or economic hardship, or minorities displaced within (rather than outside) the artificial boundaries of postcolonial states.[27] Meanwhile, refortified national borders secured Europe and the United States from what the American senator Pat McCarran called a "flood of undesirables." In a nativist retreat reflective of the reactionary reversals of the 1950s, the US Immigration and Nationality Act (1952) prioritized white Europeans over Asian, African, and Latin American migrants,[28] while Britain's Commonwealth Immigrants Act (1962) erected barriers against colonial subjects from Africa and Asia, much like antisemitic quotas had cordoned off Jewish refugees in World War II. The United States, in a Cold War context, offered sanctuary to favored anti-Communist groups – Hungarians (1956), Cubans (1959), and Vietnamese (1975–9) – while Britain granted asylum to Anglo-Egyptians (1956) and Ugandan Asians (1972) as a lingering imperial duty. Yet the amorphous majority, especially those associated with poverty or disease, found no equivalent to Truman's 1948 amnesty of European DPs. In the process, refugee camps transformed from interim measures of emergency relief into technologies of "flow management" that externalized national borders by warehousing the majority of the world's displaced at a distance, in postcolonial Africa and Asia, where tenuous economies and fragile political orders proved ill-equipped to relieve them.

However tragic for those displaced, postcolonial upheavals also presented administrative opportunities. Founded in 1950 with a limited temporal and geographic scope, the UNHCR transformed in 1967 into a permanent agency with global remit. Largely funded by and, to a degree, serving the interests of Europe and North America, the UNHCR coordinated an expanding industry of private NGOs, like Oxfam and CARE, from its metropolitan center in Geneva. Administered by waves of ex-colonial officials who repackaged paternalistic attitudes and colonial "civilizing missions" in the relief of marginal and racialized groups,[29] such organizations embraced the resettlement of displaced populations in organized camps that could be effectively managed by external agencies – a logic shared, more coercively, by the *regroupements* of colonial counterinsurgencies (chap. 7). In this context, the international aid sector, in coordination and sometimes in conflict with host countries, institutionalized a postwar regime of enclosed, demarcated camps – one that still exists today. As a standardized component of refugee management, humanitarian containment has proven effective at monitoring displaced populations and forestalling a mass exodus to Europe and North America. But as the pages that follow suggest, refugee camps have often failed to alleviate distress, protect the vulnerable, or secure human rights.

Civilizing Missions

If African and Middle Eastern refugees were "uncivilized" intruders in the West, or an unwelcome, destabilizing, and potentially dangerous presence in postcolonial states, a liberal "colonialism of compassion," from the 1960s until today, has steadily rendered them agentless victims, and as problems to be managed by Western expertise. By conceiving itself, amid the contentious conflicts of civil war and decolonization, as a "purely humanitarian organization," the UNHCR effectively depoliticized the targets of its care. Yet in place of permanent political or legal solutions, including repatriation, resettlement, or internationally recognized statehood, the UNHCR progressively embraced the distribution of *in situ* aid and the promise of "development" and "rehabilitation." Though well-meaning, such measures arguably constitute a postcolonial version of the "white man's burden" that keeps refugees "in their place," confined to Asia and Africa, while offering conduits for the spread of Western "civilization" abroad.

As stateless and therefore rightless aberrations, victims of "nationalism's fiction of an unproblematic link between territory and identity,"[30] refugees in the final decades of the twentieth century were regular targets of therapeutic intervention, of "care, cure, and control" as a UNHCR spokesperson put it.[31] Like at prisons and workhouses, sewing, shoemaking, and soap-making workshops at Palestinian camps offered vocational training, while the relocation of refugees to remote valleys has fostered the cultivation of barren Arabian deserts. The Indian government's "Project Daya" (1958) likewise placed partition refugees on marginal land inhabited by Aboriginal tribes as part of a state-directed project of internal colonization – one that followed, ironically, in British imperial footsteps with its emphasis on road and canal construction.

In Africa, likewise, UNHCR camps emerged as tools of modernization that would settle uprooted populations in disciplined agricultural communities. Once again, tribal and nomadic populations would experience the "sedenterist bias" of concentrating powers, Liisa Malkki comments.[32] And once again, work would be a vehicle of "civilizational uplift." In the 1970s, for example, the UNHCR provided Sudan with $7 million in development funds to employ Ethiopian and Eritrean refugees on hydroelectric dams and other infrastructure projects. Rwandans encamped in Tanzania likewise built schools, roads, and hospitals in a project that resembled earlier "villagization" schemes (chap. 7), though refugees objected that they were "placed in the middle of nowhere" amid "thick forests inhabited by wild animals" and directed to grow grain along with cash crops like coffee and tobacco for export. "We cultivate a lot, they eat a lot," one resident complained: "We have become their slaves."[33]

At times, exploitation has overshadowed rehabilitation, particularly in cases where UNHCR officials have had to negotiate with strained or hostile receiving states. In the 1990s, authorities in Tanzania expressed skepticism about providing secondary education to camp residents: "[T]hey think if we are educated, we will not cultivate anymore," refugees reported.[34] At Salala IDP camp in Liberia, meanwhile, a government official in 2001 accepted World Food Programme rations while contracting inmate labor to multinational corporations. Every morning, trucks transported inmates to nearby rubber plantations operated by the Firestone Tire Company, where they worked for 50 cents a day – a neoliberal iteration, perhaps, of colonial-era rubber production in French and Belgian West Africa (chap. 2).[35]

In other cases, host countries have denied refugees the right to work outside of camp – save for remote or unappealing infrastructure projects – or to participate in the local economy. In 1979, security forces in Sudan blamed Eritrean refugees for crime and prostitution, denying them access to jobs or education. Citing the "threat to our moral values and public decency," police then ordered the evacuation of the city of Khartoum and relocated Eritreans to spatially segregated camps.[36] Fearful that displaced foreigners would take jobs from locals at lower rates of pay, Tanzania similarly launched "a concerted programme" in the 1990s "to round up Burundian refugees … forcing large numbers into camps … and depriving them of wage-earning opportunities."[37] And at Kenya's sprawling Dadaab (1991–present), a massive UNHCR complex that exemplifies the tensions of modern humanitarian relief, Somali refugees have even coined a new word, *buugis*, to describe the interminable act of waiting, suspended in time. Without meaningful employment or prospects for the future, they become spectators to their own lives rather than protagonists in them.

Chewing betel nut and playing video games, many now suffer from low self-esteem and pathological dependency: "I am just like a child now. I don't know where I am, I don't know where to go," a Dadaab resident reported.[38] According to gendered divisions of labor, however, women often spend busy days collecting firewood (see figure 8.3), waiting for rations, cooking, and caring for children. UNHCR programs facilitate educational opportunities normally unavailable to Somali girls, but mothers, daughters, and wives spend an average of four hours a day queuing at centralized ration stations within fenced compounds. And while the UNHCR endeavors to "liberate" Muslim women from "harmful cultural practices" like genital mutilation – an animating objective of liberal intervention – camps often fail to protect them from sexual violence. This is especially true at Kakuma, another Kenyan camp, where men, who outnumber women by a ratio of 2.7 to 1, find outlets in sexual aggression. When women report rapes to the Kenyan police, however, the response is unsympathetic: "You are raping our trees" (the quest for firewood is unending), "so you got what you deserved."[39]

Humanitarian initiatives to inculcate democracy, transparency, and other liberal reforms have likewise met limited success. Though "mock elections" promise to prepare refugees for future independence, such ventures are often compromised, the anthropologist Michel Agier argues, by the aid sector's reluctance to afford refugee councils authority over camp finances, and by an essential fear that relinquishing institutional control to inmates will "threaten the order of the camp" and "lead it to unravel, like an uprising can topple a government." Highlighting this central anxiety, UNHCR administrators at Tobanda, Sierra Leone, justified the replacement in 2003 of a charismatic refugee representative chosen by his peers with a more pliant alternative by stating the camp did "not need democracy in order to function."[40]

Genuine compassion motivates individual aid workers, who make great sacrifices in challenging and often dangerous conditions: amid genocide and war, camps often save lives. But paternalistic interventions, however well-intentioned, suggest the essential incompatibility between camps and human rights. Efforts to foster self-government are therefore based on familiar delusions. Indeed, the violation of freedom of movement, the defining feature of encampment, is the "precursor to violations of all other human rights," refugee scholar Guglielmo Verdirame asserts.[41] It is thus that protests against rations and unclean water are sometimes met with tear gas and rubber bullets. It is thus that nation states, "incapable of providing a law" to the stateless, have "transferred the whole matter to the police," as Hannah Arendt declared.[42] And it is thus that promises to institute refugee self-governance "in five to six years," repeated for decades at refugee camps across the former colonial world, echo the justifications of liberal empire: that European governments were preparing colonial societies for independence, only they were "not yet ready."[43]

The Logic of the Workhouse

Whatever their humanitarian mandates, modern refugee camps facilitate practices of counting, classification, and control. Refugees invariably evoke a "double suspicion," Agier comments: "that of being a refugee" and "that of being a false refugee."[44] Rather than guarantee comfort and security, leaky tents, modular huts, and unappealing subsistence rations reanimate a preemptive logic of "less eligibility" inherited from Victorian workhouses (chap. 1). By mandating residency in exchange for assistance, camps filter the deserving from the undeserving, while militating against an enduring anxiety of capitalist political economy – that of misdirected charity. In Malaysia, accordingly, Vietnamese "boat people" faced an "archipelago of closed camps" in the 1970s that incarcerated them in warehouses, army barracks, and prisons previously reserved for drug addicts and juvenile delinquents. One inmate spoke of her "social death" and her camp as "hell," where the "gate will lock behind me." The hope, for Malaysian authorities, was "that word would get back to Vietnam and discourage ... others who were thinking of following in their footsteps."[45] According to a familiar dynamic of deterrence, only the truly persecuted would accept such conditions of relief, just as only the truly destitute would submit to workhouse confinement. Camps, then, were spaces for those who were "dead already, maybe not physically, but psychologically and socially."[46]

For those desperate enough to trade freedom for encampment, additional measures of segregation and surveillance await. Upon entry, refugees are registered and subjected to biometric monitoring and political "screenings." Though outwardly sympathetic to ongoing Palestinian displacement, authorities in Lebanon and Jordan, fearful of extremists, have subjected refugees to regular political interrogations. In Thailand and Indonesia, likewise, camps helped American authorities in the 1970s to process and filter out Khmer and Vietcong Communists while identifying the supposedly desirable and industrious for resettlement overseas, much as European DP camps did after World War II. Camps in Tanzania similarly classified and segregated refugees from the Rwandan genocide (1994) according to political affiliation and tribal allegiance, a process designed to curb further ethnic violence, which was widespread as rival Hutu and Tutsi militias mingled in the same camps, but also to facilitate better policing and surveillance. Such practices are now extrapolated globally. Functioning as nets, camps capture and filter inmates, identifying potential security threats, gathering political and biographical information, which the UNHCR often shares with state security agencies, and administering aid to genuine cases of need.

Camp architecture also facilitates discipline and control. Concentrated behind wire, refugees are largely invisible to global publics. Yet camps are highly panoptic spaces that make alien agglomerations legible to state authorities and international agencies: with long rows of tents that afford little private space, Dadaab in Kenya constituted "one of the most tightly monitored spaces on the planet," a UNHCR official remarked in 2010.[47] Wide avenues and geometric boulevards (figure 8.3), visible in aerial photographs, facilitate exercises in counting and calculating – a fulfillment of the Benthamite prison (chap. 1) and of colonial aspirations "to create a human landscape of perfect visibility." Highlighting the confrontational, quasi-military nature of camp management as it developed in the 1990s, the ethnographer Jennifer Hyndman observed periodic roll calls, enforced by armed police, which corralled inmates into fenced counting centers, where UNHCR officials stamped serial numbers on refugees' hands, conducted iris scans, and issued biometric ration cards. Such operations prevented refugees from claiming double rations – suspicions they were cheating the system were omnipresent – but they reminded Somali residents of "the slavery of their people under Arab rule."[48]

Camps also enforce sanitary surveillance. There is "nothing more practical than a camp for carrying out a medical screening or a vaccination campaign," Agier points out.[49] Medical policing and UN health initiatives present significant advances over squalid nineteenth-century colonial enclosures. Yet even with modern medicine, the mass and chaotic concentration of refugees has led to epidemic outbreaks, like at Mugunga in Congo, where 50,000 died of cholera in 1994. Hygienic priorities also recall practices of exclusion pioneered at plague lazarettos and industrial lockhouses for suspected prostitutes, along with visions of disease and crime projected onto refugees and asylum-seekers in both world wars. Before it detained suspects in the global war on terror (chap. 7), the American army base

FIGURE 8.3 With monotonous architecture and bleak surroundings, camps are non-places, latitudinal coordinates in the desert. Such, at least, is the view from the perspective of the state and the expert. Geometric aerial photographs, a widely disseminated visual trope (*above*), render Dadaab's human population invisible. On the ground, inmates navigate messier realities (*below*) than suggested by the perspective of the state and the planner. (Source: UNHCR.)

at Camp Bulkeley, Guantanamo, housed Haitian refugees suspected of carrying HIV – an act that highlighted enduring associations between mobile Black bodies and sexual and moral degeneration. Though the government "euphemistically refer[red] to its Guantanamo operation as a 'humanitarian camp,'" a US judge in 1993 maintained "it [was] nothing more than an HIV prison camp."[50]

REFUGEE SHELTERS

Refugee camps have often repurposed other carceral sites like POW camps and political prisons. Tolumbat in Egypt functioned, variously, as a convalescent camp, a military detention center and, after World War II, a UN refugee camp. Disused warehouses, army barracks, and workhouses, as well as hotels and health resorts, accommodated wartime DPs, while Egypt's Moses Wells, a camp for East Europeans fleeing Nazi violence, was originally a quarantine station for pilgrims returning from Mecca. In the Philippines, meanwhile, a refugee camp for Vietnamese boat people on the Palawan Islands previously housed lepers before transforming, under American administration, into the Iwahig Penal Colony (chap. 1). Perhaps most provocatively, repurposed Nazi *Konzentrationslager* highlight a shared genealogy between refugee camps and other sites of confinement, though their genocidal origins warn against the limits of meaningful comparison.

Humanitarian agencies also establish purpose-built campsites. Before erecting a camp, UNHCR workers complete "Multi-Sectoral Site Assessment Forms" detailing water supply, drainage, soil conditions, and proximity to food, fuel, and functioning health facilities. Humanitarian containment has thus become an established profession, with its own standards of expertise. UN catalogs outline simple, cost-effective structures like semicylindrical frame tents, inspired by World War I Nissen huts (figure 3.3) and communal marquee tents, previously used at Baquba in interwar Iraq (figure 8.2). As emergency shelter transitions into more permanent infrastructure, the UN recommends an array of modular housing units. Updating the basic A-frame military hut, a lightweight plastic design by the Swedish multinational IKEA advertises easy assembly in multiple languages.[51] Why is it, then, that inmates often prefer to construct their own shelters with local materials and Indigenous designs?

The Logic of the Prison

The last decades of the twentieth century showcased the coercive potential of humanitarian containment. But the twenty-first century has only
fortified the nexus between humanitarianism and security. In the wake of
September 11, 2001, the Anglo-American invasions of Afghanistan (2001)
and Iraq (2003), and the Russian-backed airstrikes of the Syrian Civil War
(2011–present) have fueled Islamic extremism while creating a burgeoning
refugee crisis matched only by the upheavals of World War II. Since the
1980s, meanwhile, trickle-down economics have placed housing, education, and medical services in America and parts of Europe under growing
strain. Yet as they flee international drone strikes, homegrown violence,
and threats to their economic and physical security, refugees and migrants
(as they are now increasingly called) have transformed, in Western minds,
from agentless victims into violent suspects and economic burdens.

As sensational terror attacks in Paris (2015), Brussels (2016), and
Manchester (2017) enflamed anxieties about Islamic extremism in the 2010s,
a proliferation of walls and fences physically partitioned the world. Europe
and America resettle only a small portion of the global refugee population:
324,000 in the United States in 2019 (less than 0.1 percent of its total population) and 2.7 million in the EU (0.6 percent of its population).[52] Collectively
housing more than 8 million refugees, meanwhile, countries like Turkey,
Jordan, and Lebanon have transformed, in the first decades of the new mil-
lennium, into a giant holding zone: a "supercamp" of continental propor-
tions, as the scholar Kjersti Berg puts it.[53] And in the years since Europeans
dismantled the Berlin Wall (1989) and guaranteed free movement across
internal borders, the European Union has ironically transformed into "a
gated continent"[54] that consigns huge numbers of Syrians, Iraqis, Afghans,
and other "undesirables" to squalid camps on its periphery. Yet it bears
observing that those who commit terrorism on European soil are mostly
EU citizens with known terror links rather than refugees displaced by violence in their home countries.

In this new world of walls, border patrols, and rigid visa restrictions,
spatial and experiential distance has severed human connection. In 2015,
Hungary, Europe's most xenophobic country (though once a source of
refugees after the 1956 Soviet invasion), built a four-meter barrier of con-
certina wire patrolled by soldiers, who directed Middle Eastern asylum-
seekers to purpose-built camps that resembled high-security prisons.
Dehumanizing conditions aimed to punish and deter – in one instance,

the correspondent Patrick Kingsley reports, border guards threw food at crowds of caged Syrians and Afghans "as if they [were] monkeys in a zoo."[55] The racial motives are explicit: the Hungarian president Viktor Orbán (1963–) proclaimed that Europeans should not become peoples of "mixed race." Echoing the fascism of previous generations, a resurgent far right in Europe has even likened refugees to cockroaches and "feral humans," or to the "barbarian invaders" that dismantled the Roman Empire.[56]

Antimigrant sentiment is by no means confined to the West, however. India, Iran, and Saudi Arabia have also erected border fences. And in 2023, the latter, a wealthy nation that holds fewer refugees (a mere 320 in 2019) than almost any nation in the world, stands accused of killing hundreds of Ethiopian asylum-seekers on its southern frontier.[57] Grappling with social and economic turmoil and saddled with an outsized share of global refugee relief, host states like Egypt, Turkey, and Jordan have likewise turned against asylum-seekers. "Go back to your own country," an Egyptian supermarket worker yelled at Hayam al-Souki, a Syrian refugee, while a government official, seemingly revolted by her presence, demanded she talk to him from the other side of the room.[58] Located on the frontlines of America's global war on terror, Jordan, coordinating with the UNHCR and supported by EU and North American foreign aid, has increasingly blurred the lines between humanitarian relief and military policing. A poll released on September 11, 2012, indicated 80 percent of Jordanians wanted all Syrians confined inside closed camps – a justification for security forces to raid unofficial settlements and incarcerate undocumented migrants behind wire. At Za'taari, a desert camp so inhospitable that not even camels can survive, refugees feel they "are living in a prison" and being treated "worse than animals." Jordanian architects and private security advisors contracted by the UNHCR have likewise designed the remote Azraq camp, a "model facility" opened in 2014, to purposefully maximize control over what officials consider "a potentially unruly population." Such practices end "any pretence," the political scientist Sophia Hoffmann concludes, "that the camp is anything other than a prison facility." With the exception of those who can afford "bail" of US$15,000, anyone leaving faces "severe consequences," a welcome pamphlet warns.[59]

In moments of crisis, today's refugees even face violence that resembles the counterinsurgencies and civil conflicts that first displaced them. Once again, Arendt might note, host states have replicated the practices of persecutors. Following a 2013 terror attack at Nairobi's exclusive Westgate Shopping Center, Kenyan authorities conflated Somali refugees, including women and children, with the Islamist Al Shabaab terror group from which many had fled. As tensions flared – "I've never seen a public mood like it," a Kenyan journalist confided – Somalis transformed from neighbors into "invaders." In a postcolonial rendition of Britain's Operation Anvil (chap. 7), Kenyan police, under President Uhuru Kenyatta, son of Jomo Kenyatta, rounded up ethnic Somalis in Nairobi's Eastleigh neighborhood and confined them in Kasarani soccer stadium – or "Kasarani concentration camp," as activists labeled it. Those who failed document checks and political screenings were then removed to Dadaab. Such was the case for "Fish," a Somali university student who had bribed his way out of previous raids, but whose luck and money ran out in April 2014: *Panda Gari!* ("get in the van!"), police yelled, as he joined his compatriots in camp.[60] The survivors of Britain's Mau Mau-era camps thus became agents of a new system of mass confinement.

As tenuous distinctions between refugee relief and political internment dissolved, Dadaab's population swelled above 400,000, making it world history's largest camp. Enforcing categorical distinctions between "us" and "them," "citizen" and "other," its barbed-wire and thorn-hedge perimeter now operates according to the "same principles that guide a prison," a Human Rights Watch observer notes. Even aid workers came to fear those they were tasked with helping. Operating in a new climate of fear, heightened by sporadic Al Shabaab attacks on Western officials, the UNHCR diverted money in 2015 from rations and shelter to reinforce its own offices with blast walls, steel gates, and razor wire: the barrier was so high that aid workers could no longer see out of their compound.[61] Elsewhere, the humanitarian aid sector's embrace of big data and GPS – the same technology that governs Chinese "smart camps" in Xinjiang (chap. 7) – has erected a "digital wall" around refugees at Azraq. Outsourcing the work of humanitarian assistance to cost-saving apps that collect intimate information about the movement, habits, diet, and health of inmates, aid workers have become bureaucrats who rarely leave their desks. The separation between helper and victim is complete.[62]

Migrant Detention

With repatriation ever less likely, camp life increasingly untenable, and migrant routes closed off by formidable border gates, some refugees pay human traffickers to secure transit to authoritarian petrostates like Qatar, condemned by Amnesty International as a contemporary "slave state." In what is certainly a new circuit of twenty-first-century indentured labor, migrants live in cockroach-infested work camps where they build the glittering city of Doha and the football stadiums of the 2022 World Cup. With its reliance on cheap and rightless workers, whose passports and documents are confiscated upon intake, the mantra of "development," of economic growth and proliferating skyscrapers, thus contains a capacity for violence, the critic Vinay Lal warns, that may underlie the "concentration camps of the future."[63]

From afar, America remains "a city on a hill," however unreachable, much as it was for Jewish refugees in World War II. Indeed, the residents of Dadaab spend their days dreaming of life in Minneapolis, much as refugees and forced migrants displaced by gang violence in Mexico or by economic and political turmoil in Venezuela dream of Miami. Yet such journeys are fraught with danger: treacherous jungle and desert crossings along with exploitation by human traffickers. Like Viktor Orbán's Hungary, meanwhile, the United States has reembraced the rhetoric of ethnic purity. With wild fantasies about shooting asylum-seekers in the legs and digging snake-and-alligator-filled pits to entrap them, President Donald Trump (1947–) described a 2018 "migrant caravan" of women and children from central America as an "invasion of our country." Declaring a National Emergency (the first on domestic soil since September 11, 2001), he then commissioned a 3,145-kilometer border wall, while deploying 5,200 federal troops to the southern border. "Our military is waiting for you," he tweeted.[64]

Yet while only 79 kilometers of the promised wall has materialized, the quest to "liberate" southwestern towns from an "occupation" of "illegal immigrants" appropriates the military rhetoric that framed earlier episodes of encampment. Between 1993 and 2017, the controversial Arizona sheriff Joe Arpaio illegally profiled undocumented Latin American migrants and asylum-seekers, detaining them in "Tent City," a canvas prison in the Sonoran desert that he explicitly called a "concentration camp," and where inmates were forced to wear pink underwear in an act of ritualistic emasculation (figure 8.4).[65] Though he was a combative vigilante, Arpaio's approach has been steadily normalized as Immigration and Customs Enforcement (ICE) squads, equipped with military-grade weapons first developed to fight Communist insurgents overseas, conduct night-time raids in America's ethnic neighborhoods. The consequent mass arrest of "criminal aliens" and their prolonged detention has fused criminal justice and immigration enforcement into a single carceral network, scholars of America's prison industrial complex have charged.[66] Meanwhile, Donald Trump's promises in 2023 to build giant military camps for migrants who

FIGURE 8.4 "Tent City." The US Department of Justice concluded Sheriff Joe Arpaio's migrant roundups constituted the worst case of racial profiling in US history. Though convicted of criminal contempt, Arpaio's presidential pardon in 2020 served to endorse his methods. (Source: Getty Images.)

were "poisoning the blood" of America suggest Arpaio's model may be expanded should the former president be re-elected.[67]

Controversial flashpoints highlight the shocking conditions of American migrant detention. Between 2017 and 2019, an internal Homeland Security Report concluded, unsafe and filthy barracks, racist abuse, sexual humiliation, and the pepper-spraying of mentally ill detainees constituted "barbaric practices[s]" that "clearly violated[ed] ... basic principles of humanity."[68] In particular, the preemptive separation of children from their parents, a policy that deterred refugees from entering the country to seek asylum (a right guaranteed by UN charter), gave rise to facilities like Texas's Ursula detention camp. Nicknamed "the dog kennel," it incarcerated minors in chain-link pens while denying them basic necessities like toothbrushes, showers, and soap. Continuities with earlier episodes of encampment soon emerged. As Trump-affiliated spokesmen cited the internment of Japanese Americans as legal precedent for race-based registries and bans, the federal government repurposed Fort Sill, Oklahoma, formerly a Japanese internment camp and earlier a site of Indigenous confinement (chaps. 2 and 7), as a migrant detention facility. As non-citizens, however, asylum-seekers face additional hardships: "at least I and other children were not pulled screaming from our mothers' arms," the activist and World War II Japanese internment camp survivor George Takei observed.[69] As the chapters of this book attest, children often bear the brunt of encampment, whether in the concentration camps of the South African War or the separation of families at residential schools, slave plantations, and the Soviet Gulag.[70]

"Fortress Australia," once a destination for convicts, indentured laborers, and other outcast populations (chap. 1), has likewise developed a network of repressive detention facilities to entrap would-be asylum-seekers. In the first decades of the twenty-first century, naval ships patrol the waters of the South Pacific, intercepting suspected migrants, including large numbers of refugees fleeing Syria and Afghanistan, and detaining them for up to ten years at offshore processing facilities far from legal and humanitarian oversight. Located in remote deserts or impoverished island nations like Nauru, to which Australia now outsources detention, such institutions have "ceased to be mere detention centers," critics like the Australian Court of Appeals judge Stephen Charles argues, "they are now concentration camps."[71] Bearing witness to a "system designed to ... produce suffering," Dr. Peter Young, a former healthcare director, concurred: "When people go to prison they go through a recognized independent judicial process. It's not arbitrary." Moreover, "those with mental health problems generally improve [in prison] ... What we see in detention is the opposite ... they get sicker." Though vaccinations have prevented communicable diseases like smallpox and measles from killing in mass numbers, psychological trauma has reached epidemic levels. The self-harm and sensational self-immolation of inmates at Nauru illustrates what the Royal Australian College of Psychiatrists describes as the "severe and detrimental effects" of "prolonged detention."[72]

Conclusion

From Dadaab to Za'taari, and from Palestine to Nauru, today's refugees face a diverse network of contemporary camps, in which humanitarian concerns intersect with discourses of racism, security, and political economy. Just as prisons and workhouses (chap. 1) placed vagrants and rootless criminals into social quarantine, modern refugee camps have extrapolated the dynamics of exclusion to a planetary scale. And while dedicated aid workers struggle to provide shelter and safety, the steady criminalization of asylum-seekers and the consequent militarization of humanitarian containment has unsettled tenuous distinctions between "refugee camps," "migrant camps," and "concentration camps." The scholar Barbara Harell-Bond maintains that "[t]here is an innate contradiction between keeping people in camps and respecting human rights," not only because camps "constitute a unique setting for the arbitrary exercise of power," but because the international system denies rights to those without a stable, functioning government to guarantee their interests.[73] Meanwhile, the international community's indifference toward marginalized populations – abetted by their detention in distant camps, where they are largely invisible – has forestalled the imagination of alternate solutions.

Despite their plight, however, refugees do not suffer in silence. They are not passive victims. Though they inhabit a new regime of twenty-first-century camps, one that emerged despite postwar invocations of "never again," they also fight at the vanguard, in a new battle for rights – to residency, to work, to social and political life – which emanate not from their national citizenship or immigration documents (which many lack), but from the fact that they are human. To abolish the boundaries of the camp would be to abolish the boundaries of caste, class, race, and nation. Yet however futile or "misty-eyed," as the Australian prime minister John Howard put it, the insistence "I am human" emanates from behind the wire. Though inmates speak different languages and practice different cultures and faiths, they forge new identities and new solidarities that remind those on the outside of a shared and essential humanity. As Riaz, a refugee at the self-settled "jungle" camp in Calais in northern France put it, "I help others because our lives here are important and equally so are other people's lives." Immersed within a diverse and cosmopolitan camp community of Somalis and Syrians, Muslims and Christians, he vowed "to help [others] because we all survive as one human race. We all are or could be friends or relatives."[74]

Notes

1 Sophie Hardach, "The Refugees Housed at Dachau," *The Guardian*, September 19, 2015, https://www.theguardian.com/world/2015/sep/19/the-refugees-who-live-at-dachau.

2 Kirsten McConnachie, "Camps of Containment: A Genealogy of the Refugee Camp," *Humanity* 7, no. 3 (2016): 397–412.

3 Hannah Arendt, "We Refugees," in *The Jewish Writings*, ed. Jerome Kohn and Ron F. Feldman (New York: Schocken Books, 2008), 265.

4 Guglielmo Verdirame and Barbara Harrell-Bond, *Rights in Exile: Janus-Faced Humanitarianism* (New York: Berghahn, 2005).

5 Caroline Shaw, *Britannia's Embrace: Modern Humanitarianism and the Imperial Origins of Refugee Relief* (Oxford: Oxford University Press, 2015).

6 Ed Mynott, "Nationalism, Racism and Immigration Control: From Anti-racism to Anti-capitalism," in *From Immigration Controls to Welfare Controls*, ed. Steve Cohen, Beth Humphries, and Ed Mynott (London: Routledge, 2002), 14.

7 Aidan Forth, *Barbed-Wire Imperialism: Britain's Empire of Camps, 1876–1903* (Berkeley: University of California, 2017), 49.

8 Laura Belik, "Mobilizing Labor for Infrastructure in Northeast Brazil, 1915–1932," in *The Routledge Handbook of Infrastructure Design: Global Perspectives from Architectural History*, ed. Joseph Heathcott (New York: Routledge, 2022), 76–84.

9 Forth, *Barbed-Wire Imperialism*, 106.

10 Shaw, *Britannia's Embrace*, 214.

11 Tehila Sasson, "From Empire to Humanity: The Russian Famine and the Imperial Origins of International Humanitarianism," *Journal of British Studies* 55, no. 3 (July 2016): 519.

12 Forth, *Barbed-Wire Imperialism*, 222.

13 Peter Gatrell, *The Making of the Modern Refugee* (Oxford: Oxford University Press, 2013), 35, 32, 34.

14 Matthew Stibbe, "Civilian Internment and Civilian Internees in Europe," *Immigrants and Minorities* 26, no. 1–2 (2008): 65.

15 Gatrell, *Modern Refugee*, 58, 67, 64.

16 Michelle Tusan, "The Concentration Camp as Site of Refuge: The Rise of the Refugee Camp and the Great War in the Middle East," *Journal of Modern History* 93, no. 4 (2021): 828.

17 H.H. Austin, *The Baqubah Refugee Camp: An Account of Work on Behalf of the Persecuted Assyrian Christians* (London: The Faith Press, 1920), chap. 2. See also Benjamin White, "The Global Origins of the Modern Refugee Camp: Military Humanitarianism and Colonial Occupation at Baquba, Iraq, 1918–1920," in *Continental Encampment: Genealogies of Humanitarian Containment in the Middle East and Europe*, ed. John Knudsen and Kjersti G. Berg (New York: Berghahn, 2023), 43–67.

18 Don Gilmor, Achille Michaud, and Pierre Turgeon, *Canada: A People's History*, vol. 2 (Toronto: McClelland & Stewart, 2002), 145.

19 Gatrell, *Modern Refugee*, 101.

20 Arendt paraphrased in Gatrell, *Modern Refugee*, 77.

21 Liisa Malkki, "Refugees and Exile: From 'Refugee Studies' to the National Order of Things," *Annual Review of Anthropology* 24 (1995): 499–500.

22 William Hitchcock, *The Bitter Road to Freedom: A New History of the Liberation of Europe* (New York: Free Press, 2008), 320.

23 Escape through a hole in the perimeter fence did, however, permit visits to the town of Katowice, an impossibility under Nazi rule. Primo Levi, *The Reawakening*, trans. Stuart Woolf (New York: Touchstone, 1995), 70.

24 Roni Mikel-Arieli, "Cycles of Incarceration: From the 'Third Reich' through British Mandatory Palestine to Mauritius," in *Internment Refugee Camps: Historical and Contemporary Perspectives*, ed. Gabriele Anderl, Linda Erker and Christoph Reinprecht (Bielefeld: Transcript, 2023), 217, 226.

25 Gatrell, *Modern Refugee*, 103.

26 Gatrell, *Modern Refugee*, 168, 119.

27 Laura Robson, "Towards a Shared Practice of Encampment: An Historical Investigation of UNRWA and the UNHCR to 1967," *Journal of Refugee Studies* (2023): 13, https://doi.org/10.1093/jrs/feado45.

28 Maddalena Marinari, "Divided and Conquered: Immigration Reform Advocates and the Passage of the 1952 Immigration and Nationality Act," *Journal of American Ethnic History* 35, no. 3 (2016): 12.

29 Tehila Sasson, *The Solidarity Economy: Nonprofits and the Making of Neoliberalism after Empire* (Princeton: Princeton University Press, 2024).

30 Yến Lê Espiritu, "Refugee," in *Keywords for Asian American Studies*, ed. Cathy J. Schlund-Vials, Linda Trinh Võ, and K. Scott Wong (New York: NYU Press, 2015), 208.

31 Michel Agier, *Managing the Undesirables: Refugee Camps and Humanitarian Governance* (Cambridge: Polity, 2011), 144.

32 Liisa Malkki, "National Geographic: The Rooting of Peoples and the Territorialization of National Identity among Scholars and Refugees," *Cultural Anthropology* 7, no. 1 (1992): 31.

33 Liisa Malkki, *Purity and Exile: Violence, Memory, and National Cosmology among Hutu Refugees in Tanzania* (Chicago: University of Chicago Press, 1995), 119–20.

34 Malkki, *Purity and Exile*, 119–20.

35 Agier, *Managing the Undesirables*, 57–8.

36 Gaim Kibreab, "Resistance, Displacement, and Identity: The Case of Eritrean Refugees in Sudan," *Canadian Journal of African Studies* 34, no. 2 (2000): 278–9.

37 Gatrell, *Modern Refugee*, 245.

38 Merrill Smith, "Warehousing Refugees: A Denial of Rights, a Waste of Humanity," *World Refugee Survey* 2004 (Washington DC: US Committee for Refugees and Immigrants, 2004), 42.

39 Jennifer Hyndman, *Managing Displacement: Refugees and the Politics of Humanitarianism* (Minneapolis: University of Minnesota Press, 2000), 136.

40 Michel Agier, "Humanity as an Identity and Its Political Effects (A Note on Camps and Humanitarian Government)," *Humanity* 1, no. 1 (2010): 29.

41 Verdirame and Harrell-Bond, *Janus-Faced Humanitarianism*, 334.

42 Hannah Arendt, *The Origins of Totalitarianism* (New York: Harcourt, 1968), 287.

43 Hyndman, *Managing Displacement*, 139.

44 Agier, *Managing the Undesirables*, 111.

45 Gatrell, *Modern Refugee*, 208.

46 Patrick Kingsley, *The New Odyssey: The Story of Europe's Refugee Crisis* (London: Guardian Faber, 2016), 127.

47 Ben Rawlence, *City of Thorns: Nine Lives in the World's Largest Refugee Camp* (London: Picador, 2016), 113.

48 Hyndman, *Managing Displacement*, 124, 128.

49 Agier, *Managing the Undesirables*, 66.

50 A. Naomi Paik, "Carceral Quarantine at Guantanamo: Legacies of US Imprisonment of Haitian Refugees, 1991–1994," *Radical History Review* 115 (2013): 142.

51 Shelter Design Catalogue, UNHCR, accessed July 12, 2022, https://sheltercluster. s3.eu-central-1.amazonaws.com/public/4Biii%20-%20UNHCR%202016%20-%20 Shelter%20Design%20Catalogue.pdf.

52 "Refugee Population by Country or Territory of Asylum," accessed October 2, 2023, https://data.worldbank.org/indicator/SM.POP.REFG.

53 John Knudsen and Kjersti G. Berg, "Introduction" in Knudsen and Berg, *Continental Encampment*, 4.

54 Matthew Carr, *Fortress Europe: Dispatches from a Gated Continent* (New York: New Press, 2016).

55 Kingsley, *New Odyssey*, 267.

56 Jon Stone, "Katie Hopkins' Migrant 'Cockroaches' Article Resembles Pro-Genocide Propaganda," *Independent*, April 24, 2015, https://www.independent.co.uk/news/uk /politics/katie-hopkins-migrant-cockroaches-column-resembles-progenocide-propaganda -says-the-un-10201959.html.

57 "They Fired on Us Like Rain," Human Rights Watch, accessed August 22, 2023, https://www.hrw.org/report/2023/08/21/they-fired-us-rain/saudi-arabian-mass-killings-ethiopian-migrants-yemen-saudi.

58 Kingsley, *New Odyssey*, 104.

59 Suraina Pasha, "Humanitarianism, Securitization, and Containment in Jordan's Za'atari Refugee Camp," *British Journal of Sociology* 72, no. 4 (2021): 1145, 1148; Sophia Hoffmann, "Humanitarian Security in Jordan's Azraq Camp," *Security Dialogue* 48, no. 2 (2017): 103, 107, 108.

60 Rawlence, *City of Thorns*, 341.

61 Rawlence, *City of Thorns*, 113, 173.

62 Hoffman, "Humanitarian Security," 105; Keren Weitzberg, "Machine-Readable Refugees," *London Review of Books*, September 14, 2020, https://www.lrb.co.uk/blog/2020/september/machine-readable-refugees.

63 Vinay Lal, "The Concentration Camp and Development: The Pasts and Future of Genocide," *Patterns of Prejudice* 39, no. 20 (2005): 220.

64 Jennifer Jacobs and Justin Sink, "US to Send 5,200 Troops to Border as Migrant Caravan Nears," *Bloomberg News*, October 29, 2018, https://www.bloomberg.com/news/articles/2018-10-29/trump-is-said-to-plan-ordering-about-5-000-troops-to-border?in_source=embedded-checkout-banner.

65 Valeria Fernandez, "Arizona's 'Concentration Camp': Why Was Tent City Kept Open for 24 Years?," *The Guardian*, August 21, 2017, https://www.theguardian.com/cities/2017/aug/21/arizona-phoenix-concentration-camp-tent-city-jail-joe-arpaio-immigration.

66 Robert T. Chase, ed., *Caging Borders and Carceral States: Incarcerations, Immigration Detentions, and Resistance* (Chapel Hill: University of North Carolina Press, 2019).

67 Rebecca Shabad, "Trump on 'Poisoning the Blood' Remarks: 'I Never Knew That Hitler Said It,'" *NBC News*, December 22, 2023, https://www.nbcnews.com/politics/donald-trump/trump-poisoning-blood-remarks-never-knew-hitler-said-rcna130958; Charlie Savage, Maggie Haberman, and Jonathan Swan, "Sweeping Raids, Giant Camps and Mass Deportations: Inside Trump's 2025 Immigration Plans," *New York Times*, November 11, 2023, https://www.nytimes.com/2023/11/11/us/politics/trump-2025-immigration-agenda.html.

68 Tom Dreisbach, "Government's Own Experts Found 'Barbaric' and 'Negligent' Conditions in ICE Detention," *NPR*, August 16, 2023, https://www.npr.org/2023/08/16/1190767610/ice-detention-immigration-government-inspectors-barbaric-negligent-conditions.

69 George Takei, "'At Least During the Internment …' Are Words I Thought I'd Never Utter," *Foreign Policy*, June 19, 2018, https://foreignpolicy.com/2018/06/19/at-least-during-the-internment-are-words-i-thought-id-never-utter-family-separation-children-border/. Amid widespread criticism, the administration abandoned its plans to use Fort Sill.

70 Wilson Bell, "The Dreadful History of Children in Concentration Camps," *The Conversation*, June 20, 2018, https://theconversation.com/the-dreadful-history-of-children-in-concentration-camps-98549.

71 Stephen Charles, "Our Detention Centres Are Concentration Camps and Must Be Closed," *Sydney Morning Herald*, May 4, 2016, https://www.smh.com.au/opinion/our-detention-centres-are-intentionally-cruel-and-must-be-closed-20160504-golro4.html.

72 David Marr and Oliver Laughland, "Australia's Detention Regime Sets Out to Make Asylum-Seekers Suffer, Says Chief Immigration Psychiatrist," *The Guardian*, August 4, 2014, https://www.theguardian.com/world/2014/aug/05/-sp-australias-detention-regime-sets-out-to-make-asylum-seekers-suffer-says-chief-immigration-psychiatrist.

73 Verdirame and Harrell-Bond, *Janus-Faced Humanitarianism*, 271.

74 Calais Writers, *Voices from the "Jungle": Stories from the Calais Refugee Camp* (London: Pluto Press, 2017), 164.

Conclusion: Remembering and Forgetting

Whether for refugees or racial enemies, political prisoners or social undesirables, men, women, or children, camps are central features of the modern world. Arising from earlier institutions of confinement like prisons and workhouses, slave plantations and native reservations, they proliferated throughout the twentieth century and across the global landscape. At times, camps have been instruments of social engineering and rehabilitation, at other times of genocide and brutal retribution, and, still more commonly, of chaos and neglect. Though often depicted as instruments of totalitarian power – of the Holocaust in particular – camps are also products of colonial conquest, military occupation, and even humanitarian intervention. The diversity and ubiquity of camps across the modern world and across the ideological spectrum complicates efforts, from philosophers and historians alike, to define "the camp" according to a singular paradigm or unifying theory. Nonetheless, common themes hold together a diverse panorama. Languages of military combat (of invasions and enemies), of medicine (inmates, invariably, are a biopolitical threat, a contagion polluting the body politic), and even of gardening (the fencing off or cultivation of weeds) have framed numerous encampment operations. Discourses of race, often inherited from the colonial world, and the dynamics of revolution – where mass confinement, forced labor, and even genocide are justified as the means of a utopian end – have also underpinned many episodes of encampment, which invariably happen in moments of perceived emergency – of war, famine, political upheaval – or what the philosopher Giorgio Agamben calls a "state of exception."

Camps, ultimately, are microcosms of the societies that create them – of their aspirations and insecurities, their ideologies and inequalities. At base, the massive range of camps in the modern world stems from a fundamental need to control and contain the built and human environment – and from the corruption and brutality that often results. Marginalized inmates, identified as dangerous or suspect, and invariably stripped of rights, have suffered immensely. But they have also resisted and lived to bear witness. As constituent "others," they reveal the social, political, racial, and gendered prejudices that fostered their encampment, while their vulnerability underlines the abuse authorities often commit in total institutions where authority reigns unchecked. As historical artifacts, moreover, camps mark the rise and fall of nations and empires, of war and peace, of social crisis and political change. They take a central place in the narratives of modern history, and they highlight the transnational exchange of ideas and institutions, of technological transformation – from mud huts and primitive tents to barbed-wire barracks and high-tech "smart camps" – and of recurring patterns of repression and resistance. And though camps are the subjects of history, their memory informs culture and politics in the present. What, by way of conclusion, are the politics of remembering (and forgetting) encampment? How has the history and commemoration of camps been used and abused? And how might the mobilization of memory prevent (or facilitate) future camps?

Memory is neither objective nor straightforward but mediated by the politics of the present and contested by multiple constituencies. Though they are designed to isolate and disempower the putatively dangerous or marginal, camps have nonetheless been crucibles for the fashioning of national, ethnic, and political identities, often forged through shared memories of suffering and persecution. Though dangerous or suspect and segregated from the comity of humankind, inmates have nonetheless asserted their own agency. As Éamon de Valera, an Irish nationalist interned after the Easter Rebellion (1916, chap. 3), noted, the "concentration of some of our best men and women in jails and camps" offered a "wonderful opportunity for political discussions."[1] Examining refugee camps as sites "of continual creative subversion and transformation," the ethnographer Liisa Malkki likewise discovered that Hutu refugees billeted at camps in Congo and Tanzania expressed exclusive forms of collective and ethnic identity when compared to those outside, who assimilated with local populations.[2]

Encampment was similarly formative for Boer women and children, victims of the twentieth century's first "concentration camps" during the South African War (1899–1902, chap. 3). Framed by a politically potent, though factually dubious, "paradigm of suffering," camp memoirs like Elizabeth Neethling's *Should We Forget?* (1903) became central texts of an emerging Afrikaner nationalism. With the erection of Bloemfontein's "Women's Monument" in 1913, official state commemoration supplanted private memory, and by the 1950s, the conversion of individual campsites into *Gedenktuin*, "gardens of memory," reconstituted inmates as nationalist martyrs united in death to country and race. By visiting these shrines, white South Africans mobilized a strategic sense of victimhood, one that emphasized the suffering of women and children while possessing and projecting power over a country increasingly contested by Black liberation forces – whose leaders, imprisoned on Robben Island or confined to segregated townships and Bantustans (chap. 7), developed their own national identity. What official commemoration left out, however, was the presence of Black Africans, who were also concentrated in British camps. Nationalism, after all, depends on forgetting history as much as remembering it. While South Africa's apartheid-era state engaged in historical "whitewashing," the Black-majority "rainbow nation" of Nelson Mandela mobilized a narrative of "mutual suffering" that reinserted the Black experience into the history of Boer War camps during the 1990s.[3] The specter of the camp has informed postcolonial politics elsewhere in Africa, too. Following Kenyan independence in 1960, the British state destroyed files relating to torture and abuse at detention camps and guarded villages, while President Kenyatta (once imprisoned as a Mau Mau leader, chap. 7) worked hard to reconcile loyalists and rebels, even going so far as to label Mau Mau "a disease which has been eradicated," and which "must never be remembered again." Amnesia served the early politics of reconciliation in war-torn Kenya: the past would be buried rather than dug up. Yet the activism of future generations brought awareness of British concentration camps back into the spotlight. Reparations claims before the British High Court in 2009, supported by Caroline Elkins, David Anderson, and other historians of Britain's "imperial gulag," resulted in a payment of £19.9 million to 5,000 Kenyan survivors, along with a public monument in Nairobi. Britain's foreign secretary, William Hague, apologized for "harsh prison regimes," "detention without trial," and "shocking levels of violence," but omitted specific details – castration with a pair of pliers, rape with a glass bottle – that generated the settlement.[4] Nonetheless, guarded statements of remorse and complacent gestures to "forgive and forget" have not significantly altered popular nostalgia in Britain, which still regards imperial history as a marker of past glory.

Legal action has also informed memory of American and Canadian concentration camps. In 1988, the Civil Liberties Act acknowledged the fundamental injustice of the evacuation, relocation, and internment of Japanese Americans and provided each survivor with $20,000 in reparations; Canada followed suit with a similar package. Activism from public figures, like the Canadian poet Joy Kogawa, whose critically acclaimed novel *Obasan* has been adapted as a children's book and lyric opera, has raised public awareness, along with the actor George Takei's graphic novel *They Called Us Enemy*, which updated an artistic form pioneered by Miné Okubo's *Citizen 13660* (chap. 7). Heeding's Okubo's opening inscription – "I hope that things can be learned from this tragic episode, for I believe it could happen again"[5] – monuments at former camps like Manzanar have reclaimed the American landscape as a space of commemoration, though their remote locations makes public visits difficult. Opened in 2022, a memorial at the Tanforan Assembly Center, now the San Bruno rail station in suburban San Francisco (through which this author regularly though unwittingly passed as a graduate student), will facilitate memory at a more accessible site.[6]

In contrast to Japanese Americans, however, redress for Black and Native Americans, victims of older yet more enduring regimes of mass confinement, has been more gradual and contentious, though memories of plantations, slave ships, and transit camps on the Trail of Tears (chap. 2) may well inform future reparations. To this end, some Native Americans have embraced the terminology of "concentration camps" to describe their own histories of forced removal and confinement,[7] while analogies between America's prison-industrial complex and the Soviet Gulag, albeit polemical, have informed serious scholarship on America's racialized "plea-to-prison pipeline."[8] In Canada, likewise, former residential schools have been rallying points for truth and reconciliation. The province of Alberta, for example, promised $1 million in funding in 2021 to build a monument commemorating residential school victims. Echoing Mau Mau survivors, however, Indigenous activists emphasize that decolonization depends on the restitution of land and property rather than the erection of monuments.

In America as elsewhere, memory is contested, and camps are fodder for contemporary culture wars. A fortified far right has propagated apologetic histories that celebrate the achievements of white settlers and plantation owners while glossing over the violence of slavery and Native removals. The report of the *1776 Project* (2021), written by conservative activists rather than professional historians, expunged narratives of racial injustice from American history even as migrant detention camps embraced racial profiling on the southern border. Meanwhile, the controversial political commentator Michelle Malkin's startling 2004 book *In Defense of Internment* defended the encampment of Japanese Americans as a template for future extrajudicial confinements, including of Arab Americans during the "war on terror." It is unclear whether "educational propagandists" have ever equated Japanese internment with Nazi death camps as Malkin contends, but the nomenclature "concentration camp" remains so tethered to the specter of Auschwitz that it elicits an emotive backlash whenever it is applied to camps for other demographics. The semantic furor that surrounded the left-wing American congresswoman Alexandria Ocasio-Cortez's comparison, on Twitter, of migrant detention facilities to "concentration camps" in 2019, or controversy over similar statements made by Pope Francis, are cases in point.[9] Yet while a euphemistic vocabulary of "relocation centers" and "detention facilities" has emerged in the United States, scholars like Roger Daniels and Andrea Pitzer argue the term "concentration camp," whose historical usage extends far beyond Nazi Germany, better captures the detention of Japanese Americans and today's racialized asylum-seekers.[10]

Such debates indicate that Nazi camps remain powerful cultural icons. For Jewish victims, as for other encamped people, *Konzentrationslager* were horrifying containers that nonetheless framed cohesive national and political identities – Auschwitz's mandate to erase Jewish inmates from history, then, was clearly counterproductive. In 1952, West Germany paid reparations to the state of Israel, as heir to Jewish victims of Nazism, of $107 million. More than money, however, collective memory of Nazi camps has facilitated a cohesive ethnic-Jewish identity among a diverse and multicultural population. Concentrating Jews from Norway to North Africa, and from Italy to Ukraine, Auschwitz, after all, constituted a "perpetual Babel" of languages and cultures, Primo Levi wrote, yet one united by narratives of shared suffering and survival. Yad Vashem, Israel's national Holocaust Museum, and Jerusalem's Chamber of the Holocaust, a site of rich Zionist symbolism, place the Nazi camp experience at the center of postwar Jewish identity, as does the memorial at Atlit, which traces the history of Jewish internment under the British Empire. Such commemorative practices help victims claim membership in a larger collectivity while processing individual trauma – as do pilgrimages to the ruined wooden barracks of Malaysian and Indonesian refugee camps undertaken by Vietnamese boat people, or visits to Khmer killing fields and the Tsitsernakaberd Armenian Genocide Memorial.

The mobilization of memory also serves an urgent moral role, for to forget the crimes of history is to risk repeating them. "Never again" adorns

Holocaust memorials across the Western world, though whether the slogan is a particular command to prevent a second Jewish Holocaust or a universal injunction against mass confinement in its many forms depends on whether one believes Nazi camps to be a singular event in human history or the especially lethal manifestation of a wider malady. Whatever the case, memories of Nazi persecution have, arguably, framed Israel's often brutal military occupation of Palestine, particularly after flashpoints of antisemitic violence, like the Hamas attacks of October 7, 2023. Never again would Jews be victims, forced out of their homes, Israeli leaders proclaim – much as memory of Boer War concentration camps, a far less brutal manifestation of encampment, fortified uncompromising measures in apartheid South Africa. Detained behind security fences and concentrated in refugee camps, meanwhile, Palestinians have ironically generated their own identity based on analogous narratives of exile and exclusion. Embracing the camp as a symbol of their oppression, Palestinian artists and activists have installed refugee tents in foreign museums to bring awareness to Palestine's plight.[11]

How have camps informed the politics of postwar Germany and Europe? Disturbing footage taken by American and Soviet forces liberating Buchenwald, Dachau, and Auschwitz featured prominently at the Nuremburg Trials (1945–6), which sentenced the Auschwitz commandant Rudolf Höss to death by hanging at a gallows facing the camp crematorium. In the aftermath of war, however, public commemoration was slow. Though bestsellers today, elegant memoirs by Primo Levi and Elie Wiesel originally struggled to find publishers. Still pockmarked with DP camps, postwar Europe (like postcolonial Kenya) was uninterested in remembering wartime traumas. Alain Resnais's award-winning film *Night and Fog* (1956), however, drew new attention to concentration camps, as did the 1960 trial of the senior Nazi official Adolf Eichmann, which induced Hannah Arendt to coin the phrase "banality of evil" to describe the emotionless, systematic way in which Nazi functionaries followed orders. As a public media spectacle, the trial triggered wider debates about antisemitism, collaboration, societal complicity, and the psychology of groupthink. The 1960s also witnessed the first academic histories of Nazi camps, while Dachau, Sachsenhausen, and other campsites were converted into museums following the resettlement of their final DP inhabitants. In the age of mass air travel, many are now major tourist sites. Visiting Auschwitz-Birkenau on a sunny summer's day is an educational but uncanny experience: orderly and enormous piles of human hair and gold teeth extracted from murder victims shock visitors into realizing the Holocaust's system and scale. Museums commemorating other sites of confinement, from Sydney's Hyde Park Barracks and Green Island penal colony in Taiwan, to the Kimberley mining museum and Victorian workhouses converted into boutique hotels offer less gruesome variations of "camp tourism."

With the exception of fringe conspiracy theorists, Europeans generally accept the facts about Nazi concentration camps. But their interpretation has generated controversy. The *Historikerstreit* ("historians' debate") of the 1980s witnessed vigorous exchanges concerning the place of camps specifically and the Holocaust more generally within German and European history. Were Nazi camps unique, or could they be compared to the Soviet Gulag and other enclosures? Did German history follow a "special path" (*Sonderweg*), or could the Nazi experience be assimilated into global and comparative histories of racial violence and mass confinement? Art Spiegelman's Pulitzer Prize-winning *Maus: A Survivor's Tale* (1991), like graphic novels by Okubo and Takei, exposed new generations to debates about memory, representation, and transgenerational trauma. And while the Jewish experience continued to dominate public commemoration, memorials recognizing homosexuals (2008), Roma and Sinti (2012), and other victims of Nazi camps have recently enriched Berlin's monumental landscape.

But does a focus on Nazi atrocities overshadow awareness of other camps and other crimes? Commemoration of *Konzentrationslager* in colonial South-West Africa has been more fleeting. An official apology in 2004 for the Nama and Herero genocide ruled out financial compensation for victims, while a 2021 statement from Germany's foreign minister was carefully crafted to avoid admission of legal culpability. It did not consult individual survivors or African community leaders, or address the lingering inequities – of land ownership and resource access – entailed by settler-colonial dispossession. The return to Namibia of human skulls, collected in concentration camps and used in Berlin for eugenic research, and the replacement of Berlin's colonial-era Ethnological Museum by the more progressive Humboldt Forum do, however, suggest future directions for reconciliation.

"Memory wars" have animated public debate elsewhere in Europe, particularly when the messy history of wartime concentration camps complicates edifying narratives of resistance and victimhood. In Poland, legislation in 2018 outlawed the term "Polish concentration camp" and criminalized discussion of Polish-Nazi collaboration. In France, however, President Jacques Chirac's official apology in 1995 for France's detention and deportation of Jewish children laid foundations for broader social awareness of French complicity in the Holocaust. Commemorative plaques now adorn public schools across the country, while films like *Les Milles* (1995) and documentaries like *Les camps du silence* (1988) or *Gurs, un silence assourdissant* (2017) depict wartime camps in France to the general public. As in Germany, however, colonial camps are largely forgotten. While revelations about brutal conditions at Algerian *regroupement* centers motivated France's political left to embrace anticolonial politics, embittered settlers returning to France formed an influential political base for the racist, far-right National Front. *Harkis*, Algerians who fought for France, have recently received compensation for their postwar dispossession. Yet French schoolbooks rarely address *regroupement* and detention camps in Algeria, prompting President Macron to concede the Algerian War "is today absent from our political memory."[12] Commemorative gaps have thus opened space for continuing practices of racial exclusion – Algerian migrants and their descendants often live in segregated *banlieue*, or urban ghettos, and face police brutality and racial profiling. Nonetheless, rival "truth inquiries," appointed by the French and Algerian governments in 2021, along with touring public art exhibits, like *Discrete Violence* (2017–18) by the architectural historian Samia Henni, or Dorothée-Myriam Kellou's recent podcast, "L'Algérie des camps," and film, *À Mansourah, tu nous as séparés* (2020), promise to bring new attention to the history of colonial concentration.[13]

Whatever its shortcomings, widespread awareness and condemnation of concentration camps in western Europe has fortified postwar liberal democracy. Driven by a sense of collective guilt and responsibility for Jewish refugees in World War II, Germany's embrace of more than a million Syrian asylum-seekers in 2015 highlighted its successful de-Nazification. Russia, unfortunately, presents a stark contrast. Condemnation and commemoration of Nazi concentration camps in Soviet-occupied Europe perpetuated heroic myths that Communism alone had defeated fascism, but it failed to recognize analogies with the Gulag, which continued to expand after World War II and even repurposed some former Nazi camps. The death of Stalin in 1953 permitted amnesties for many Gulag prisoners, but it was not until *Glasnost* reforms in the 1980s that the Soviet public embraced an honest and open discussion of Gulag crimes. To this end, the power of words cannot be understated. First published in Paris in 1974 after being smuggled out of Russia, Alexandr Solzhenitsyn's *Gulag Archipelago* constituted a powerful indictment of the Soviet regime and the concentration camps that symbolized it. In 1989, its official release in the Soviet Union arguably brought down an empire – much as revelations about camp atrocities in

Kenya and Algeria delegitimized the colonial empires of Britain and France. Recognizing unsettling parallels, American authorities at Guantanamo Bay reportedly banned the book in 2013.[14] Meanwhile, Russia's Nobel Prize-winning human rights organization Memorial documented Stalin's crimes, of which the Gulag formed the centerpiece. Throughout the 1990s, conferences gathered Gulag survivors to publicize their experiences. Moscow's Gulag History Museum opened in 2001, while a virtual Museum of the Gulag, based in St. Petersburg, assembled artifacts and testimonials. Moreover, the opening of Soviet archives to foreign historians yielded nuanced studies that confirmed some of the findings of political dissidents and polemical "Cold War warriors" like Robert Conquest, who emphasized the Gulag's unrelenting brutality, while also highlighting histories of ordinary criminals and special settlements – softer iterations of the Gulag that complicate stark contrasts between good and evil.

If 1989 promised an end to Communist camps, however, it was less than a rupture than originally hoped. The Tiananmen Square protests failed to dismantle China's repressive penal architecture, and the PRC's diplomatic cover to Pyongyang, including its opposition to a 2014 UN Investigative Committee, ensures the perpetuation of the North Korean gulag. And while politicized shrines celebrate the "revolutionary martyrs" detained at Xifeng concentration camp under Chiang Kai-shek, public commemoration of laogai life in Communist China remains confined to expatriate dissidents like Harry Wu, founder of the Laogai Museum and Research Center in Washington, DC. In a revival of Maoist dictatorship, Xi Jinping's China has increasingly criminalized dissent while rejecting criticism of China's human rights abuses as Western propaganda. Political survival in contemporary China thus depends on "knowing what not to know" – and that includes the laogai.[15] Uyghur concentration camps in Xinjiang are a direct result.

The commemoration of Soviet camps, meanwhile, was always incomplete: only one Gulag outpost (outside the city of Perm, east of Moscow) was ever transformed into a museum, while the Kolyma Peninsula remains an unmarked graveyard of exposed bones bleached by the Arctic sun. And as Vladimir Putin, empowered by his collaboration with China, North Korea, and other rogue states, embraces a renewed politics of imperial aggression, Russia has actively rehabilitated the Soviet Empire as a symbol of past greatness. To sustain the myth, Soviet-era archives (with the exception of those in Ukraine and the Baltics) are now largely closed, and Stalin regularly tops polls asking Russians to name the country's greatest historical leader. Remembering, then, can only happen when the past is the past – and in Putin's Russia, Stalinist repression, including the mass detention of political prisoners in Siberia, defines the present. Though Putin has, at times, strategically harnessed Gulag memory in the service of a nationalist narrative controlled by the state, the confiscation of Memorial's archives in 2008 was prelude to the organization's full dismantling in December 2021. Two months later, Russian troops invaded Ukraine in Europe's largest war of imperial aggression since World War II.

In the last two years, Russian detention camps in occupied Ukraine recall post-World War II filtration camps erected to register, interrogate, and indoctrinate civilians. Sorting populations by ethnicity and loyalty, they also perform an analogous function to the camps of colonial counterinsurgencies. The discovery of mass graves, of burnt corpses and bodies buried alive, exemplifies the shocking violence of Russian "cleansing" (*zachistka*) operations, prompting the Ukrainian Ministry of Defense to condemn a secret Russian torture chamber as a "mini-Auschwitz."[16] Meanwhile, the forced deportation of 1.6 million Ukrainian citizens, including 250,000 children, to the Russian hinterland recalls Stalin's forced deportations of Ukrainians, Crimeans, kulaks, and other "anti-Soviet" groups during and after World War II.

The politics of the present often frames the way we remember the past. Nonetheless, some historical accounts are more accurate than others. Nations that actively admit and learn from their mistakes, that document and discuss them, that tolerate free speech and civil society, are far less likely to repeat them, as the present-day contrast between Germany and Russia (as well as China) suggests. Yet the history of mass confinement extends far beyond the "evil empires" of the twentieth (and twenty-first) centuries. Though democratic norms and legal safeguards can limit human rights abuses, no regime has entirely escaped the camp, as the mass confinement of refugees and the migrant detention centers of Europe and America attest. This book is written in hopes that a more global history – one that examines camps not only in Soviet Russia, or Nazi Germany, or Communist China, but in democratic and colonial regimes, from Britain to South Africa, from Israel to America, from Australia to Japan – will serve the mandates of public memory, historical awareness, and ultimately, of truth, justice, and reconciliation.

Notes

1 Padraic Kenney, *Dance in Chains: Political Imprisonment in the Modern World* (Oxford: Oxford University Press, 2017), 239.

2 Liisa Malkki, *Purity and Exile: Violence, Memory, and National Cosmology among Hutu Refugees in Tanzania* (Chicago: University of Chicago Press, 1995), 237.

3 Liz Stanley, *Mourning Becomes ... Post/Memory, Commemoration and the Concentration Camps of the South African War* (Manchester: Manchester University Press, 2006).

4 "Kenya's Mau Mau Uprising: Victims Tell Their Stories," *BBC*, June 6, 2013, https://www.bbc.co.uk/news/uk-22797624; William Hague, "Statement to Parliament on Settlement of Mau Mau Claims," June 6, 2013, https://www.gov.uk/government/news/statement-to-parliament-on-settlement-of-mau-mau-claims.

5 Miné Okubo, *Citizen 13660* (New York: Columbia University Press, 1946), xii.

6 "Tanforan Memorial Project," San Bruno Community Foundation, accessed December 12, 2022, https://www.sbcf.org/tanforam-memorial#:~:text=The%20memorial%20features%20a%20replica,of%20the%208%2C000%20former%20incarcerees.

7 "About Us," Tolowa Dee-Ni' Nation, accessed December 11, 2022, https://www.tolowa-nsn.gov/35/About-Us.

8 Ruth Gilmore, *Golden Gulag: Prisons, Surplus, Crisis, and Opposition in Globalizing California* (Berkeley: University of California Press, 2007).

9 Aidan Forth, "Concentration Camps Have Deep Roots in Liberal Democracies," *The Conversation*, October 15, 2019, https://theconversation.com/concentration-camps-have-deep-roots-in-liberal-democracies-124340; Cleve R. Wootson, "Pope Francis Called Refugee Centers Concentration Camps. A Jewish Group Says There's No Comparison," *Washington Post*, April 23, 2017, https://www.washingtonpost.com/news/acts-of-faith/wp/2017/04/23/pope-francis-called-refugee-centers-concentration-camps-a-jewish-group-says-theres-no-comparison/.

10 Roger Daniels, "Words Do Matter: A Note on Inappropriate Terminology and the Incarceration of the Japanese Americans," in *Nikkei in the Pacific Northwest: Japanese Americans and Japanese Canadians in the Twentieth Century*, ed. Louis Fiset and Gail Nomura (Seattle: University of Washington Press, 2005); Pitzer quoted in Jack Holmes, "An Expert on Concentration Camps Says That's Exactly What the US Is Running at the Border," *Esquire*, June 13, 2019, https://www.esquire.com/news-politics/a27813648/concentration-camps-southern-border-migrant-detention-facilities-trump/.

11 "Emily Jacir," Station Museum of Contemporary Art, accessed December 8, 2022, https://stationmuseum.com/past-exhibitions/made-in-palestine/emily-jacir/#:~:text=Her%20refugee%20tent%2C%20rough%20and,bulldozers%20regularly%20demolish%20Palestinian%20homes; "Palestinian Art: Resilience and Inspiration," Zawyeh Gallery,accessedDecember8,2022,https://zawyeh.net/palestinian-art-resilience-and-inspiration/.

12 Nabila Ramdani, "Algeria Needs an Apology and Reparations from France – Not a History Lesson," *The Guardian*,July31,2022,https://www.theguardian.com/commentisfree/2020/jul/31/algeria-apology-reparations-france-history-emmanuel-macron.

13 Samia Henni, "Discreet Violence: Architecture and the French War in Algeria," accessed August 31, 2023, https://www.samiahenni.com/exhibits.html; Dorothée-Myriam Kellou and Thomas Dutter, "L'Algérie des Camps," October 6, 2020, in *Enquête à la 1ere personne*, produced by Pascaline Bonnet and Camille Renard, *France Culture*, podcast, https://www.radiofrance.fr/franceculture/podcasts/serie-l-algerie-des-camps.

14 Nicholas Clairmont, "US Military Prison Officials at Guantanamo Ban a Book Criticizing the Soviet Gulag System," *Politics & Current Affairs*, August 21, 2013.

15 Margaret Hillenbrand, *Negative Exposures: Knowing What Not to Know in Contemporary China* (Durham: Duke University Press, 2020).

16 Sam Sokol, "Russia Ran a 'Mini-Auschwitz' in Recently Liberated Ukrainian City, Ministry Says," *Haaretz*, October 6, 2022, https://www.haaretz.com/world-news/europe/2022-10-06/ty-article/.highlight/russia-ran-a-mini-auschwitz-in-recently-liberated-ukrainian-city-ministry-says/00000183-acaf-d57e-a79f-efffdad50000. Many Russian atrocities have been independently verified, though allegations about gold teeth pulled from torture victims is likely false.

Annotated Bibliography

Introduction

Andre Kaminski's *Konzentrationslager 1896 bis heute: Eine Analyse* (Stuttgart: W. Kohlhammer, 1982) offered an early foray into the global history of camps, as did Joël Kotek and Pierre Rigolout's more substantial *Le Siècle des Camps: Detention, concentration, extermination, cent ans de mal radical* (Paris: JC Lattes, 2000). In English, Dan Stone, *Concentration Camps: A Short History* (Oxford: Oxford University Press, 2017), and the journalist Andrea Pitzer's *One Long Night: A Global History of Concentration Camps* (New York: Little, Brown, and Company, 2017) provide general overviews, though these works are less comparative or transnational than the current book. Edited volumes like Colman Hogan and Marta Marin-Domine (eds.), *The Camp: Narratives of Internment and Exclusion* (Newcastle: Cambridge Scholars Publishing, 2007), and Alan Kramer and Bettina Greiner (eds.), *Welt der Lager: Zur "Erfolgsgeschichte" einer Institution* (Hamburg: Hamburger Edition, 2013), offer useful contributions that approach camps as diverse global institutions with histories that preceded and outlasted the totalitarian dictatorships of World War II. Charlie Hailey's *Camps: A Guide to 21st-Century Space* (Cambridge: MIT Press, 2009) challenges readers to consider the definitional boundaries of "the camp." *Behind Barbed Wire: An Encyclopedia of Concentration and Prisoner-of-War Camps* (Santa Barbara: ABC-CLIO, 2019) by Alexander Mikaberidze provides a useful reference with an international framework. The most influential theoretical works are Hannah Arendt, *The Origins of Totalitarianism* (New York: Harcourt, 1968); Zygmunt Bauman, *Modernity and the Holocaust* (Ithaca: Cornell University Press, 1989); and Giorgio Agamben's *State of Exception*, trans. Kevin Attell (Chicago: University of Chicago Press, 2005) and *Homo Sacer: Sovereign Power and Bare Life*, trans. Daniel Heller-Roazen (Stanford: Stanford University Press, 1998).

Chapter 1: Industrial Enclosure

Influenced by the historiographical trends of social history and the compelling arguments of Michel Foucault's *Discipline and Punish: Birth of the Prison*, trans. Alan Sheridan (New York: Vintage, 1995, first published in 1975), the history of prisons is well established. Michael Ignatieff's classic *A Just Measure of Pain: The Penitentiary in the Industrial Revolution, 1750–1850* (New York: Pantheon Books, 1978) roots prisons in the reformist impulses of the Enlightenment and industrial revolution. Patricia O'Brien, *The Promise of Punishment: Prisons in Nineteenth-Century France* (Princeton: Princeton University Press, 1982), and David Rothman, *Discovery of the Asylum: Social Order and Disorder in the New Republic* (New York: de Gruyter, 2002), do the same for France and America respectively. David Garland's *Punishment and Modern Society: A Study in Social Theory* (Chicago: University of Chicago Press, 1990) provides a theoretical primer. Workhouses are rooted in similar historiographical traditions. Norman Longmate, *The Workhouse* (London: Pimlico, 2003), offers a classic account; Peter Higginbotham's website www.workhouses.org.uk includes images and excerpts of relevant primary sources. Barbara Arneil's *Domestic Colonies: The Turn Inward to Colony* (Oxford: Oxford University Press, 2017) outlines the history of labor colonies, while Ann Laura Stoler's *Duress: Imperial Durabilities in Our Times* (Durham: Duke University Press, 2016) offers a theoretical assessment. In the past two decades, scholars have turned to the transnational development of prisons as instruments of social and racial control, particularly in the colonial world. Frank Dikötter and Ian Brown (eds.), *Cultures of Confinement: A History of the Prison in Africa, Asia, and Latin America* (Ithaca: Cornell University Press, 2007); Florence Bernault (ed.), *A History of Prison and Confinement in Africa* (Portsmouth, NH: Heinemann, 2003); and Peter Zinoman, *The Colonial Bastille: A History of Imprisonment in Vietnam, 1862–1940* (Berkeley: University of California Press, 2001), provide comparative, transnational insight. Though classic narratives highlight the ways in which prisons replaced older modes of punishment like execution and banishment, Christian De Vito and Alex Lichtenstein's *Global Convict Labour* (Leiden: Brill, 2015) and Clare Anderson's edited volume, *A Global History of Convicts and Penal Colonies* (London: Bloomsbury, 2018), arising out of the international research consortium "Carchipelago" (https://staffblogs.le.ac.uk/carchipelago/), establishes the penal colony as a long-lasting transnational form of punishment and exile. Anderson's volume provocatively assimilates twentieth-century practices like the Soviet Gulag into longer traditions of penal exile. Finally, Alison Bashford and Carolyn Strange (eds.), *Isolation: Places and Practices of Exclusion* (London: Routledge, 2003), provide an interdisciplinary and transnational array of essays considering a broad range of carceral institutions that preceded twentieth-century camps.

Chapter 2: Colonial Compartments

Chapter 2 assembles research from a broad range of fields. Carl Nightingale's transnational *Segregation: A Global History of Divided Cities* (Chicago: University of Chicago Press, 2012) highlights the ubiquity of segregationist practices throughout world history; David Stannard's *American Holocaust: The Conquest of the New World* (Oxford: Oxford University Press, 1992) makes sometimes polemical connections between Indigenous confinement and twentieth-century violence. Literature on slavery is immense, though an emphasis on personal narratives, as in Richard Dunn's comparative *A Tale of Two Plantations: Slave Life and Labor in Jamaica and Virginia* (Cambridge: Harvard University Press, 2014), dominates over institutional histories of the plantation as a site of confinement. Along with technical manuals listed in the endnotes, John Michael Vlach's *Back of the Big House: The Architecture of Plantation Slavery* (Chapel Hill: University of North Carolina Press, 1993) highlights plantation architecture and management. Stanley Elkins's thought-provoking but controversial comparison between slave plantations and Nazi concentration camps, *Slavery: A Problem in American Institutional and Intellectual Life* (Chicago: University of Chicago Press, 1959), is worth consideration. Markus Rediker's *The Slave Ship: A Human History* (New York: Penguin, 2008) is an influential account of the ship as a carceral site. Alex Lichtenstein's *Twice the Work of Free Labor: The Political Economy of Convict Labor in the New South* (New York: Verso, 1996), Ruth Wilson Gilmore's *The Golden Gulag: Prisons, Surplus, Crisis, and Opposition in Globalizing California* (Berkeley: University of California Press, 2007), and Michelle Alexander's bestselling *The New Jim Crow: Mass Incarceration in the Age of Colorblindness* (New York: New Press, 2020) trace continuities between slavery and prisons. The ethnic cleansing of Indigenous peoples in North America and Australia is well documented. James Daschuk's *Clearing the Plains: Disease, Politics of Starvation and the Loss of Indigenous Life* (Regina: University of Regina Press, 2019); Benjamin Madley's *An American Genocide: The United States and the California Indian Catastrophe, 1846–1873* (New Haven: Yale University Press, 2017); and Theda Perdue and Michael D. Green's classic *The Cherokee Nation and the Trail of Tears* (New York: Penguin, 2008) are influential narratives. Less scholarship is available about reserves and reservations as institutions, though N. Cole Harris, *Making Native Space: Colonialism, Resistance, and Reserves in British Columbia* (Vancouver: UBC Press, 2011), provides a thoughtful introduction. Dirk Moses's theoretically sophisticated anthology *Genocide and Settler Society: Frontier Violence and Stolen Indigenous Children in Australian History* (New York: Berghahn, 2004) and Peter Read's *Settlement: A History of Australian Indigenous Housing* (Canberra: Aboriginal Studies Press, 2000) highlight Aboriginal confinement in Australia. Residential schools have attracted intense public interest, particularly in Canada, where the *Report of the Truth and Reconciliation Commission of Canada: Volume I, Canada's Residential Schools* (Montreal: McGill-Queen's University Press, 2015) assembles the latest findings. John S. Millow, *A National Crime: The Canadian Government and the Residential School System, 1879–1986* (Winnipeg: University of Manitoba Press, 2017) and David Adams, *Education for Extinction: American Indians and the Boarding School Experience* (Lawrence: University of Kansas Press, 2000) are the best academic overviews. Alex William's film *The Pass System* (2015; http://thepasssystem.ca/) and Tim Wolochatiuk's *We Were Children* (2012; https://www.nfb.ca/film/we_were_children/) highlight the experience of those interned.

Chapter 3: Military Captivity

For the "total war" dynamics that facilitated mass confinement, see David Bell, *The First Total War: Napoleon's Europe and the Birth of Warfare as We Know It* (Boston: Houghton Mifflin, 2007) and Drew Gilpin Faust, *This Republic of Suffering: Death and the American Civil War* (New York: Alfred A. Knopf, 2009). The POW camps of the American Civil War have an enormous scholarship. R.S. Davis, *Ghosts and Shadows of Andersonville: Essays on the Secret Social Histories of America's Deadliest Prison* (Macon, GA: Mercer University Press, 2006), and James M. Gillispie, *Andersonvilles of the North: The Myths and Realities of Northern Treatment of Civil War Confederate Prisoners* (Denton, TX: University of Northern Texas Press, 2012), highlight conditions in Union and Confederate enclosures. Roger Pickenpaugh examines voices of those interned in *Captives in Blue: The Civil War Prisons of the Confederacy* (Tuscaloosa: University of Alabama Press, 2013). Contraband camps deserve more attention, though Chandra Manning, in *Troubled Refuge: Struggling for Freedom in the Civil War* (New York: Alfred A. Knopf, 2016), provides an important introduction. Concentration camps in colonial Africa have received significant attention in the past decade. For the South African War, see Aidan Forth, *Barbed-Wire Imperialism: Britain's Empire of Camps, 1876–1903* (Berkeley: University of California Press, 2017), and Elizabeth van Heyningen, *The Concentration Camps of the Anglo-Boer War: A Social History* (Auckland Park: Jacana Media, 2013); van Heyningen's comprehensive website at https://www2.lib.uct.ac.za/mss/bccd/ provides an excellent research database. David Olusoga and Casper W. Erichsen's *The Kaiser's Holocaust: Germany's Forgotten Genocide and the Colonial Roots of Nazism* (London: Faber and Faber, 2010) is the most comprehensive history of German South-West African camps; the BBC documentary *Namibia: Genocide and the Second Reich* (2005; https://www.youtube.com/watch?v=Rbon6HqzjEI) showcases many of its findings. Isabel Hull's classic *Absolute Destruction: Military Culture and the Practices of War in Imperial Germany* (Ithaca: Cornell University Press, 2006) compares British and German camps, assesses why the latter were more deadly, and suggests ways in which colonial practices informed German militarism in World War I and World War II. Jonas Kreienbaum's *A Sad Fiasco: Colonial Concentration Camps in Southern Africa, 1900–1906*, trans. Elizabeth Janik (New York: Berghahn, 2019) also compares British and German colonial camps. Articles like Jonathan Hyslop, "The Invention of the Concentration Camp: Cuba, Southern Africa and the Philippines, 1896–1907," *South African Historical Journal* 63, no. 2 (2011): 251–76; Iain Smith and Andreas Stucki, "The Colonial Development of Concentration Camps (1868–1902)," *Journal of Imperial and Commonwealth History* 39, no. 3 (2011): 417–37; and Sibylle Scheipers, "The Use of Camps in Colonial Warfare," *Journal of Imperial and Commonwealth History* 43, no. 4 (2015): 678–98, place colonial camps within the transnational framework of military counterinsurgency. Literature on military captivity in World War I is vast. Multiple publications by Matthew Stibbe, including *Civilian Internment during the First World War: A European and Global History, 1914–20* (London: Palgrave Macmillan, 2019); Heather Jones, particularly

254 | Annotated Bibliography

Violence against Prisoners of War in the First World War: Britain, France, and Germany, 1914–1920 (Cambridge: Cambridge University Press, 2013); and Alon Rachmaninov, *POWs and the Great War: Captivity on the Eastern Front* (Oxford: Berg, 2002), are influential overviews. Multiple publications by Panikos Panayi place internment within broader histories of antimigrant xenophobia; Stefan Manz, Panikos Panayi, and Matthew Stibbe (eds.), *Internment during the First World War: A Mass Global Phenomenon* (London: Routeledge, 2020), and Panayi and Manz, *Enemies in the Empire: Civilian Internment in the British Empire during the First World War* (Oxford: Oxford University Press, 2020), bring a global framework to a topic often dominated by Eurocentric narratives. Raymond Kevorkian examines camps during the Armenian genocide in Part V, chaps. 4–5 of *The Armenian Genocide: A Complete History* (London: I.B. Tauris, 2011).

Chapter 4: The Soviet Gulag

Wilson Bell assesses the rich and varied scholarship in "Gulag Historiography: An Introduction," *Gulag Studies* 2–3 (2009–10): 1–20; Michael David-Fox (ed.), *The Soviet Gulag: Evidence, Interpretation and Comparison* (Pittsburgh: Pittsburgh University Press, 2014), and Alan Barenburg and Emily Johnson (eds.), *Rethinking the Gulag: Identities, Sources, Legacies* (Bloomington: Indiana University Press, 2022), compile recent approaches. Early scholarship relied on memoirs written by political prisoners. These include Alexandr Solzhenitsyn's three-volume *The Gulag Archipelago: An Experiment in Literary Investigation*, trans. Thomas P. Whitney (New York: Harper Perennial, 1974–78), which portrayed the camps as symptoms of Soviet moral decay; so did his novel *One Day in the Life of Ivan Denisovich* (1962) and its 1970 and 2021 film adaptations. Other memoirs, many of which are cataloged at https://sarahjyoung.com/site/gulag-bibliography/gulag-bibliography-english-language-texts-and-translations/, include works by Evgenia Ginzburg, Margarete Buber-Neumann, Michael Solomon, Varlam Shalamov, Dmitry Likhachov, and Jacques Rossi. Cold War rivalries framed early scholarship by English-speaking historians, who emphasized terror and mass death. Robert Conquest's *Kolyma: The Arctic Death Camps* (London: Macmillan, 1978) inspired an era of "Cold War warriors" like Richard Pipes and Martin Malia, as well as critical accounts like Stephan Courtois et al. (eds.), *The Black Book of Communism: Crimes, Terror, Repression*, trans. Jonathan Murphy and Mark Kramer (Cambridge: Harvard University Press, 1989). The fall of the Soviet Union in 1991 provided Western and Russian scholars with unprecedented access to previously secret archives, leading to historical reevaluations that question the "totalitarian" model by highlighting historical contingency and prisoner agency; drawing attention to the plurality of criminal felons (rather than political prisoners); and opening debates regarding the economic versus political origins and function of the Gulag. Anne Appelbaum's Pulitzer Prize-winning *Gulag: A History* (New York: Anchor Books, 2004) emphasizes the role of Gulag labor within the larger Soviet economy, while Steven Barnes's revisionist *Death and Redemption: The Gulag and the Shaping of Soviet Society* (Princeton: Princeton University Press, 2011) emphasizes political education and reform. The Russian historian Oleg Khlevniuk's *The History of the Gulag: From Collectivization to the Great Terror*, trans. Vadim A. Staklo (New Haven: Yale University Press, 2004) highlights the porous boundaries between the Gulag and Soviet society. Revisionist works like Alan Barenburg's *Gulag Town, Company Town: Forced Labor and Its Legacy in Vorkuta* (New Haven: Yale University Press, 2014) and Cynthia Ruder's *Building Stalinism: The Moscow Canal and the Creation of Soviet Space* (London: Bloomsbury, 2019) remind us that life in the Gulag was connected to events outside. Mark Vincent, in *Criminal Subculture in the Gulag: Prisoner Society in the Stalinist Labour Camps* (London: Bloomsbury, 2020), examines the experience of ordinary criminals. Lynne Viola's *The Unknown Gulag: The Lost World of Stalin's Special Settlements* (Oxford: Oxford University Press, 2007) draws crucial attention to much-neglected special settlements and labor colonies. The experience of Indigenous and nomadic inmates needs further study, although Yuri Slezkine, *Arctic Mirrors: Russia and the Small Peoples of the North* (Ithaca: Cornell University Press, 1994); Robert Kindler, *Stalin's Nomads: Power & Famine in Kazakhstan*, trans. Cynthia Klohr (Pittsburgh: University of Pittsburgh Press, 2018); and Alun Thomas, *Nomads and Soviet Rule: Central Asia under Lenin and Stalin* (London: I.B. Taurus, 2018), make significant inroads. Much scholarship focuses on the 1930s; Wilson Bell's *Stalin's Gulag at War: Forced Labour, Mass Death, and Soviet Victory in the Second World War* (Toronto: University of Toronto Press, 2018) and Jeffrey Hardy's *The Gulag after Stalin: Redefining Punishment in Khrushchev's Soviet Union, 1953–1964* (Ithaca: Cornell University Press, 2016) highlight later periods. Speaking to long-term continuities, Daniel Beer's *The House of the Dead: Siberian Exile under the Tsars* (London: Penguin, 2017) examines pre-Soviet punishment, while Judith Pallot's "The Gulag as the Crucible of Russia's Twenty-First Century System of Punishment," in David-Fox, *Soviet Gulag*, highlights continuities between the Gulag and criminal punishment in Russia today. The websites https://www.gulagmemories.eu/en and https://gulaghistory .org/ highlight inmate stories and experiences. For Gulag films, see https://www.rbth.com/arts/334343-russian-movies-gulag.

Chapter 5: *Konzentrationslager*

Specialist scholarship on Nazi camps is too vast to catalog in a brief entry. Early work by Eugen Kogon, Martin Broszat, and Karin Orth first spotlighted camps as central features of Nazi violence, as did Alain Resnais's disturbing 1956 film *Night and Fog* (https://www.youtube .com/watch?v=7embprPrazQ). Jane Caplan and Nikolaus Wachsmann (eds.), *Concentration Camps in Nazi Germany: The New Histories* (London: Routledge, 2009), provides a historiographical overview along with chapters highlighting new scholarship on gender and sexuality, historical commemoration, and the relationship between camps and Nazi society. The most comprehensive account, Wachsmann's *KL: A History of the Nazi Concentration Camps* (New York: Farrar, Straus, and Giroux, 2015), does not engage with global framings but highlights the neglected early history of the camps and their relation to prisons and workhouses. Much work on Nazi camps is entangled within larger histories of the Holocaust and its attendant debates, especially the *Historikerstreit* of the 1980s, which considered the intentionality of Nazi genocide and its comparability with other historical crimes, like the Soviet Gulag. The US Holocaust Museum's seven-volume *Encyclopedia of Camps and Ghettos*, available online, examines the Nazi universe of camps, from Norway to North Africa: https://www.ushmm.org /research/publications/encyclopedia-camps-ghettos/download. Chapter 5 of this book, however, is based on emerging postcolonial reassessments as well as comparative histories of forced labor, crime and punishment, and comparative genocide that place Nazi violence, and its resulting camps, within a global context. Enzo Traverso's extended essay *The Origins of Nazi Violence*, trans. Janet Lloyd (New York: New Press, 2003) embeds *Konzentrationslager* within earlier developments at prisons and workhouses, and in the colonial world. Building on the work of Hannah Arendt, who first argued for a relationship between Nazism and imperialism in Part II of *The Origins of Totalitarianism*, Jürgen Zimmerer's various works, including *From Windhoek to Auschwitz?: On the Relationship between Colonialism and the Holocaust* (Boston: De Gruyter, 2023), are postcolonial analyses that place Nazi camps within longer trajectories of imperial conquest and occupation.

The "Africa to Auschwitz" thesis, highlighted in the last chapters of Olusoga and Erichsen's *Kaiser's Holocaust* and in Benjamin Madley's article "From Africa to Auschwitz: How German South-West Africa Incubated Ideas and Methods Adopted and Developed by the Nazis in Eastern Europe," *European History Quarterly* 35, no. 3 (2005): 429–64, has been criticized, however, by Robert Gerwarth and Stephan Malinowski, "Hannah Arendt's Ghosts: Reflections on the Disputable Path from Windhoek to Auschwitz," *Central European History* 42, no. 2 (2009): 279–300. Nonetheless, the comparative history of genocide challenges readers to consider how Nazi camps are connected to – and disconnected from – larger global trends. See, for example, Dirk Moses (ed.), *Empire, Colony, Genocide: Conquest, Occupation, and Subaltern Resistance in World History* (New York: Berghahn, 2009); James Whiteman, *Hitler's American Model: The United States and the Making of Nazi Race Law* (Princeton: Princeton University Press, 2017); Carroll P. Kakel, *The American West and the German East: A Comparative and Interpretive Perspective* (New York: Palgrave, 2011); and H. Glenn Perry, *Kindred by Choice: Germans and American Indians since 1800* (Chapel Hill: University of North Carolina Press, 2013). Emil Janning's 1941 film *Ohm Krüger* (https://www.youtube.com/watch?v=sA4B8gTwaGo) highlights the place of British concentration camps in Nazi propaganda, as does Paul Moore's "'And What Concentration Camps Those Were!': Foreign Concentration Camps in Nazi Propaganda, 1933–9," *Journal of Contemporary History* 45, no. 3 (2010): 649–74. For comparison between Nazi camps and the Soviet Gulag, see Alan Barenberg, "Forced Labour in Nazi Germany and the Stalinist Soviet Union," in *The Cambridge World History of Slavery*, ed. D. Eltis et al. (Cambridge: Cambridge University Press, 2017); and Dietrich Beyrau, "Camp Worlds and Forced Labor: A Comparison of the National Socialist and Soviet Camp Systems," in David-Fox (ed.), *Soviet Gulag*.

Chapter 6: Asian Archipelagos

Scholarship on East Asian camps is a growth area, though it lacks the historiographical depth of the Nazi and Soviet regimes. Sensational memoirs by Allied POWs, such as John Coast's *Railroad of Death: The Original, Classic Account of the "River Kwai" Railway* (1946) along with David Lean's Academy Award-winning 1957 film *The Bridge on the River Kwai* have dominated our understanding of Japanese POW camps, though Sarah Kovner's *Prisoners of the Empire: Inside Japanese POW Camps* (Cambridge: Harvard University Press, 2020) suggests conditions were not always as scandalous as these testimonies imply. Apart from the atrocities of Unit 731, detailed by Sheldon Harris, *Factories of Death: Japanese Biological Warfare, 1932–1945* (London: Routledge, 2002), Japanese camps for Chinese and other Asian populations await their dedicated English-language historian. Scholarship on GMD camps under Chiang Kai-shek is largely overshadowed by the much larger laogai camps, though pertinent information can be found in Klaus Mühlhahn's "The Dark Side of Globalization: The Concentration Camps in Republican China in Global Perspective," *World History Connected* 6, no. 1 (2009), and Frank Dikötter's *Crime, Punishment and the Prison in Modern China* (New York: Columbia University Press, 2002). In contrast to the Soviet Union after 1991, Chinese archives are largely off-limits to Western historians, leading to a reliance on the testimony of political dissidents like Harry Wu, who ultimately founded the Laogai Research Foundation in Washington, DC: https://laogairesearch.org/. Inmate testimonies include Hongda Harry Wu and Carolyn Wakeman, *Bitter Winds: A Memoir of My Years in China's Gulag* (New York: Wiley, 1994); Chinese-French dissident Bao Ruo-Wang (Jean Pasqualini) and Rudolph Chelminski's *Prisoner of Mao* (New York: Coward, McCann & Geoghegan, 1973); Zhang Xianliang, *Grass Soup*, trans. Martha Avery (Boston: David R. Godine, 1995); Pu Ning, *Red in Tooth and Claw: Twenty-Six Years in Communist Chinese Prisons* (New York: Grove Press, 1994); and Liu Zongren, *Hard Time: 30 Months in a Chinese Labor Camp*, ed. Erik Noyes and James J. Wang (San Francisco: China Books, 1995). Harry Wu's *Laogai: The Chinese Gulag* (New York: Routledge, 1992) is a useful overview, while Nicole Kempton, ed., *Laogai: The Machinery of Repression* (New York: Umbrage Editions, 2009), offers vivid illustrations. Wu came to prominence in several documentaries (https://m.imdb.com/name/nm2916166/fullcredits), including a *60 Minutes* special (1992) in which he traveled back to China to take secret video footage. As an activist, however, Wu's work should be balanced with more critical assessments by professional historians. Klaus Mühlhahn's *Criminal Justice in China: A History* (Cambridge: Harvard University Press, 2009), and Philip Williams and Yenna Wu's *Great Wall of Confinement: The Chinese Prison Camp through Contemporary Fiction and Reportage* (Berkeley: University of California Press, 2004) are comprehensive monographs that place laogai within longer-term international perspectives. James D. Seymour and Richard Anderson offer a regional study of China's northwest in *New Ghosts, Old Ghosts: Prisons and Labor Reform Camps in China* (Armonk, NY: M.E. Sharpe, 1998). Information on North Korea, a closed police state with no public access to archives, relies almost entirely on memoirs by dissidents, particularly Kang Chol-Hwan and Pierre Rigoulot's *The Aquariums of Pyongyang: Ten Years in the North Korean Gulag*, trans. Yair Reiner (New York City: Basic Books, 2001). Blaine Harden's *Escape from Camp 14: One Man's Remarkable Odyssey from North Korea to Freedom in the West* (New York: Penguin, 2012) spotlights harrowing conditions in "irredeemable" camps, though the author usefully challenges readers to consider the reliability of inmate testimony. Sungmin Cho provides a scholarly overview in "The Origins and Evolution of the North Korean Prison Camps: A Comparison with the Soviet Gulag," in David-Fox, *The Soviet Gulag*. The 2014 *Report of the Commission of Inquiry on Human Rights in the Democratic People's Republic of Korea*, available at https://www.ohchr .org/en/hr-bodies/hrc/co-idprk/commission-inquiryon-h-rin-dprk, has assembled chronological and geographical details and inmate testimonies.

Chapter 7: (Post)colonial Concentration

Japanese American internment camps have a dedicated literature. Alice Yang Murray's *What Did the Internment of Japanese Americans Mean?* (Boston: Bedford/St. Martin's, 2000) includes primary source excerpts and guidance for further reading. Roger Daniels's *Concentration Camps USA: Japanese Americans and World War II* (New York: Holt, Rinehart, and Winston, 1971, updated in 1993 to include the Canadian experience) and Greg Robinson's *A Tragedy of Democracy: Japanese Confinement in North America* (New York: Columbia University Press, 2009) provide landmark overviews. Laleh Khalili's *Time in the Shadows: Confinement in Counterinsurgencies* (Stanford: Stanford University Press, 2013) places counterinsurgency camps from the late nineteenth century to the Cold War and postcolonial periods into an integrated transnational rubric. Though not specifically about camps, general histories of counterinsurgency, written by military historians like Daniel Marston and Carter Malkasian (eds.), *Counterinsurgency in Modern Warfare* (Oxford: Osprey, 2010), and Usman A. Tar (ed.), *The Routledge Handbook of Counterterrorism and Counterinsurgency in Africa* (Abingdon: Routledge, 2021), are also useful. Robert Cribb, Christina Twomey, and Sandra Wilson (eds.), *Detention Camps in Asia: The Conditions of Confinement in Modern Asian History* (Leiden: Brill, 2022), examines Malaya, Burma, Indonesia, and elsewhere. For encampment in Palestine, Kenya, and Malaya, see Caroline Elkins's *Legacy of Violence: A History of the British Empire* (New York: Alfred A. Knopf, 2022). Tan Teng Phee's *Behind Barbed Wire: Chinese New Villages during the Malayan*

Emergency, 1948–1960 (Petaling Jaya: Strategic Information and Research Development Centre, 2020) is a specialist synopsis. Elkins's Pulitzer Prize-winning *Imperial Reckoning: The Untold Story of Britain's Gulag in Kenya* (New York: Henry Holt, 2005) is the most influential account of Kenyan camps, though David Anderson's *Histories of the Hanged: The Dirty War in Kenya and the End of Empire* (New York: W.W. Norton, 2005) is an excellent history of the overall conflict. Marshall Clough, *Mau Mau Memoirs: History, Memory, and Politics* (Boulder, CO: L. Rienner, 1998), introduces primary source material; Wambui Otieno's memoir, *Mau Mau's Daughter: A Life History* (Boulder, CO: L. Rienner, 1998), showcases the inmate experience of a prominent feminist politician. Much work on Algerian *regroupement* is in French. Co-written by Abdelmayet Sayad and the famous sociologist Pierre Bourdieu, *The Uprooting: The Crisis of Traditional Agriculture in Algeria*, ed. Paul A. Silverstein, trans. Susan Emanuel (Cambridge: Polity Press, 2015), examines the dynamics of space and power in the camps. A.A. Heggoy, *Insurgency and Counterinsurgency in Algeria* (Bloomington: Indiana University Press, 1972), and Neil Macmaster, *War in the Mountains: Peasant Society and Counterinsurgency in Algeria, 1918–1958* (Oxford: Oxford University Press, 2020), situate *regroupement* within broader wartime narratives. Scholarship on Uyghur concentration camps in China is an emerging field, currently dominated by anthropologists and political scientists. Darren Byler's scholarship, based on challenging ethnographic research, is particularly useful because it places camps in Xinjiang within a broader ethnographic and comparative context. See *Terror Capitalism: Uyghur Dispossession and Masculinity in a Chinese City* (Durham: Duke University Press, 2021) and *In the Camps: China's High-Tech Penal Colony* (New York: Columbia Global Reports, 2021). For Guantanamo Bay, Amy Kaplan's "Where Is Guantanamo?," *American Quarterly* 57, no. 3 (2005): 831–58, and A.N. Paik, "Carceral Quarantine at Guantanamo: Legacies of US Imprisonment of Haitian Refugees, 1991–1994," *Radical History Review* 115 (2013): 142–68, place the camp within broader histories of colonialism, racism, and internment. The NPR debate "Guantanamo Bay: A 'Gulag of Our Times' or 'A Model Facility'?" offers lively comparative insight: https://www.democracynow.org/2005/6/1/guantanamo_bay_a_gulag_of_our.

Chapter 8: Humanitarian Containment

Social scientists have dominated scholarship on refugee camps, but their research, focused on the present, often ignores longer histories of humanitarian containment. Peter Gatrell's *The Making of the Modern Refugee* (Oxford: Oxford University Press, 2013) is an indispensable guide to the shifting refugee experience over time. Forth, *Barbed-Wire Imperialism*, traces the prehistory of refugee camps in colonial India and South Africa; Kirsten McConnachie traces a wide-ranging, long-durée history in "Camps of Containment: A Genealogy of the Refugee Camp," *Humanity* 7, no. 3 (2016): 397–412. *Continental Encampment: Genealogies of Humanitarian Containment in the Middle East and Europe*, ed. John Knudsen and Kjersti G. Berg (New York: Berghahn, 2023), spotlights the fallout of World War I in the Middle East as a watershed moment in the global dissemination and standardization of refugee camps. The related website, https://www.cmi.no/projects/2181-supercamp-genealogies-of-humanitarian -containment#blog, hosted by Norway's Chr. Michelsen Institute, features thoughtful articles and blogposts. Gabriele Anderl, Linda Erker, and Christoph Reinprecht (eds.), *Internment Refugee Camps: Historical and Contemporary Perspectives* (Bielefeld: Transcript, 2023), compiles historical and contemporary scholarship on migrants and refugee camps, highlighting parallels to modern practice. Liisa Malkki highlights the ambiguities of the camp as a site of both care and control in *Purity and Exile: Violence, Memory, and National Cosmology among Hutu Refugees in Tanzania* (Chicago: University of Chicago Press, 1995) and in various other articles cited throughout the chapter. Jennifer Hyndman, *Managing Displacement: Refugees and the Politics of Humanitarianism* (Minneapolis: University of Minnesota Press, 2000), and Guglielmo Verdirame and Barbara Harrell-Bond, *Rights in Exile: Janus-Faced Humanitarianism* (New York: Berghahn, 2005), do the same. Based on ethnographic research in Africa, Michel Agier, *Managing the Undesirables: Refugee Camps and Humanitarian Government*, trans. David Fernbach (Cambridge: Polity Press, 2011), engages with the philosopher Giorgio Agamben's paradigm of the camp, but does not place refugee internment within a historical context. Irit Katz, *The Common Camp: Architecture of Power and Resistance in Israel-Palestine* (Minneapolis: University of Minnesota Press, 2022), and Irit Katz, Diana Martin, and Claudio Minca (eds.), *Camps Revisited: Multifaceted Spatialities of a Modern Political Technology* (London: Rowman & Littlefield, 2018), examine the space, architecture, and geography of refugee camps and related institutions. Many works engage with Hannah Arendt's influential essay "We Refugees," in *The Jewish Writings*, ed. Jerome Kohn and Ron F. Feldman (New York: Schocken Books, 2008), which considers the vulnerability of "stateless" populations in an era of nation states. Journalistic accounts highlight the plight of those uprooted by the 2015 Syrian migrant crisis; see Ben Rawlence, *City of Thorns: Nine Lives in the World's Largest Refugee Camp* (London: Picador, 2016); Matthew Carr, *Fortress Europe: Dispatches from a Gated Continent* (New York: The New Press, 2016); Patrick Kinsgley, *The New Odyssey: The Story of Europe's Refugee Crisis* (London: Guardian Faber, 2016); and Calais Writers, *Voices from the "Jungle": Stories from the Calais Refugee Camp* (London: Pluto Press, 2017). Robert T. Chase (ed.), *Caging Borders and Carceral States: Incarcerations, Immigration Detentions, and Resistance* (Chapel Hill: University of North Carolina Press, 2019), examines the growing nexus between migrant detention and America's prison industrial complex. Documentary series like Christina Clusiau and Shaul Schwarz's *Immigration Nation*, and Emma Freeman and Jocelyn Moorhouse's *Stateless*, both released on Netflix in 2020, show-case the dynamics of migrant detention in the United States and Australia respectively.

Conclusion: Remembering and Forgetting

For the contested politics of memory in South Africa, see Liz Stanley, *Mourning Becomes ... Post/memory, Commemoration and the Concentration Camps of the South African War* (Manchester: Manchester University Press, 2006). For Japanese American internment, see Alice Yang Murray, *Historical Memories of the Japanese American Internment and the Struggle for Redress* (Stanford: Stanford University Press, 2007). Zuzanna Bogomił considers commemoration in *Gulag Memories: The Rediscovery and Commemoration of Russia's Repressive Past*, trans. Philip Palmer (New York: Berghahn Books, 2018), as does Alan Barenberg and Emily Johnson's *Rethinking the Gulag*. Harold Marcuse assesses memory of Nazi camps in *Legacies of Dachau: The Uses and Abuses of a Concentration Camp, 1933–2001* (Cambridge: Cambridge University Press, 2008). Memories of encampment in the Global South deserve further attention. Caroline Elkins compares Kenya and South Africa – in each case, colonial archives documenting the experi-ence of Black inmates were destroyed – in "Reckoning with the Past: The Contrast between the Kenyan and South African Experiences," *Social Dynamics* 26, no. 2 (2000): 8–28. Liisa Malkki's *Purity and Exile* examines identity formation and memory in African refugee camps, while Julie Peteet, *Landscape of Hope and Despair: Palestinian Refugee Camps* (Philadelphia: University of Pennsylvania Press, 2005), explores the process in Palestine. Concentration camps feature prominently at the US Holocaust Museum in Washington, DC (https://www.ushmm.org/) and Yad Vashem in Jerusalem (https://yadvashem.org/). Many campsites have been converted into memorials; visits to Dachau (https://www.kz-gedenkstaette-dachau.de/en/), Sachsenhausen (https://www.sachsenhausen-sbg.de/), or Auschwitz (https://www.auschwitz.org/en/) are moving and disturbing. Access to Russian memorials is challenging, but researchers can consult the (state-curated) website of the Moscow Gulag Museum (https://gmig.ru/en/) and the Czech-based Gulag Virtual Museum (https://gulag.online/en). In America, the Andersonville (https://www.nps.gov/ande/index.htm) and Manzanar (https://www.nps.gov/manz/index.htm) National Historic Sites commemorate Japanese American internment and Civil War POW camps respectively, while in South Africa, *Gedenktuin*, or "Gardens of Memory" at former concentration camps (https://www.sawarmemorials.ed.ac.uk/concentration-camps-of-the-south-african-war-1899-1902/concampmemorials/), serve as nationalist shrines to white Afrikaners but have largely effaced the Black African experience. The War Museum in Bloemfontein (https://wmbr.org.za/) has gradually changed its focus since the end of apartheid. When visiting any museum or monument, visitors should think critically about potential bias and the way historical narratives are sometimes presented in a selective, politicized, or emotive way.

Index

Page numbers in italics denote figures.

265

Milton Keynes UK
Ingram Content Group UK Ltd.
UKHW020847310524
443451UK00011B/577

9 781487 588281